American Political Rhetoric

American Political Rhetoric
A Reader

Third Edition

Edited by

Peter Augustine Lawler
and
Robert Martin Schaefer

Rowman & Littlefield Publishers, Inc.

ROWMAN & LITTLEFIELD PUBLISHERS, INC.

Published in the United States of America
by Rowman & Littlefield Publishers, Inc.
4720 Boston Way, Lanham, Maryland 20706

3 Henrietta Street
London, WC2E 8LU, England

Copyright © 1995 by Rowman & Littlefield Publishers, Inc.

An excerpt from Richard M. Nixon, *Beyond Peace*, ©1994 Richard M. Nixon, is reprinted by permission of Random House, Inc.

Excerpts from Alexis de Tocqueville, *Democracy in America*, ed. J. P. Mayer, trans. George Lawrence, ©1988 HarperCollins, are reprinted by permission of HarperCollins.

British Cataloging in Publication Information Available

Library of Congress Cataloging-in-Publication Data

American political rhetoric : a reader / edited by Peter Augustine
Lawler and Robert Martin Schaefer. – 3rd ed.
p.   cm.
1. United States–Constitutional history–Sources. 2. United
States–Politics and government–Sources.   I. Lawler, Peter
Augustine.   II. Schaefer, Robert Martin.
JK21.A462   1995   320.973–dc20   95-7428   CIP

ISBN 0–8476–8047–9 (pbk. : alk. paper)

Printed in the United States of America

The paper used in this publication meets the minimum requirements of American National Standard for Information Sciences—Permanence of Paper for Printed Library Materials, ANSI Z39.48–1984.

Contents

Acknowledgments

We want to thank the many thoughtful men and women who have studied American politics with us at Berry College and the University of Mobile. They have given us the opportunity, encouragement, and incentive to produce this revised and expanded third edition.

We also want to thank Berry College and the University of Mobile for providing assistance in the various stages of production. At Berry, Vickie Ford and Kathy Gann did a great deal of the word processing and much of the proofreading. Matt Barrett and Jen Siebels did most of the research and contributed editorial assistance. Jason Robertson read the proofs with a fresh eye. At Mobile, Allison Knight's fine computer and copyediting skills proved to be invaluable. We also thank Dr. Cathy A. Broadwell, a kind friend and *defensor pacis*.

Once again, we enjoyed working with the friendly, competent, and always accessible people at Rowman and Littlefield. In particular we thank Jon Sisk, Jennifer Ruark, Julie Kirsch, and Lynn Gemmell.

We follow Tocqueville's advice when we remember that no study of American politics is complete without an acknowledgment of the superiority of American women. We are especially grateful to four of them: Rita, Catherine, Terri, and Maggie.

Introduction

As a way of introducing students to the study of American politics, this book presents some of the best examples of American political rhetoric. We do not consider rhetoric to be empty words or merely propaganda. Statesmen use rhetoric to persuade citizens to support particular policies. Their goal, of course, is political success. But a statesman's pursuit of success through rhetoric is never simple. Inevitably, in an effort to persuade, a statesman appeals to self-interest. But citizens can also be moved morally, through the articulation of, and appeal to, principle. They listen to reason and respond to reasonable appeals that oppose or moderate selfish desires and blind inclinations. The study of rhetoric is the study of the diverse human motivations that constitute political life. Most importantly, it can be seen as a study of the diverse and irreducible components of the human soul.

In a democracy, the words of statesmen should be evaluated critically by citizens. The premise of this book is that students of American politics are, first of all, citizens. Our intention is to lead them to become better citizens.

Political scientists usually criticize America today for the quality of its citizenship. They claim citizens have become apathetic and easily deceived, or are not really citizens at all. But they also explain that even what seems to be the activity of citizens is, in reality, determined by social or economic forces that are not political at all.

James Q. Wilson, one of America's most distinguished political scientists, wrote *The Moral Sense* to recapture the perspective of the citizen.[1] He presented scientific evidence for Aristotle's position that human beings, by nature, are fitted to become social and responsible beings. They must acquire virtue through habituation and attachment to others in order to act freely. Wilson wrote against the reigning scientific view that human beings are naturally asocial and

irresponsible. Human freedom is freedom from the illusions and constraints that society imposes on us. This scientific skepticism, present
in most of the study of political science today, denies that there is
any foundation for the citizen's perception of his freedom and responsibility.

With the preparation of this text, we have, in effect, rejected
scientific reductionism. We say, with Wilson, that one cause of the
decline of citizenship is the popularization of scientific skepticism.
Citizens have been taught to distrust not only politicians but also
their own judgment. We believe that situation can be improved. The
perspectives of citizenship and statesmanship genuinely exist and
so can be rehabilitated in our time.

Some might call the rhetorical approach to the study of politics
idealistic. Idealism has come to mean a pure and apolitical moral-
ism or utopianism. But rhetoric is practical and partisan. Because it
aims at political success, it is more realistic than idealistic. It mod-
erates idealism with knowledge of what is possible for human beings
here and now.

Rhetoric, through its intention to persuade, is also opposed to the
seemingly pure realism of pragmatism. Success itself is not a standard. Principle must be articulated and applied, because there are
almost always better or worse alternatives available, and because
citizens rightly distrust the unprincipled use of power. Statesmen
always know that pragmatism is unrealistic, and that realism and
idealism are apolitical extremes. The rhetorical approach is distinc-
tively political. It means to miss as little of political reality as
possible.

This book is intended to supplement more than replace the American government textbook. Its principles of organization can readily
be modified by an instructor to accompany almost any textbook. It,
for good reason, is rather short. The selections are to be read carefully and discussed thoroughly.

We are pleased to recommend another text we have edited, *The
American Experiment: Essays on the Theory and Practice of Liberty*.[2] Among its many features is that it is informed by much the
same approach to the study of politics as this book. It is also the
work of many hands and so holds the student's interest with its
diversity.

This is the third edition of *American Political Rhetoric*. It has
become both larger and better. New features of this edition include
sections on gender and foreign policy, and much greater coverage

of the presidency, Congress, and the judiciary. These changes have come, in part, from the helpful suggestions of those who have used the book over the years.

Notes

1. James Q. Wilson, *The Moral Sense* (New York: Free Press, 1993).
2. Peter Augustine Lawler and Robert Martin Schaefer, *The American Experiment: Essays on the Theory and Practice of Liberty* (Lanham, Md.: Rowman & Littlefield, 1994).

1

Founding Principles

The selections in this chapter are accounts of the founding or basic principles of political order in the United States. They, above all else, determine the form of government that was and is still chosen to shape the American way of life.

THE DECLARATION OF INDEPENDENCE, IN CONGRESS, JULY 4, 1776. THE UNANIMOUS DECLARATION OF THE THIRTEEN UNITED STATES OF AMERICA

This is the argument supporting the assertion of independence by the thirteen American colonies in 1776. The principles on which this argument is based are held to be valid not merely for eighteenth-century Anglo-Americans, but for all human beings at all times and in all places. It is these rational or "self-evident" truths—not some irrational tradition or culture— that give Americans coherence as a political community.

When in the Course of human Events, it becomes necessary for one People to dissolve the Political Bands which have connected them with another, and to assume among the Powers of the Earth, the separate and equal Station to which the Laws of Nature and of Nature's God entitle them, a decent Respect to the Opinions of Mankind requires that they should declare the causes which impel them to the Separation.—We hold these Truths to be self-evident, that all Men are created equal, that they are endowed by their Creator with certain unalienable Rights, that among these are Life, Liberty, and the Pursuit of Happiness—That to secure these Rights, Governments are instituted among Men, deriving their just Powers from the Consent of the Governed—That whenever any Form of

1

Government becomes destructive of these Ends, it is the Right of the People to alter or to abolish it, and to institute new Government, laying its Foundation on such Principles and organizing its Powers in such Form, as to them shall seem most likely to effect their Safety and Happiness. Prudence, indeed, will dictate that Governments long established should not be changed for light and transient Causes; and accordingly all Experience hath shown, that Mankind are more disposed to suffer, while Evils are sufferable, than to right themselves by abolishing the Forms to which they are accustomed. But when a long Train of Abuses and Usurpations, pursuing invariably the same Object, evinces a Design to reduce them under absolute Despotism, it is their Right, it is their Duty, to throw off such Government, and to provide new Guards for their future Security. Such has been the patient Sufferance of these Colonies; and such is now the Necessity which constrains them to alter their former Systems of Government. The History of the present King of Great-Britain is a History of repeated Injuries and Usurpations, all having in direct Object the Establishment of an absolute Tyranny over these States. To prove this, let Facts be submitted to a candid World.—He has refused his Assent to Laws, the most wholesome and necessary for the public Good.—He has forbidden his Governors to pass Laws of immediate and pressing Importance, unless suspended in their Operation till his Assent should be obtained; and when so suspended, he has utterly neglected to attend to them. —He has refused to pass other Laws for the Accommodation of large Districts of People, unless those People would relinquish the Right of Representation in the Legislature, a Right inestimable to them and formidable to Tyrants only.—He has called together Legislative Bodies at Places unusual, uncomfortable, and distant from the Depository of their public Records, for the sole Purpose of fatiguing them into Compliance with his Measures.—He has dissolved Representative Houses repeatedly, for opposing with manly Firmness his Invasions on the Rights of the People.—He has refused for a long Time, after such Dissolutions, to cause others to be elected; whereby the Legislative Powers, incapable of Annihilation, have returned to the People at large for their exercise; the State remaining in the mean time exposed to all the Dangers of Invasion from without, and Convulsions within.—He has endeavoured to prevent the Population of these States; for that Purpose obstructing the Laws for Naturalization of Foreigners; refusing to pass others to encourage their Migration hither, and raising the Conditions of new

Appropriation of Lands.—He has obstructed the Administration of Justice, by refusing his Assent to Laws for establishing Judiciary Powers.—He has made Judges dependent on his Will alone, for the Tenure of their Offices, and the Amount and Payment of their Salaries.—He has erected a Multitude of new Offices, and sent hither Swarms of Officers to harrass our People, and eat out their Substance.—He has kept among us, in Times of Peace, Standing Armies, without the consent of our Legislatures.—He has affected to render the Military independent of and superior to the Civil Power. —He has combined with others to subject us to a Jurisdiction foreign to our Constitution, and unacknowledged by our Laws; giving his Assent to their Acts of pretended Legislation:—For quartering large Bodies of Armed Troops among us:—For protecting them, by a mock Trial, from Punishment for any Murders which they should commit on the Inhabitants of these States:—For cutting off our Trade with all Parts of the World:—For imposing Taxes on us without our Consent:—For depriving us in many Cases, of the Benefits of Trial by Jury:—For transporting us beyond Seas to be tried for pretended Offences:—For abolishing the free System of English Laws in a neighbouring Province, establishing therein an arbitrary Government, and enlarging its Boundaries, so as to render it at once an Example and fit Instrument for introducing the same absolute Rule into these Colonies:—For taking away our Charters, abolishing our most valuable Laws, and altering fundamentally the Forms of our Governments:—For suspending our own Legislatures, and declaring themselves invested with Power to legislate for us in all Cases whatsoever.—He has abdicated Government here, by declaring us out of his Protection and waging War against us.—He has plundered our Seas, ravaged our Coasts, burnt our Towns, and destroyed the Lives of our People.—He is at this Time, transporting large Armies of foreign Mercenaries to compleat the Works of Death, Desolation and Tyranny, already begun with circumstances of Cruelty and Perfidy, scarcely paralleled in the most barbarous Ages, and totally unworthy the Head of a civilized Nation.—He has constrained our fellow Citizens taken Captive on the high Seas to bear Arms against their Country, to become the Executioners of their Friends and Brethren, or to fall themselves by their Hands.—He has excited domestic Insurrections amongst us, and has endeavoured to bring on the Inhabitants of our Frontiers, the merciless Indian Savages, whose known Rule of Warfare, is an undistinguished Destruction, of all Ages, Sexes and Conditions.—In every stage of these Oppressions we have Petitioned for Redress in the most humble Terms: Our repeated Petitions have been answered only by repeated Injury. A Prince, whose Character is thus marked by every act which may define a Tyrant, is unfit to be the Ruler of a free People. Nor have we been wanting in Attentions to our British Brethren. We have warned them from Time to Time of Attempts by their Legislature to extend an unwarrantable Jurisdiction over us. We have reminded them of the Circumstances of our Emigration and Settlement here. We have appealed to their native Justice and Magnanimity, and we have conjured them by the Ties of our common Kindred to disavow these Usurpations, which, would inevitably interrupt our Connections and Correspondence. They too have been deaf to the Voice of Justice and of Consanguinity. We must, therefore, acquiesce in the Necessity, which denounces our Separation, and hold them, as we hold the rest of Mankind, Enemies in War, in Peace, Friends.

We, therefore, the Representatives of the United States of America, in General Congress, Assembled, appealing to the Supreme Judge of the World for the Rectitude of our Intentions, do, in the Name, and by Authority of the good People of these Colonies, solemnly Publish and Declare, That these United Colonies are, and of Right ought to be, Free and Independent States; that they are absolved from all Allegiance to the British Crown, and that all political Connection between them and the State of Great-Britain, is and ought to be totally dissolved; and that as Free and Independent States, they have full Power to levy War, conclude Peace, contract Alliances, establish Commerce, and to do all other Acts and Things which Independent States may of right do. And for the support of this Declaration, with a firm Reliance on the Protection of divine Providence, we mutually pledge to each other our Lives, our Fortunes, and our sacred Honor.

ALEXIS DE TOCQUEVILLE, *DEMOCRACY IN AMERICA* (1835)

Tocqueville's reflections on America of the 1830s remain the best account of democracy as not merely a form of government but also a way of life. This Frenchman's book is indispensable for understanding comprehensively the American political order. The selection below is one of a very few exceptions to the rule in this book of considering only the writings of American statesmen.

Social State of the Anglo-Americans

THE SOCIAL STATE is commonly the result of circumstances, sometimes of laws, but most often of a combination of the two. But once it has come into being, it may itself be considered as the prime cause of most of the laws, customs, and ideas which control the nation's behavior; it modifies even those things which it does not cause.

Therefore one must first study their social state if one wants to understand a people's laws and mores.

The Striking Feature in the Social Condition of the Anglo-Americans Is That It Is Essentially Democratic

There are many important things to be said about the social condition of the Anglo-Americans, but one feature dominates all the others.

The social state of the Americans is eminently democratic. It has been like that ever since the birth of the colonies but is even more so now.

I said that a high degree of equality prevailed among the immigrants who first settled on the coast of New England. In that part of the states even the seeds of aristocracy were never planted. There only intellectual power could command influence, and the people came to respect certain names as symbols of enlightenment and virtue. The views of some citizens carried such weight that if it had invariably passed from father to son, their influence might reasonably have been called aristocratic.

That was the case to the east of the Hudson. To the southwest of that river and right down to the Floridas, things were different.

Great English landowners had come to settle in most of the states southwest of the Hudson. They brought with them aristocratic principles, including the English law of inheritance. I have explained the reasons that made it impossible ever to establish a powerful aristocracy in America. Those reasons applied southwest of the Hudson too, but with less force than to the east thereof. In the South one man and his slaves could cultivate a wide extent of land. So there were rich landowners in that part of the country. But their influence was not exactly aristocratic, in the sense in which that word is used in Europe, for they had no privileges, and the use of slaves meant that they had no tenants and consequently no patronage. However, the great landowners south of the Hudson did form an upper class, with its own ideas and tastes, and in general it did concentrate political activity in its hands. It was a sort of aristocracy not very different from the bulk of the people whose passions and interests it easily embraced, arousing neither love nor hate. It was, to conclude, weak and unlikely to last. That was the class which, in the South, put itself at the head of the rebellion; it provided the best leaders of the American Revolution.

At that time society was shaken to the core. The people, in whose name the war had been fought, became a power and wanted to act on their own; democratic instincts awoke; the English yoke had been broken, and a taste for every form of independence grew; little by little the influence of individuals ceased to carry weight; customs and laws began to march in step toward the same goal.

But it was the law of inheritance which caused the final advance of equality.

I am surprised that ancient and modern writers have not attributed greater importance to the laws of inheritance and their effect on the progress of human affairs. They are, it is true, civil laws, but they should head the list of all political institutions, for they have an unbelievable influence on the social state of peoples, and political laws are no more than the expression of that state. Moreover, their way of influencing society is both sure and uniform; in some sense they lay hands on each generation before it is born. By their means man is armed with almost supernatural power over the future of his fellows. When the lawgiver has once fixed the law of inheritance, he can rest for centuries; once the impulse has been given to his handiwork, he can take his hand away; the mechanism works by its own power and apparently spontaneously aims at the goal indicated beforehand. If it has been drafted in a certain way, it assembles, concentrates, and piles up property, and soon power too, in the hands of one man; in a sense it makes an aristocracy leap forth from the ground. Guided by other principles and directed toward other goals, its effect is even quicker; it divides, shares, and spreads property and power; then sometimes people get frightened at the speed of its progress; despairing of stopping its motion, men seek at least to put obstacles and difficulties in its way; there is an attempt to balance its action by measures of opposite tendency. But all in vain! It grinds up or smashes everything that stands in its way; with the continual rise and fall of its hammer strokes, everything is reduced to a fine, impalpable dust, and that dust is the foundation for democracy. When the law of inheritance allows or, *a fortiori*, ordains the equal sharing of a father's property among his children, the results are of two sorts, which need to be distinguished, though they both tend toward the same end.

Owing to the law of inheritance, the death of each owner causes a revolution in property; not only do possessions change hands, but their very nature is altered, as they are continually broken up into smaller fractions. That is the direct physical effect of the law. So in countries where equal shares are the rule, property, particularly landed property, has a permanent tendency to grow less. However, the effects of such legislation would only be felt in the fullness of time if the effects of the law were simply left to work themselves out, for in families with not more than two children (and the average of families with a population pattern such as France is said to be only three), those children sharing their father's and their mother's fortune would not be poorer than either of the latter individually.

But the rule of equal shares does not affect only the fate of property; it also affects the very soul of the landowner and brings his passions into play. It is these indirect effects which rapidly break up great fortunes, especially landed property.

In nations where the law of inheritance is based on primogeniture, landed estates generally pass undivided from one generation to another. Hence family feeling finds a sort of physical expression in the land. The family represents the land, and the land the family, perpetuating its name, origin, glory, power, and virtue. It is an imperishable witness to the past and a precious earnest of the future.

When the law ordains equal shares, it breaks that intimate connection between family feeling and preservation of the land; the land no longer represents the family, for, as it is bound to be divided up at the end of one or two generations, it is clear that it must continually diminish and completely disappear in the end or if fortune favors them, may still hope to be no less rich than their parent, but they cannot expect to possess the same lands; their wealth is bound to be composed of different elements from his.

Now, as soon as landowners are deprived of their strong sentimental attachment to the land, based on memories and pride, it is certain that sooner or later they will sell it, for they have a powerful pecuniary interest in so doing, since other forms of investment earn a higher rate of interest and liquid assets are more easily used to satisfy the passions of the moment.

Once divided, great landed estates do not come together again; for, proportionately, a smallholder gets a better income from his fields than a great landlord from his, and so he sells it too at a much higher price. Thus the same economic calculation which induced the rich man to sell vast properties will even more powerfully dissuade him from buying up small holdings to make a great one again.

What passes for family feeling is often based on an illusion of personal selfishness; a man seeks to perpetuate himself and, in some sense, to make himself immortal through his great-grandchildren. Where family feeling is at an end, personal selfishness turns again to its real inclinations. As the family is felt to be a vague, indeterminate, uncertain conception, each man concentrates on his immediate convenience; he thinks about getting the next generation established in life, but nothing further. Hence a man does not seek to perpetuate his family, or at least he seeks other means than landed estates to do so.

Thus the law of inheritance not only makes it difficult for families to retain the same domains intact, but takes away their wish to try to do so and, in a sense, leads them to cooperate with the law in their own ruin.

The law of equal shares progresses along two paths: by acting upon things, it affects persons; by acting on persons, it has its effect on things.

By both these means it strikes at the root of landed estates and quickly breaks up both families and fortunes.

It is certainly not for us, Frenchmen of the nineteenth century, who are daily witness of the political and social changes caused by the law of inheritance, to doubt its power. Every day we see its influence coming and going over our land, knocking down the walls of our houses in its path, and throwing down the fences of our fields. But though the law of inheritance has done much among us, it still has much to do. Our memories, thoughts, and habits still put substantial obstacles in its way.

In the United States its work of destruction has almost been brought to an end. It is there that one can study its chief effects.

The English law concerning succession to property was abolished in almost all the states at the time of the Revolution. The law of entail was so modified that it hardly put any restraint on the free sale of land.

The first generation passed away; land began to be divided. As time passed, the change grew faster and faster. Now, hardly sixty years later, the aspect of society is already hard to recognize; the families of the great landowners have almost mingled with the common mass. In the state of New York, where formerly there were many, only two still keep their heads above the waters which are ready to swallow them too. The sons of these wealthy citizens are now merchants, lawyers, or doctors. Most of them have fallen into the most complete obscurity. The last trace of hereditary ranks and distinctions has been destroyed; the law of inheritance has everywhere imposed its dead level.

It is not that in the United States, as everywhere, there are no rich; indeed I know no other country where love of money has such a grip on men's hearts or where stronger scorn is expressed for the theory of permanent equality of property. But wealth circulates there with incredible rapidity, and experience shows that two successive generations seldom enjoy its favors.

This picture, which some may think overdrawn, would give only a very imperfect impression of what goes on in the new states of the West and Southwest.

At the end of the last century a few bold adventurers began to penetrate into the Mississippi valley. It was like a new discovery of America; soon most of those who were immigrating went there; previously unheard of communities suddenly sprang up in the wilderness. States that had not even been named a few years before took their places in the American Union. It is in the West that one can see democracy in its most extreme form. In these states, in some sense improvisations of fortune, the inhabitants have arrived only yesterday in the land where they dwell.

They hardly know one another, and each man is ignorant of his neighbor's history. So in that part of the American continent the population escapes the influence not only of great names and great wealth but also of the natural aristocracy of education and probity. No man there enjoys the influence and respect due to a whole life spent publicly in doing good. There are inhabitants already in the new states of the West, but not as yet a society.

But it is not only fortunes that are equal in America; equality to some extent affects their mental endowments too.

I think there is no other country in the world where, proportionately to population, there are so few ignorant and so few learned individuals as in America.

Primary education is within reach of all; higher education is hardly available to anybody.

That is easily understood and is indeed the necessary consequence of what has been said before.

Almost all Americans enjoy easy circumstances and can so easily acquire the basic elements of human knowledge.

There are few rich men in America; hence almost all Americans have to take up some profession. Now, every profession requires an apprenticeship. Therefore the Americans can devote only the first years of life to general education; at fifteen they start on a career, so their education generally ends at the age when ours begins. If it is continued beyond that point, it aims only at some specialized and profitable objective; science is studied in the same spirit as one takes up a trade; and only matters of immediate and recognized practical application receive attention.

In America most rich men began by being poor; almost all men of leisure were busy in their youth; as a result, at the age when one might have a taste for study, one has not the time; and when time is available, the taste has gone.

So there is no class in America in which a taste for intellectual pleasures is transmitted with hereditary wealth and leisure and which holds the labors of the mind in esteem.

Both the will and the power to engage in such work are lacking.

A middling standard has been established in America for all human knowledge. All minds come near to it, some by raising and some by lowering their standards.

As a result one finds a vast multitude of people with roughly the same ideas about religion, history, science, political economy, legislation, and government.

Intellectual inequalities come directly from God, and man cannot prevent them existing always.

But it results from what we have just been explaining, that, though mental endowments remain unequal as the Creator intended, the means of exercising them are equal.

Therefore, in America now the aristocratic element, which was from the beginning weak, has been, if not destroyed, at least made feebler still, so that one can hardly attribute to it any influence over the course of things.

On the other hand, time, circumstances, and laws have made the democratic element not merely preponderant but, one might say, exclusive.

One cannot trace any family or corporate influence; it is often hard even to discover any durable individual influence.

So the social state of America is a very strange phenomenon. Men there are nearer equality in wealth and mental endowments, or, in other words, more nearly equally powerful, than in any other country of the world or in any other age of recorded history.

Political Consequences of the Social State of the Anglo-Americans

It is easy to deduce the political consequences of such a social state.

By no possibility could equality ultimately fail to penetrate into the sphere of politics as everywhere else. One cannot imagine that men should remain perpetually unequal in just one respect though equal in all others; within a certain time they are bound to become equal in all respects.

Now, I know of only two ways of making equality prevail in the political sphere; rights must be given either to every citizen or to nobody.

So, for a people who have reached the Anglo-Americans' social state, it is hard to see any middle course between the sovereignty of all and the absolute power of one man.

One must not disguise it from oneself that the social state I have just described may lead as easily to the one as to the other of those results.

There is indeed a manly and legitimate passion for equality which rouses in all men a desire to be strong and respected. This passion tends to elevate the little man to the rank of the great. But the human heart also nourishes a debased taste for equality, which leads the weak to want to drag the strong down to their level and which induces men to prefer equality in servitude to inequality in freedom. It is not that peoples with a democratic social state naturally scorn freedom; on the contrary, they have an instinctive taste for it. But freedom is not the chief and continual object of their desires; it is equality for which they feel an eternal love; they rush on freedom with quick and sudden impulses, but if they miss their mark they resign themselves to their disappointment; but nothing will satisfy them without equality, and they would rather die than lose it.

On the other hand, when the citizens are all more or less equal, it becomes difficult to defend their freedom from the encroachments of power. No one among them being any longer strong enough to struggle alone with success, only the combination of the forces of all is able to guarantee liberty. But such a combination is not always forthcoming.

So, nations can derive either of two great political consequences from the same social state; these consequences differ vastly from each other, but both originate from the same fact.

The Anglo-Americans who were the first to be faced with the above-mentioned alternatives were lucky enough to escape absolute power. Circumstances, origin, education, and above all mores allowed them to establish and maintain the sovereignty of the people.

THE NORTHWEST ORDINANCE (1787)

The Northwest Ordinance, passed by the Continental Congress in 1787 and the first U.S. Congress in 1789, organized the territory north of the Ohio River, which was later divided into states. It is often cited by those who do not believe that the separation of church and state also means a complete separation between religion and the state.

. . . And, for extending the fundamental principles of civil and religious liberty, which form the basis whereon these republics, their laws and constitutions are erected; to fix and establish those principles as the basis of all laws, constitutions, and governments, which forever hereafter shall be formed in the said territory: to provide also for the establishment of States, and permanent government therein, and for their admission to a share in the federal councils on an equal footing with the original States, at as early periods as may be consistent with the general interest:

It is hereby ordained and declared by the authority aforesaid, That the following articles shall be considered as articles of compact between the original States and the people and the States in the said territory and forever remain unalterable, unless by common consent, to wit:

ART. 1.   No person, demeaning himself in a peaceable and orderly manner shall ever be molested on account of his mode of worship or religious sentiments, in the said territory.

ART. 2.   The inhabitants of the said territory shall always be entitled to the benefits of the writ of *habeas corpus*, and of the trial by jury; of a proportionate representation of the people in the legislature; and of judicial proceedings according to the course of the common law. All persons shall be bailable, unless for capital offences, where the proof shall be evident or the presumption great. All fines shall be moderate; and no cruel or unusual punishments shall be inflicted. No man shall be deprived of his liberty or property, but by the judgement of his peers or the law of the land; and, should the public exigencies make it necessary, for the common preservation, to take any person's property, or to demand his particular services, full compensation shall be made for the same. And, in the just preservation of rights and property, it is understood and declared, that no law ought ever to be made, or have force in said territory, that shall, in any manner whatever, interfere with or affect private contracts or engagements, *bona fide*, and without fraud, previously formed.

ART. 3. Religion, morality, and knowledge being necessary to good government and the happiness of mankind, schools and the means of education shall forever be encouraged. The utmost good faith shall always be observed towards the Indians; their lands and property shall never be taken from them without their consent; and, in their property, rights, and liberty, they shall never be invaded or disturbed, unless in just and lawful wars authorized by Congress; but laws founded in justice and humanity, shall from time to time be made for preventing wrongs being done to them, and for preserving peace and friendship with them. . . .

FEDERALIST 9

The Federalist is a series of 85 papers that were originally published (1787–88) in the New York City press in support of the election of delegates to the New York State ratifying convention for the Constitution. The papers were later collected into book form. They were written by Alexander Hamilton, James Madison, and John Jay, but all published under the pseudonym "Publius." The use of one pseudonym suggests an effort by the authors to present a wholly consistent perspective in the various papers, and in this they achieved a remarkable measure of success.

The Federalist was written with at least two audiences in mind. First, it was intended as a piece of campaign literature or propaganda, to achieve the immediate result of constitutional ratification. Second, it was intended to preserve the force of the Constitution by showing thoughtful individuals in future generations the Constitution's full purpose. So the papers were written quickly, but very carefully.

A Firm Union will be of the utmost moment to the peace and liberty of the States as a barrier against domestic faction and insurrection. It is impossible to read the history of the petty Republics of Greece and Italy, without feeling sensations of horror and disgust at the distractions with which they were continually agitated, and at the rapid succession of revolutions, by which they were kept in a state of perpetual vibration, between the extremes of tyranny and anarchy. If they exhibit occasional calms, these only serve as short-lived contrasts to the furious storms that are to succeed. If now and then intervals of felicity open themselves to view, we behold them with a mixture of regret arising from the reflection that the pleasing scenes before us are soon to be overwhelmed by the tempestuous waves of sedition and party-rage. If momentary rays of glory break forth from the gloom, while they dazzle us with their transient and fleeting brilliancy, they at the same time admonish us to lament that the vices of government should pervert the direction and tarnish the lustre of those bright talents and exalted endowments, for which the favored soils, that produced them, have been so justly celebrated.

From the disorders that disfigure the annals of those republics, the advocates of despotism have drawn arguments, not only against the forms of republican government, but against the very principles of civil liberty. They have decried all free government, as inconsistent with the order of society, and have indulged themselves in malicious exultation over its friends and partisans. Happily for mankind, stupendous fabrics reared on the basis of liberty, which have flourished for ages, have in a few glorious instances refuted their gloomy sophisms. And, I trust, America will be the broad and solid foundation of other edifices not less magnificent, which will be equally permanent monuments of their errors.

But it is not to be denied that the portraits, they have sketched of republican government, were too just copies of the originals from which they were taken. If it had been found impracticable, to have devised models of a more perfect structure, the enlightened friends to liberty would have been obliged to abandon the cause of that species of government as indefensible. The science of politics, however, like most other sciences, has received great improvement. The efficacy of various principles is now well understood, which were either not known at all, or imperfectly known to the ancients. The regular distribution of power into distinct departments—the introduction of legislative balances and checks—the institution of courts composed of judges, holding their offices during good behavior—the representation of the people in the legislature by deputies of their own election—these are either wholly new discoveries or have made their principal progress towards perfection in modern times. They are means, and powerful means, by which the excellencies of republican government may be retained and its imperfections lessened or avoided. To this catalogue of circumstances, that tend to the amelioration of popular systems of civil government, I shall venture, however novel it may appear to some, to add one more on a principle, which has been made the foundation of an objection to the New Constitution, I mean the ENLARGEMENT OF THE ORBIT within which such systems are to revolve either in respect to the dimensions of a single State, or to the consolidation of several smaller States into one great confederacy. The latter is that which immediately concerns the object under consideration. It will however be of use to examine the principle in its application to a single State which shall be attended to in another place.

The utility of a confederacy, as well to suppress faction and to guard the internal tranquility of States, as to increase their external force and security, is in reality not a new idea. It has been practiced upon in different countries and ages, and has received the sanction of the most applauded writers, on the subject of politics. The opponents of the *plan* proposed have with great assiduity cited and circulated the observations of Montesquieu on the necessity of a contracted territory for a republican government. But they seem not to have been apprised of the sentiments of that great man expressed in another part of his work, nor to have adverted to the consequences of the principles to which they subscribe, with such ready acquiescence.

When Montesquieu recommends a small extent for republics, the standards he had in view were of dimensions, far short of the limits of almost every one of these States. Neither Virginia, Massachusetts, Pennsylvania, New York, North Carolina, nor Georgia, can by any means be compared with the models, from which he reasoned and to which the terms of his description apply. If we therefore take his ideas on this point, as the criterion of truth, we shall be driven to the alternative, either of taking refuge at once in the arms of monarchy, or of splitting ourselves into an infinity of little jealous, clashing, tumultuous commonwealths, the wretched nurseries of unceasing discord and the miserable objects of universal pity or contempt. Some of the writers, who have come forward on the other side of the question, seem to have been aware of the dilemma; and have even been bold enough to hint at the division of the larger States, as a desirable thing. Such an infatuated policy, such a desperate expedient, might, by the multiplication of petty offices, answer the view of men, who possess not qualifications to extend their influence beyond the narrow circles of personal intrigue, but it would never promote the greatness or happiness of the people of America. . . .

FEDERALIST 10

Among the numerous advantages promised by a well-constructed Union, none deserves to be more accurately developed than its tendency to break and control the violence of faction. The friend of popular governments never finds himself so much alarmed for their character and fate as when he contemplates their propensity to this dangerous vice. He will not fail, therefore, to set a due value on any plan which, without violating the principles to which he is attached, provides a proper cure for it. The instability, injustice, and confusion introduced into the public councils have, in truth, been the mortal diseases under which popular governments have everywhere perished, as they continue to be the favorite and fruitful topics from which the adversaries to liberty derive their most specious declamations. The valuable improvements made by the American constitutions on the popular models, both ancient and modern, cannot certainly be too much admired; but it would be an unwarrantable partiality to contend that they have as effectually obviated the danger on this side, as was wished and expected. Complaints are everywhere heard from our most considerate and virtuous citizens, equally the friends of public and private faith and of public and personal liberty, that our governments are too unstable, that the public good is disregarded in the conflicts of rival parties, and that measures are too often decided, not according to the rules of justice and the rights of the minor party, but by the superior force of an interested and overbearing majority. However anxiously we may wish that these complaints had no foundation, the evidence of known facts will not permit us to deny that they are in some degree true. It will be found, indeed, on a candid review of our situation, that some of the distresses under which we labor have been erroneously charged on the operation of our governments; but it will be found, at the same time, that other causes will not alone account for many of our heaviest misfortunes; and, particularly, for that prevailing and increasing distrust of public engagements and alarm for private rights which are echoed from one end of the continent to the other. These must be chiefly, if not wholly, effects of the unsteadiness and injustice with which a factious spirit has tainted our public administration.

By a faction I understand a number of citizens, whether amounting to a majority or minority of the whole, who are united and actuated by some common impulse of passion, or of interest, adverse to the rights of other citizens, or to the permanent and aggregate interests of the community.

There are two methods of curing the mischiefs of faction: the one, by removing its causes; the other, by controlling its effects.

There are again two methods of removing the causes of faction: the one, by destroying the liberty which is essential to its existence; the other, by giving to every citizen the same opinions, the same passions, and the same interests.

It could never be more truly said than of the first remedy that it was worse than the disease. Liberty is to faction what air is to fire, an ailment without which it instantly expires. But it could not be a less folly to abolish liberty, which is essential to political life, because it nourishes faction than it would be to wish the annihilation of air, which is essential to animal life, because it imparts to fire its destructive agency.

The second expedient is as impracticable as the first would be unwise. As long as the reason of man continues fallible, and he is at liberty to exercise it, different opinions will be formed. As long as the connection subsists between his reason and his self-love, his opinions and his passions will have a reciprocal influence on each other; and the former will be objects to which the latter will attach themselves. The diversity in the faculties of men, from which the rights of property originate, is not less an insuperable obstacle to a uniformity of interests. The protection of these faculties is the first object of government. From the protection of different and unequal faculties of acquiring property, the possession of different degrees and kinds of property immediately results; and from the influence of these on the sentiments and views of the respective proprietors ensues a division of the society into different interests and parties.

The latent causes of faction are thus sown in the nature of man; and we see them everywhere brought into different degrees of activity, according to the different circumstances of civil society. A zeal for different opinions concerning religion, concerning government, and many other points, as well of speculation as of practice; an attachment to different leaders ambitiously contending for preeminence and power; or to persons of other descriptions whose fortunes have been interesting to the human passions, have, in turn, divided mankind into parties, inflamed them with mutual animosity, and rendered them much more disposed to vex and oppress each other than to co-operate for their common good. So strong is this propensity of mankind to fall into mutual animosities that where no substantial occasion presents itself the most frivolous and fanciful distinctions have been sufficient to kindle their unfriendly passions and excite their most violent conflicts. But the most common and durable source of factions has been the various and unequal distribution of property. Those who hold and those who are without property have ever formed distinct interests in society. Those who are creditors, and those who are debtors, fall under a like discrimination. A landed interest, a manufacturing interest, a mercantile interest, a moneyed interest, with many lesser interests, grow up of necessity in civilized nations, and divide them into different classes, actuated by different sentiments and views. The regulation of these various and interfering interests forms the principal task of modern legislation and involves the spirit of party and faction in the necessary and ordinary operations of government.

No man is allowed to be a judge in his own cause, because his interest would certainly bias his judgment, and, not improbably, corrupt his integrity. With equal, nay with greater reason, a body of men are unfit to be both judges and parties at the same time; yet what are many of the most important acts of legislation but so many judicial determinations, not indeed concerning the rights of single persons, but concerning the rights of large bodies of citizens? And what are the different classes of legislators but advocates and parties to the causes which they determine? Is a law proposed concerning private debts? It is a question to which the creditors are parties on one side and the debtors on the other. Justice ought to hold the balance between them. Yet the parties are, and must be, themselves the judges; and the most numerous party, or in other words, the most powerful faction must be expected to prevail. Shall domestic manufacturers be encouraged, and in what degree, by restrictions on foreign manufacturers? are questions which would be differently decided by the landed and the manufacturing classes, and probably by neither with a sole regard to justice and the public good. The apportionment of taxes on the various descriptions of property is an act which seems to require the most exact impartiality; yet there is, perhaps, no legislative act in which greater opportunity and temptation are given to a predominant party to trample on the rules of justice. Every shilling with which they overburden the inferior number is a shilling saved to their own pockets.

It is in vain to say that enlightened statesmen will be able to adjust these clashing interests and render them all subservient to the public good. Enlightened statesmen will not always be at the helm. Nor, in many cases, can such an adjustment be made at all without taking into view indirect and remote considerations, which will rarely prevail over the immediate interest which one party may find in disregarding the rights of another or the good of the whole.

The inference to which we are brought is that the causes of faction cannot be removed and that relief is only to be sought in the means of controlling its *effects*.

If a faction consists of less than a majority, relief is supplied by the republican principle, which enables the majority to defeat its sinister views by regular vote. It may clog the administration, it may convulse the society; but it will be unable to execute and mask its violence under the forms of the Constitution. When a majority is included in a faction, the form of popular government, on the other hand, enables it to sacrifice to its ruling passion or interest both the public good and the rights of other citizens. To secure the public good and private rights against the danger of such a faction, and at the same time to preserve the spirit and the form of popular government, is then the great object to which our inquiries are directed. Let me add that it is the great desideratum by which alone this form of government can be rescued from the opprobrium under which it has so long labored and be recommended to the esteem and adoption of mankind.

By what means is this object attainable? Evidently by one of two only. Either the existence of the same passion or interest in a majority at the same time must be prevented, or the majority, having such coexistent passion or interest, must be rendered, by their number and local situation, unable to concert and carry into effect schemes of oppression. If the impulse and the opportunity be suffered to coincide, we well know that neither moral nor religious motives can be relied on as an adequate control. They are not found to be such on the injustice and violence of individuals, and lose their efficacy in proportion to the number combined together, that is, in proportion as their efficacy becomes needful.

From this view of the subject it may be concluded that a pure democracy, by which I mean a society consisting of a small number of citizens, who assemble and administer the government in person, can admit of no cure for the mischiefs of faction. A common passion or interest will, in almost every case, be felt by a majority of the whole; a communication and concert results from the form of government itself; and there is nothing to check the inducements to sacrifice the weaker party or an obnoxious individual. Hence it is that such democracies have ever been spectacles of turbulence and contention; have ever been found incompatible with personal security or the rights of property; and have in general been as short in their lives as they have been violent in their deaths. Theoretic politicians, who have patronized this species of government, have erroneously supposed that by reducing mankind to a perfect equality in their political rights, they would at the same time be perfectly equalized and assimilated in their possessions, their opinions, and their passions.

A republic, by which I mean a government in which the scheme of representation takes place, opens a different prospect and promises the cure for which we are seeking. Let us examine the points in which it varies from pure democracy, and we shall comprehend both the nature of the cure and the efficacy which it must derive from the Union.

The two great points of difference between a democracy and a republic are: first, the delegation of the government, in the latter, to a small number of citizens elected by the rest; secondly, the greater number of citizens and greater sphere of country over which the latter may be extended.

The effect of the first difference is, on the one hand, to refine and enlarge the public views by passing them through the medium of a chosen body of citizens, whose wisdom may best discern the true interest of their country and whose patriotism and love of justice will be least likely to sacrifice it to temporary or partial considerations. Under such a regulation it may well happen that the public voice, pronounced by the representatives of the people, will be more consonant to the public good than if pronounced by the people themselves, convened for the purpose. On the other hand, the effect may be inverted. Men of factious tempers, of local prejudices, or of sinister designs, may, by intrigue, by corruption, or by other means, first obtain the suffrages, and then betray the interests of the people. The question resulting is, whether small or extensive republics are most favorable to the election of proper guardians of the public weal; and it is clearly decided in favor of the latter by two obvious considerations.

In the first place it is to be remarked that however small the republic may be the representatives must be raised to a certain number in order to guard against the cabals of a few; and that however large it may be they must be limited to a certain number in order to guard against the confusion of a multitude. Hence, the number of representatives in the two cases not being in proportion to that of the constituents, and being proportionally greatest in the small republic, it follows that if the proportion of fit characters be not less in the large than in the small republic, the former will present a greater option, and consequently a greater probability of a fit choice.

In the next place, as each representative will be chosen by a greater number of citizens in the large than in the small republic, it will be more difficult for unworthy candidates to practice with success the vicious arts by which elections are too often carried; and the suffrages of the people being more free, will be more likely to center on men who possess the most attractive merit and the most diffusive and established characters.

It must be confessed that in this, as in most other cases, there is a mean, on both sides of which inconveniences will be found to lie. By enlarging too much the number of electors, you render the representative too little acquainted with all their local circumstances and lesser interests; as by reducing it too much, you render him unduly attached to these, and too little fit to comprehend and pursue great and national objects. The federal Constitution forms a happy combination in this respect; the great and aggregate interests being referred to the national, the local and particular to the State legislatures.

The other point of difference is the greater number of citizens and extent of territory which may be brought within the compass of republican than of democratic government; and it is this circumstance principally which renders factious combinations less to be dreaded in the former than in the latter. The smaller the society, the fewer probably will be the distinct parties and interests composing it; the fewer the distinct parties and interests, the more frequently will a majority be found of the same party; and the smaller the number of individuals composing a majority, and the smaller the compass within which they are placed, the more easily will they concert and execute their plans of oppression. Extend the sphere and you take in a greater variety of parties and interests; you make it less probable that a majority of the whole will have a common motive to invade the rights of other citizens; or if such a common motive exists, it will be more difficult for all who feel it to discover their own strength and to act in unison with each other. Besides other impediments, it may be remarked that, where there is a consciousness of unjust or dishonorable purposes, communication is always checked by distrust in proportion to the number whose concurrence is necessary.

Hence, it clearly appears that the same advantage which a republic has over a democracy in controlling the effects of faction is enjoyed by a large over a small republic—is enjoyed by the Union over the States composing it. Does this advantage consist in the substitution of representatives whose enlightened views and virtuous sentiments render them superior to local prejudices and to schemes of injustice? It will not be denied that the representation of the Union will be most likely to possess these requisite endowments.

Does it consist in the greater security afforded by a greater variety of parties, against the event of any one party being able to outnumber and oppress the rest? In an equal degree does the increased variety of parties comprised within the Union increase this security. Does it, in fine, consist in the greater obstacles opposed to the concert and accomplishment of the secret wishes of an unjust and interested majority? Here again the extent of the Union gives it the most palpable advantage.

The influence of factious leaders may kindle a flame within their particular States but will be unable to spread a general conflagration through the other States. A religious sect may degenerate into a political faction in a part of the Confederacy; but the variety of sects dispersed over the entire face of it must secure the national councils against any danger from that source. A rage for paper money, for an abolition of debts, for an equal division of property, or for any other improper or wicked project, will be less apt to pervade the whole body of the Union than a particular member of it, in the same proportion as such a malady is more likely to taint a particular county or district than an entire State.

In the extent and proper structure of the Union, therefore, we behold a republican remedy for the diseases most incident to republican government. And according to the degree of pleasure and pride we feel in being republicans ought to be our zeal in cherishing the spirit and supporting the character of federalists.

FEDERALIST 47

Having reviewed the general form of the proposed government and the general mass of power allotted to it, I proceed to examine the particular structure of this government, and the distribution of this mass of power among its constituent parts.

One of the principal objections inculcated by the more respectable adversaries to the Constitution is its supposed violation of the political maxim that the legislative, executive, and judiciary departments ought to be separate and distinct. In the structure of the federal government no regard, it is said, seems to have been paid to this essential precaution in favor of liberty. The several departments of power are distributed and blended in such a manner as at once to destroy all symmetry and beauty of form, and to expose some of the essential parts of the edifice to the danger of being crushed by the disproportionate weight of other parts.

No political truth is certainly of greater intrinsic value, or is stamped with the authority of more enlightened patrons of liberty than that on which the objection is founded. The accumulation of all powers, legislative, executive, and judiciary, in the same hands, whether of one, a few, or many, and whether hereditary, self-appointed, or elective, may justly be pronounced the very definition of tyranny. Were the federal Constitution, therefore, really chargeable with this accumulation of power, or with a mixture of powers, having a dangerous tendency to such an accumulation, no further arguments would be necessary to inspire a universal reprobation of the system. I persuade myself, however, that it will be made apparent to everyone that the charge cannot be supported, and that the maxim on which it relies has been totally misconceived and misapplied. In order to form correct ideas on this important subject it will be proper to investigate the sense in which the preservation of liberty requires that the three great departments of power should be separate and distinct.

The oracle who is always consulted and cited on this subject is the celebrated Montesquieu. If he be not the author of this invaluable precept in the science of politics, he has the merit at least of displaying and recommending it most effectually to the attention of mankind. Let us endeavor, in the first place, to ascertain his meaning on this point.

The British Constitution was to Montesquieu what Homer has been to the didactic writers on epic poetry. As the latter have considered the work of the immortal bard as the perfect model from which the principles and rules of the epic art were to be drawn, and by which all similar works were to be judged, so this great political critic appears to have viewed the Constitution of England as the standard, or to use his own expression, as the mirror of political liberty; and to have delivered, in the form of elementary truth, the several characteristic principles of that particular system. That we may be sure, then, not to mistake his meaning in this case, let us recur to the source from which the maxim was drawn.

On the slightest view of the British Constitution, we must perceive that the legislative, executive, and judiciary departments are by no means totally separate and distinct from each other. The executive magistrate forms an integral part of the legislative authority. He alone has the prerogative of making treaties with foreign sovereigns which, when made, have, under certain limitations, the force of legislative acts. All the members of the judiciary department are appointed by him, can be removed by him on the address of the two Houses of Parliament, and form, when he pleases to consult them, one of his constitutional councils. One branch of the legislative department forms also a great constitutional council to the executive chief, as, on another hand, it is the sole depositary of judicial power in cases of impeachment, and is invested with the supreme appellate jurisdiction in all other cases. The judges, again, are so far connected with the legislative department as often to attend and participate in its deliberations, though not admitted to a legislative vote.

From these facts, by which Montesquieu was guided, it may clearly be inferred that in saying "There can be no liberty where the legislative and executive powers are united in the same person, or body of magistrates," or, "if the power of judging be not separated from the legislative and executive powers," he did not mean that these departments ought to have no partial agency in, or no control over, the acts of each other. His meaning, as his own words import, and still more conclusively as illustrated by the example in his eye, can amount to no more than this, that where the whole power of one department is exercised by the same hands which possess the whole power of another department, the fundamental principles of a free constitution are subverted. This would have been the case in the constitution examined by him, if the king, who is the sole executive magistrate, had possessed also the complete legislative power, or the supreme administration of justice; or if the entire legislative body had possessed the supreme judiciary, or the supreme executive authority. This, however, is not among the vices of that constitution. The magistrate in whom the whole executive power resides cannot of himself make a law, though he can put a negative on every law; nor administer justice in person, though he has the appointment of those who do administer it. The judges can exercise no executive prerogative, though they are shoots from the executive stock; nor any legislative function, though they may be advised by the legislative councils. The entire legislature can perform no judiciary act, though by the joint act of two of its branches the judges may be removed from their offices, and though one of its branches is possessed of the judicial power in the last resort. The entire legislature, again, can exercise no executive prerogative, though one of its branches constitutes the supreme executive magistracy, and another, on the impeachment of a third, can try and condemn all the subordinate officers in the executive department.

The reasons on which Montesquieu grounds his maxim are a further demonstration of his meaning. "When the legislative and executive powers are united in the same person or body," says he, "there can be no liberty, because apprehensions may arise lest the same monarch or senate should enact tyrannical laws to execute them in a tyrannical manner." Again: "Were the power of judging joined with the legislative, the life and liberty of the subject would be exposed to arbitrary control, for the judge would then be the legislator. Were it joined to the executive power, the judge might behave with all the violence of an oppressor." Some of these reasons are more fully explained in other passages; but briefly stated as they are here they sufficiently establish the meaning which we have put on this celebrated maxim of this celebrated author.

If we look into the constitutions of the several States we find that, notwithstanding the emphatical and, in some instances, the unqualified terms in which this axiom has been laid down, there is not a single instance in which the several departments of power have been kept absolutely separate and distinct. New Hampshire, whose constitution was the last formed, seems to have been fully aware of the impossibility and inexpediency of avoiding any mixture whatever of these departments, and has qualified the doctrine by declaring "that the legislative, executive, and judiciary powers ought to be kept as separate from, and independent of, each other as the nature of a free government will admit; or as is consistent with that chain of connection that binds the whole fabric of the constitution in one indissoluble bond of unity and amity." Her constitution accordingly mixes these departments in several respects. The Senate, which is a branch of the legislative department, is also a judicial tribunal for the trial of impeachments. The President, who is the head of the executive department, is the presiding member also of the Senate; and, besides an equal vote in all cases, has a casting vote in case of a tie. The executive head is himself eventually elective every year by the legislative department, and his council is every year chosen by and from the members of the same department. Several of the officers of state are also appointed by the legislature. And the members of the judiciary department are appointed by the executive department.

The constitution of Massachusetts has observed a sufficient though less pointed caution in expressing this fundamental article of liberty. It declares "that the legislative department shall never exercise the executive and judicial powers, or either of them; the executive shall never exercise the legislative and judicial powers, or either of them; the judicial shall never exercise the legislative and executive powers, or either of them." This declaration corresponds precisely with the doctrine of Montesquieu, as it has been explained, and is not in a single point violated by the plan of the convention. It goes no farther than to prohibit any one of the entire departments from exercising the powers of another department. In the very Constitution to which it is prefixed, a partial mixture of powers has been admitted. The executive magistrate has a qualified negative on the legislative body, and the Senate, which is a part of the legislature, is a court of impeachment for members both of the executive and judiciary departments. The members of the judiciary department, again, are appointable by the executive department, and removable by the same authority on the address of the two legislative branches. Lastly, a number of the officers of government are annually appointed by the legislative department. As the appointment to offices, particularly executive offices, is in its nature an executive function, the compilers of the Constitution have, in this last point at least, violated the rule established by themselves.

I pass over the constitutions of Rhode Island and Connecticut, because they were formed prior to the Revolution and even before the principle under examination had become an object of political attention.

The constitution of New York contains no declaration on this subject, but appears very clearly to have been framed with an eye to the danger of improperly blending the different departments. It gives, nevertheless, to the executive magistrate, a partial control over the legislative department; and, what is more, gives a like control to the judiciary department; and even blends the executive and judiciary departments in the exercise of this control. In its council of appointment members of the legislative are associated with the executive authority, in the appointment of officers, both executive and judiciary. And its court for the trial of impeachments and correction of errors is to consist of one branch of the legislature and the principal members of the judiciary department.

The constitution of New Jersey has blended the different powers of government more than any of the preceding. The governor, who is the executive magistrate, is appointed by the legislature; is chancellor and ordinary, or surrogate of the State; is a member of the Supreme Court of Appeals, and president, with a casting vote, of one of the legislative branches. The same legislative branch acts again as executive council to the governor, and with him constitutes the Court of Appeals. The members of the judiciary department are appointed by the legislative department, and removable by one branch of it, on the impeachment of the other.

According to the constitution of Pennsylvania, the president, who is the head of the executive department, is annually elected by a vote in which the legislative department predominates. In conjunction with an executive council, he appoints the members of the judiciary department and forms a court of impeachment for trial of all officers, judiciary as well as executive. The judges of the Supreme Court and justices of the peace seem also to be removable by the legislature; and the executive power of pardoning, in certain cases, to be referred to the same department. The members of the executive council are made EX OFFICIO justices of peace throughout the State.

In Delaware, the chief executive magistrate is annually elected by the legislative department. The speakers of the two legislative branches are vice-presidents in the executive department. The executive chief, with six others appointed, three by each of the legislative branches, constitutes the Supreme Court of Appeals; he is joined with the legislative department in the appointment of the other judges. Throughout the States it appears that the members of the legislature may at the same time be justices of the peace; in this State, the members of one branch of it are EX OFFICIO justices of the peace; as are also the members of the executive council. The principal officers of the executive department are appointed by the legislative; and one branch of the latter forms a court of impeachments. All officers may be removed on address of the legislature.

Maryland has adopted the maxim in the most unqualified terms; declaring that the legislative, executive, and judicial powers of government ought to be forever separate and distinct from each other. Her constitution, notwithstanding, makes the executive magistrate appointable by the legislative department; and the members of the judiciary by the executive department.

The language of Virginia is still more pointed on this subject. Her constitution declares "that the legislative, executive, and judiciary departments shall be separate and distinct; so that neither exercises the powers properly belonging to the other; nor shall any person exercise the powers of more than one of them at the same time, except that the justices of county courts shall be eligible to either House of Assembly." Yet we find not only this express exception with respect to the members of the inferior courts, but that the chief magistrate, with his executive council, are appointable by the legislature; that two members of the latter are triennially displaced at the pleasure of the legislature; and that all the principal offices, both executive and judiciary, are filled by the same department. The executive prerogative of pardon, also, is in one case vested in the legislative department.

The constitution of North Carolina, which declares "that the legislative, executive, and supreme judicial powers of government ought to be forever separate and distinct from each other," refers, at the same time, to the legislative department, the appointment not only of the executive chief, but all the principal officers within both that and the judiciary department.

In South Carolina, the constitution makes the executive magistracy eligible by the legislative department. It gives to the latter, also, the appointment of the members of the judiciary department, including even justices of the peace and sheriffs; and the appointment of officers in the executive department, down to captains in the army and navy of the State.

In the constitution of Georgia where it is declared "that the legislative, executive, and judiciary departments shall be separate and distinct, so that neither exercise the powers properly belonging to the other," we find that the executive department is to be filled by appointments of the legislature; and the executive prerogative of pardon to be finally exercised by the same authority. Even justices of the peace are to be appointed by the legislature.

In citing these cases, in which the legislative, executive, and judiciary departments have not been kept totally separate and distinct, I wish not to be regarded as an advocate for the particular organizations of the several State governments. I am fully aware that among the many excellent principles which they exemplify they carry strong marks of the haste, and still stronger of the inexperience, under which they were framed. It is but too obvious that in some instances the fundamental principle under consideration has been violated by too great a mixture, and even an actual consolidation of the different powers; and that in no instance has a competent provision been made for maintaining in practice the separation delineated on paper. What I have wished to evince is that the charge brought against the proposed Constitution of violating the sacred maxim of free government is warranted neither by the real meaning annexed to that maxim by its author, nor by the sense in which it has hitherto been understood in America. This interesting subject will be resumed in the ensuing paper.

FEDERALIST 48

It was shown in the last paper that the political apothegm there examined does not require that the legislative, executive, and judiciary departments should be wholly unconnected with each other. I shall undertake, in the next place, to show that unless these departments be so far connected and blended as to give to each a constitutional control over the others, the degree of separation which the maxim requires, as essential to a free government, can never in practice be duly maintained.

It is agreed on all sides that the powers properly belonging to one of the departments ought not to be directly and completely administered by either of the other departments. It is equally evident that none of them ought to possess, directly or indirectly, an overruling influence over the others in the administration of their respective powers. It will not be denied that power is of an encroaching nature and that it ought to be effectually restrained from passing the limits assigned to it. After discriminating, therefore, in theory, the several classes of power, as they may in their nature be legislative, executive, or judiciary, the next and most difficult task is to provide some practical security for each, against the invasion of the others. What this security ought to be is the great problem to be solved.

Will it be sufficient to mark, with precision, the boundaries of these departments in the constitution of the government, and to trust to these parchment barriers against the encroaching spirit of power? This is the security which appears to have been principally relied on by the compilers of most of the American constitutions. But experience assures us that the efficacy of the provision has been greatly overrated; and that some more adequate defense is indispensably necessary for the more feeble against the more powerful members of the government. The legislative department is everywhere extending the sphere of its activity and drawing all power into its impetuous vortex.

The founders of our republics have so much merit for the wisdom which they have displayed that no task can be less pleasing than that of pointing out the errors into which they have fallen. A respect for truth, however, obliges us to remark that they seem never for a moment to have turned their eyes from the danger, to liberty, from the overgrown and all-grasping prerogative of an hereditary magistrate, supported and fortified by an hereditary branch of the legislative authority. They seem never to have recollected the danger from legislative usurpations, which, by assembling all power in the same hands, must lead to the same tyranny as is threatened by executive usurpations.

In a government where numerous and extensive prerogatives are placed in the hands of an hereditary monarch, the executive department is very justly regarded as the source of danger, and watched with all the jealousy which a zeal for liberty ought to inspire. In a democracy, where a multitude of people exercise in person the legislative functions and are continually exposed, by their incapacity for regular deliberation and concerted measures, to the ambitious intrigues of their executive magistrates, tyranny may well be apprehended, on some favorable emergency, to start up in the same quarter. But in a representative republic where the executive magistracy is carefully limited, both in the extent and the duration of its power; and where the legislative power is exercised by an assembly, which is inspired by a supposed influence over the people with an intrepid confidence in its own strength; which is sufficiently numerous to feel all the passions which actuate a multitude, yet not so numerous as to be incapable of pursuing the objects of its passions by means which reason prescribes; it is against the enterprising ambition of this department that the people ought to indulge all their jealousy and exhaust all their precautions.

The legislative department derives a superiority in our governments from other circumstances. Its constitutional powers being at once more extensive, and less susceptible of precise limits, it can, with the greater facility, mask, under complicated and indirect measures, the encroachments which it makes on the co-ordinate departments. It is not unfrequently a question of real nicety in legislative bodies whether the operation of a particular measure will, or will not, extend beyond the legislative sphere. On the other side, the executive power being restrained within a narrower compass and being more simple in its nature, and the judiciary being described by landmarks still less uncertain, projects of usurpation by either of these departments would immediately betray and defeat themselves. Nor is this all: as the legislative department alone has access to the pockets of the people, and has in some constitutions full discretion, and in all a prevailing influence, over the pecuniary rewards of those who fill the other departments, a dependence is thus created in the latter, which gives still greater facility to encroachments of the former.

I have appealed to our own experience for the truth of what I advance on this subject. Were it necessary to verify this experience by particular proofs, they might be multiplied without end. I might collect vouchers in abundance from the records and archives of every State in the Union. But as a more concise and at the same time equally satisfactory evidence, I will refer to the example of two States, attested by two unexceptionable authorities.

The first example is that of Virginia, a State which, as we have seen, has expressly declared in its constitution that the three great departments ought not to be intermixed. The authority in support of it is Mr. Jefferson, who, besides his other advantages for remarking the operation of the government, was himself the chief magistrate of it. In order to convey fully the ideas with which his experience had impressed him on this subject it will be necessary to quote a passage of some length from his very interesting *Notes on the State of Virginia.* "All the powers of government, legislative, executive, and judiciary, result to the legislative body. The concentrating of these in the same hands is precisely the definition of despotic government. It will be no alleviation that these powers will be exercised by a plurality of hands, and not by a single one. One hundred and seventy-three despots would surely be as oppressive as one. Let those who doubt it turn their eyes on the republic of Venice. As little will it avail us that they are chosen by ourselves. An elective despotism was not the government we fought for; but one which should not only be founded on free principles, but in which the powers of government should be so divided and balanced among several bodies of magistracy as that no one could transcend their legal limits without being effectually checked and restrained by the others. For this reason that convention which passed the ordinance of government laid its foundation on this basis, that the legislative, executive, and judiciary departments should be separate and distinct, so that no person should exercise the powers of more than one of them at the same time. But no barrier was provided between these several powers. The judiciary and the executive members were left dependent on the legislative for their subsistence in office, and some of them for their continuance in it. If, therefore, the legislature assumes executive and judiciary powers, no opposition is likely to be made; nor, if made, can be effectual; because in that case they may put their proceedings into the form of acts of Assembly, which will render them obligatory on the other branches. They have accordingly, in many instances, decided rights which should have been left to judiciary controversy, and the direction of the executive, during the whole time of their session, is becoming habitual and familiar."

The other State which I shall have for an example is Pennsylvania; and the other authority, the Council of Censors, which assembled in the years 1783 and 1784. A part of the duty of this body, as marked out by the Constitution, was "to inquire whether the Constitution had been preserved inviolate in every part; and whether the legislative and executive branches of government had performed their duty as guardians of the people, or assumed to themselves, or exercised, other or greater powers than they are entitled to by the Constitution." In the execution of this trust, the council were necessarily led to a comparison of both the legislative and executive proceedings with the constitutional powers of these departments; and from the facts enumerated, and to the truth of most of which both sides in the council subscribed, it appears that the Constitution had been flagrantly violated by the legislature in a variety of important instances.

A great number of laws had been passed violating, without any apparent necessity, the rule requiring that all bills of a public nature shall be previously printed for the consideration of the people; although this is one of the precautions chiefly relied on by the Constitution against improper acts of the legislature.

The constitutional trial by jury had been violated and powers assumed which had not been delegated by the Constitution.

Executive powers had been usurped.

The salaries of the judges, which the Constitution expressly requires to be fixed, had been occasionally varied; and cases belonging to the judiciary department frequently drawn within legislative cognizance and determination.

Those who wish to see the several particulars falling under each of these heads may consult the journals of the council which are in print. Some of them, it will be found, may be imputable to peculiar circumstances connected with the war; but the greater part of them may be considered as the spontaneous shoots of an ill-constituted government.

It appears, also, that the executive department had not been innocent of frequent breaches of the Constitution. There are three observations, however, which ought to be made on this head: first, a great proportion of the instances were either immediately produced by the necessities of the war, or recommended by Congress or the commander-in-chief; second, in most of the other instances they conformed either to the declared or the known sentiments of the legislative department; third, the executive department of Pennsylvania is distinguished from that of the other States by the number of members composing it. In this respect, it has as much affinity to a legislative assembly as to an executive council. And being at once exempt from the restraint of an individual responsibility for the acts of the body, and deriving confidence from mutual example and joint influence, unauthorized measures would, of course, be more freely hazarded, than where the executive department is administered by a single hand, or by a few hands.

The conclusion which I am warranted in drawing from these observations is that a mere demarcation on parchment of the constitutional limits of the several departments is not a sufficient guard against those encroachments which lead to a tyrannical concentration of all the powers of government in the same hands.

FEDERALIST 49

The author of the *Notes on the State of Virginia* [Thomas Jefferson], quoted in the past paper, has subjoined to that valuable work the draught of a constitution, which had been prepared in order to be laid before a convention expected to be called in 1783, by the legislature, for the establishment of a constitution for that commonwealth. The plan, like everything from the same pen, marks a turn of thinking, original, comprehensive, and accurate; and is the more worthy of attention as it equally displays a fervent attachment to republican government and an enlightened view of the dangerous propensities against which it ought to be guarded. One of the precautions which he proposes, and on which he appears ultimately to rely as a palladium to the weaker departments of power against the invasions of the stronger, is perhaps altogether his own, and as it immediately relates to the subject of our present inquiry, ought not to be overlooked.

His proposition is "that whenever any two of the three branches of government shall concur in opinion, each by the voices of two thirds of their whole number, that a convention is necessary for altering the Constitution, or correcting breaches of it, a convention shall be called for the purpose."

As the people are the only legitimate fountain of power, and it is from them that the constitutional charter, under which the several branches of government hold their power, is derived, it seems strictly consonant to the republican theory to recur to the same original authority, not only whenever it may be necessary to enlarge, diminish, or new-model the powers of government, but also whenever any one of the departments may commit encroachments on the chartered authorities of the others. The several departments being perfectly co-ordinate by the terms of their common commission, neither of them, it is evident, can pretend to an exclusive or superior right of settling the boundaries between their respective powers; and how are the encroachments of the stronger to be prevented, or the wrongs of the weaker to be redressed, without an appeal to the people themselves, who, as the grantors of the commission, can alone declare its true meaning, and enforce its observance?

There is certainly great force in this reasoning, and it must be allowed to prove that a constitutional road to the decision of the people ought to be marked out and kept open, for certain great and extraordinary occasions. But there appear to be insuperable objections against the proposed recurrence to the people, as a provision in all cases for keeping the several departments of power within their constitutional limits.

In the first place, the provision does not reach the case of a combination of two of the departments against the third. If the legislative authority, which possesses so many means of operating on the motives of the other departments, should be able to gain to its interest either of the others, or even one third of its members, the remaining department could derive no advantage from this remedial provision. I do not dwell, however, on this objection, because it may be thought to lie rather against the modification of the principle, than against the principle itself.

In the next place, it may be considered as an objection inherent in the principle that as every appeal to the people would carry an implication of some defect in the government, frequent appeals would, in great measure, deprive the government of that veneration which time bestows on everything, and without which perhaps the wisest and freest governments would not possess the requisite stability. If it be true that all governments rest on opinion, it is no less true that the strength of opinion in each individual, and its practical influence on his conduct, depend much on the number which he supposes to have entertained the same opinion. The reason of man, like man himself, is timid and cautious when left alone, and acquires firmness and confidence in proportion to the number with which it is associated. When the examples which fortify opinion are ancient as well as numerous, they are known to have a double effect. In a nation of philosophers, this consideration ought to be disregarded. A reverence for the laws would be sufficiently inculcated by the voice of an enlightened reason. But a nation of philosophers is as little to be expected as the philosophical race of kings wished for by Plato. And in every other nation, the most rational government will not find it a superfluous advantage to have the prejudices of the community on its side.

The danger of disturbing the public tranquility by interesting too strongly the public passions is a still more serious objection against a frequent reference of constitutional questions to the decision of the whole society. Notwithstanding the success which has attended the revisions of our established forms of government and which does so much honor to the virtue and intelligence of the people of America, it must be confessed that the experiments are of too ticklish a nature to be unnecessarily multiplied. We are to recollect that all the existing constitutions were formed in the midst of a danger which repressed the passions most unfriendly to order and concord; of an enthusiastic confidence of the people in their patriotic leaders, which stifled the ordinary diversity of opinions on great national questions; of a universal ardor for new and opposite forms, produced by a universal resentment and indignation against the ancient government; and whilst no spirit of party connected with the changes to be made, or the abuses to be reformed, could mingle its leaven in the operation. The future situations in which we must expect to be usually placed do not present any equivalent security against the danger which is apprehended.

But the greatest objection of all is that the decisions which would probably result from such appeals would not answer the purpose of maintaining the constitutional equilibrium of the government. We have seen that the tendency of republican governments is to an aggrandizement of the legislative at the expense of the other departments. The appeals to the people, therefore, would usually be made by the executive and judiciary departments. But whether made by one side or the other, would each side enjoy equal advantages on the trial? Let us view their different situations. The members of the executive and judiciary departments are few in number, and can be personally known to a small part only of the people. The latter, by the mode of their appointment, as well as by the nature and permanence of it, are too far removed from the people to share much in their prepossessions. The former are generally the objects of jealousy and their administration is always liable to be discolored and rendered unpopular. The members of the legislative department, on the other hand, are numerous. They are distributed and dwell among the people at large. Their connections of blood, of friendship, and of acquaintance embrace a great proportion of the most influential part of the society. The nature of their public trust implies a personal influence among the people, and that they are more immediately the confidential guardians of the rights and liberties of the people. With these advantages it can hardly be supposed that the adverse party would have an equal chance for a favorable issue.

But the legislative party would not only be able to plead their cause most successfully with the people. They would probably be constituted themselves the judges. The same influence which had gained them an election into the legislature would gain them a seat in the convention. If this should not be the case with all, it would probably be the case with many, and pretty certainly with those leading characters, on whom everything depends in such bodies. The convention, in short, would be composed chiefly of men who had been, who actually were, or who expected to be, members of the department whose conduct was arraigned. They would consequently be parties to the very question to be decided by them.

It might, however, sometimes happen, that appeals would be made under circumstances less adverse to the executive and judiciary departments. The usurpations of the legislature might be so flagrant and so sudden, as to admit of no specious coloring. A strong party among themselves might take side with the other branches. The executive power might be in the hands of a peculiar favorite of the people. In such a posture of things, the public decision might be less swayed by prepossessions in favor of the legislative party. But still it could never be expected to turn on the true merits of the question. It would inevitably be connected with the spirit of pre-existing parties, or of parties springing out of the question itself. It would be connected with persons of distinguished character and extensive influence in the community. It would be pronounced by the very men who had been agents in, or opponents of, the measures to which the decision would relate. The passions, therefore, not the reason, of the public would sit in judgment. But it is the reason, alone, of the public, that ought to control and regulate the government. The passions ought to be controlled and regulated by the government.

We found in the last paper that mere declarations in the written Constitution are not sufficient to restrain the several departments within their legal rights. It appears in this that occasional appeals to the people would be neither a proper nor an effectual provision for that purpose. How far the provisions of a different nature contained in the plan above quoted might be adequate I do not examine. Some of them are unquestionably founded on sound political principles, and all of them are framed with singular ingenuity and precision.

FEDERALIST 51

To what expedient, then, shall we finally resort, for maintaining in practice the necessary partition of power among the several departments as laid down in the Constitution? The only answer that can be given is that as all these exterior provisions are found to be inadequate the defect must be supplied, by so contriving the interior structure of the government as that its several constituent parts may, by their mutual relations, be the means of keeping each other in their proper places. Without presuming to undertake a full development of this important idea I will hazard a few general observations which may perhaps place it in a clearer light, and enable us to form a more correct judgment of the principles and structure of the government planned by the convention.

In order to lay a due foundation for that separate and distinct exercise of the different powers of government, which to a certain extent is admitted on all hands to be essential to the preservation of liberty, it is evident that each department should have a will of its own; and consequently should be so constituted that the members of each should have as little agency as possible in the appointment of the members of the others. Were this principle rigorously adhered to, it would require that all the appointments for the supreme executive, legislative, and judiciary magistracies should be drawn from the same fountain of authority, the people, through channels having no communication whatever with one another. Perhaps such a plan of constructing the several departments would be less difficult in practice than it may in contemplation appear. Some difficulties, however, and some additional expense would attend the execution of it. Some deviations, therefore, from the principle must be admitted. In the constitution of the judiciary department in particular, it might be inexpedient to insist rigorously on the principle: first, because peculiar qualifications being essential in the members, the primary consideration ought to be to select that mode of choice which best secures these qualifications; second, because the permanent tenure by which the appointments are held in that department must soon destroy all sense of dependence on the authority conferring them.

It is equally evident that the members of each department should be as little dependent as possible on those of the others for the emoluments annexed to their offices. Were the executive magistrate, or the judges, not independent of the legislature in this particular, their independence in every other would be merely nominal.

But the great security against a gradual concentration of the several powers in the same department consists in giving to those who administer each department the necessary constitutional means and personal motives to resist encroachments of the others. The provision for defense must in this, as in all other cases, be made commensurate to the danger of attack. Ambition must be made to counteract ambition. The interest of the man must be connected with the constitutional rights of the place. It may be a reflection on human nature that such devices should be necessary to control the abuses of government. But what is government itself but the greatest of all reflections on human nature? If men were angels, no government would be necessary. If angels were to govern men, neither external nor internal controls on government would be necessary. In framing a government which is to be administered by men over men, the great difficulty lies in this: you must first enable the government to control the governed; and in the next place oblige it to control itself. A dependence on the people is, no doubt, the primary control on the government; but experience has taught mankind the necessity of auxiliary precautions.

This policy of supplying, by opposite and rival interests, the defect of better motives, might be traced through the whole system of human affairs, private as well as public. We see it particularly displayed in all the subordinate distributions of power, where the constant aim is to divide and arrange the several offices in such a manner as that each may be a check on the other—that the private interest of every individual may be a sentinel over the public rights. These inventions of prudence cannot be less requisite in the distribution of the supreme powers of the State.

But it is not possible to give to each department an equal power of self-defense. In republican government, the legislative authority necessarily predominates. The remedy for this inconvenience is to divide the legislature into different branches; and to render them, by different modes of election and different principles of action, as little connected with each other as the nature of their common functions and their common dependence on the society will admit. It may even be necessary to guard against dangerous encroachments by still further precautions. As the weight of the legislative authority requires that it should be thus divided, the weakness of the executive may require, on the other hand, that it should be fortified. An absolute negative on the legislature appears, at first view, to be the natural defense with which the executive magistrate should be armed. But perhaps it would be neither altogether safe nor alone sufficient. On ordinary occasions it might not be exerted with the requisite firmness, and on extraordinary occasions it might be perfidiously abused. May not this defect of an absolute negative be supplied by some qualified connection between this weaker department and the weaker branch of the stronger department, by which the latter may be led to support the constitutional rights of the former, without being too much detached from the rights of its own department?

If the principles on which these observations are founded be just, as I persuade myself they are, and they be applied as a criterion to the several State constitutions, and to the federal Constitution, it will be found that if the latter does not perfectly correspond with them, the former are infinitely less able to bear such a test.

There are, moreover, two considerations particularly applicable to the federal system of America, which place that system in a very interesting point of view.

First. In a single republic, all the power surrendered by the people is submitted to the administration of a single government; and the usurpations are guarded against by a division of the government into distinct and separate departments. In the compound republic of America, the power surrendered by the people is first divided between two distinct governments, and then the portion allotted to each subdivided among distinct and separate departments. Hence a double security arises to the rights of the people. The different governments will control each other, at the same time that each will be controlled by itself.

Second. It is of great importance in a republic not only to guard the society against the oppression of its rulers, but to guard one part of the society against the injustice of the other part. Different interests necessarily exist in different classes of citizens. If a majority be united by a common interest, the rights of the minority will be insecure. There are but two methods of providing against this evil: the one by creating a will in the community independent of the majority—that is, of the society itself; the other, by comprehending in the society so many separate descriptions of citizens as will render an unjust combination of a majority of the whole very improbable, if not impracticable. The first method prevails in all governments possessing an hereditary or self-appointed authority. This, at best, is but a precarious security; because a power independent of the society may as well espouse the unjust views of the major as the rightful interests of the minor party, and may possibly be turned against both parties. The second method will be exemplified in the federal republic of the United States. Whilst all authority in it will be derived from and dependent on the society, the society itself will be broken into so many parts, interests and classes of citizens, that the rights of individuals, or of the minority, will be in little danger from interested combinations of the majority. In a free government the security for civil rights must be the same as that for religious rights. It consists in the one case in the multiplicity of interests, and in the other in the multiplicity of sects. The degree of security in both cases will depend on the number of interests and sects; and this may be presumed to depend on the extent of country and number of people comprehended under the same government.

This view of the subject must particularly recommend a proper federal system to all the sincere and considerate friends of republican government, since it shows that in exact proportion as the territory of the Union may be formed into more circumscribed Confederacies, or States, oppressive combinations of a majority will be facilitated; the best security, under the republican forms, for the rights of every class of citizen, will be diminished; and consequently the stability and independence of some member of the government, the only other security, must be proportionally increased. Justice is the end of government. It is the end of civil society. It ever has been and ever will be pursued until it be obtained, or until liberty be lost in the pursuit. In a society under the forms of which the stronger faction can readily unite and oppress the weaker, anarchy may as truly be said to reign as in a state of nature, where the weaker individual is not secured against the violence of the stronger; and as, in the latter state, even the stronger individuals are prompted, by the uncertainty of their condition, to submit to a government which may protect the weak as well as themselves; so, in the former state, will the more powerful factions or parties be gradually induced, by a like motive, to wish for a government which will protect all parties, the weaker as well as the more powerful. It can be little doubted that if the State of Rhode Island was separated from the Confederacy and left to itself, the insecurity of rights under the popular form of government within such narrow limits would be displayed by such reiterated oppressions of factious majorities that some power altogether independent of the people would soon be called for by the voice of the very factions whose misrule had proved the necessity of it. In the extended republic of the United States, and among the great variety of interests, parties, and sects which it embraces, a coalition of a majority of the whole society could seldom take place on any other principles than those of justice and the general good; whilst there being thus less danger to a minor from the will of a major party, there must be less pretext, also, to provide for the security of the former, by introducing into the government a will not dependent on the latter, or, in other words, a will independent of the society itself. It is no less certain than it is important, notwithstanding the contrary opinions which have been entertained, that the larger the society, provided it lie within a practicable sphere, the more duly capable it will be of self-government. And happily for the republican cause, the practicable sphere may be carried to a very great extent by a judicious modification and mixture of the federal principle.

CENTINEL, LETTER I (PHILADELPHIA) *INDEPENDENT JOURNAL* (1787)

Centinel is the pseudonym of an Anti-Federalist author, probably Samuel Bryan. The Anti-Federalists opposed the ratification of the Constitution, primarily because they thought that the large republic could secure neither liberty nor democracy. They put a greater emphasis on the equality and virtue of citizens for the preservations of liberty than did The Federalist.

. . . [W]e see the house of representatives are on the part of the people to balance the senate, who I suppose will be composed of the *better sort, the well born, etc.* The number of the representatives (being only one for every 30,000 inhabitants) appears to be too few, either to communicate the requisite information of the wants, local circumstances, and sentiments of so extensive an empire, or to prevent corruption and undue influence in the exercise of such great powers. The term for which they are to be chosen is too long to preserve a due dependence and accountability to their constituents, and the mode and places of their election are not sufficiently ascertained; for as Congress have the control over both, they may govern the choice by ordering the *representatives* of a *whole* state to be *elected in one* place and that too may be the most *inconvenient*.

The senate, the great efficient body in this plan of government, is constituted on the most unequal principles. The smallest state in the union has equal weight with the great states of Virginia, Massachusetts or Pennsylvania. The Senate, besides its legislative functions, has a very considerable share in the Executive; none of the principal appointments to office can be made without its advice and consent. The term and mode of its appointment will lead to permanency; the members are chosen for six years, the mode is under the control of Congress, and as there is no exclusion by rotation, they may be continued for life, which, from their extensive means of influence, would follow of course. The President, who would be a mere pageant of state, unless he coincides with the view of the Senate, would either become the head of the aristocratic junto in that body or its minion; besides, their influence being the most predominant could best secure his re-election to office. And from his power of granting pardons, he might screen from punishment the most treasonable attempts on the liberties of the people when instigated by the Senate.

From this investigation into the organization of this government, it appears that it is devoid of all responsibility or accountability to the great body of the people, and that so far from being a regular balanced government, it would be in practice a *permanent ARISTOCRACY*.

The framers of it, actuated by the true spirit of such a government, which ever abominates and suppresses all free inquiry and discussion, have no provision for the *liberty of the press*, that grand *palladium of freedom and scourge of tyrants*; but observed a total silence on that head. . . .

[Our] situation is represented to be so critically dreadful that,

however reprehensible and exceptionable the proposed plan of government may be, there is no alternative between the adoption of it and absolute ruin. My fellow citizens, things are not at that crisis. It is the argument of tyrants. The present distracted state of Europe secures us from injury on that quarter, as to domestic dissensions, we have not so much to fear from them, as to precipitate us in this form of government, without it is a safe and a proper one. For remember, of all *possible* evils, that of *despotism* is the *worst* and the most to be *dreaded*. . . .

A republican or free government can only exist where the body of the people are virtuous and where property is pretty equally divided; in such a government the people are the sovereign and their sense or opinion is the criterion of every public measure. When this ceases to be the case, the nature of the government is changed, and an aristocracy, monarchy or despotism will rise on its ruin. The highest responsibility is to be attained in a simple structure of government, for the great body of the people never steadily attend to the operations of government and for want of due information are liable to be imposed on. If you complicate the plan by various orders, the people will be perplexed and divided in their sentiments about the source of abuses or misconduct; some will impute it to the Senate, others to the house of representatives, and so on, that the interposition of the people may be rendered imperfect or perhaps wholly abortive. But if imitating the constitution of Pennsylvania, you vest all of the legislative power in one body of men (separating the executive and judicial) elected for a short period, and necessarily excluded by rotation from permanency, and guarded from precipitancy and surprise by delays imposed on its proceedings, you will create the most perfect responsibility, for then whenever the people feel a grievance they cannot mistake the authors and will apply the remedy with certainty and effect, discarding them at the next election. This tie of responsibility will obviate all the dangers apprehended from a single legislature, and will best secure the rights of the people.

Having premised this much, I shall now proceed to the examination of the proposed plan of government, and I trust, shall make it appear to the meanest capacity, that it has none of the essential requisites of a free government. . . .

The late revolution having effaced in a great measure all former habits and the present institutions are so recent that there exists not that great reluctance to innovation, so remarkable in old communities, and which accords with reason, for the most comprehensive mind cannot foresee the full operation of material changes on civil polity; it is the genius of the common law to resist innovation.

The wealthy and ambitious, who in every community think they have a right to lord it over their fellow creatures, have availed themselves very successfully to this favorable disposition; for the people thus unsettled in their sentiments have been prepared to accede to any extreme of government. All the distresses and difficulties they experience, proceeding from various causes, have been ascribed to the impotency of the present confederation, and thence they have been led to expect full relief from the adoption of the proposed system of government, and in the other event, immediate ruin and annihilation as a nation. These characters flatter themselves that they have lulled all distrust and jealousy of their new plan by gaining the concurrence of the two men in whom America has the highest confidence [George Washington and Benjamin Franklin], and now triumphantly exult in the completion of their long meditated schemes of power and aggrandizement. I would be very far from insinuating that the two illustrious personages alluded to have not the welfare of their country at heart, but that the unsuspecting goodness and zeal of the one has been imposed on in a subject of which he must be necessarily inexperienced from his other arduous engagements; and that the weakness and indecision attendant on old age, has been practiced on in the other. . . .

JAMES MADISON, *ON PROPERTY* (1792)

This essay, which defines property in more comprehensive language than is usually used today, illuminates precisely what government protects—its "first object"—according to Federalist *10. Here we have Madison's perception of the relationship between economic and moral or religious liberty.*

This term in its particular application means "that dominion which one man claims and exercises over the external things of the world, in exclusion of every other individual."

In its larger and juster meaning, it embraces every thing to which a man may attach a value and have a right; and which leaves to every one else the like advantage.

In the former sense, a man's land, or merchandise, or money is called his property.

In the latter sense, a man has a property in his opinions and the free communication of them.

He has a property of peculiar value in his religious opinions, and in the profession and practice dictated by them.

He has a property very dear to him in the safety and liberty of his person.

He has an equal property in the free use of his faculties and free choice of the objects on which to employ them.

In a word, as a man is said to have a right to his property, he may be equally said to have a property in his rights.

Where an excess of power prevails, property of no sort is duly respected. No man is safe in his opinions, his person, his faculties, or his possessions.

Where there is an excess of liberty, the effect is the same, tho' from an opposite cause.

Government is instituted to protect property of every sort; as well that which lies in the various rights of individuals, as that which the term particularly expresses. This being the end of government, that alone is a *just* government, which *impartially* secures to every man, whatever is his *own*.

According to this standard of merit, the praise of affording a just securing to property, should be sparingly bestowed on a government which, however scrupulously guarding the possessions of individuals, does not protect them in the enjoyment and communication of their opinions, in which they have an equal, and in the estimation of some, a more valuable property.

More sparingly should this praise be allowed to a government, where a man's religious rights are violated by penalties, or fettered by tests, or taxed by a hierarchy. Conscience is the most sacred of all property; other property depending in part on positive law, the exercise of that, being a natural and unalienable right. To guard a man's house as his castle, to pay public and enforce private debts with the most exact faith, can give no title to invade a man's conscience which is more sacred than his castle, or to withhold from it that debt of protection, for which the public faith is pledged, by the very nature and original conditions of the social pact.

That is not a just government, nor is property secure under it, where the property which a man has in his personal safety and personal liberty, is violated by arbitrary seizures of one class of citizens for the service of the rest. A magistrate issuing his warrants to a press gang, would be in his proper functions in Turkey or Indostan, under appellations proverbial of the most complete despotism.

That is not a just government, nor is property secure under it, where arbitrary restrictions, exemptions, and monopolies deny to part of its citizens that free use of their faculties, and free choice of their occupations, which not only constitute their property in the general sense of the word; but are the means of acquiring property strictly so called. What must be the spirit of legislation where a manufacturer of cloth is forbidden to bury his own child in a linen shroud, in order to favour his neighbour who manufactures woolen cloth; where the manufacturer and wearer of woolen cloth are again forbidden the economical use of buttons of that material, in favor of the manufacturer of buttons of other materials!

A just security to property is not afforded by that government, under which unequal taxes oppress one species of property and reward another species: where arbitrary taxes invade the domestic sanctuaries of the rich, and excessive taxes grind the faces of the poor; where the keenness and competitions of want are deemed an insufficient spur to labor, and taxes are again applied, by an unfeeling policy, as another spur; in violation of that sacred property, which Heaven, in decreeing man to earn his bread by the sweat of his brow, kindly reserved to him, in the small repose that could be spared from the supply of his necessities.

If there be a government then which prides itself in maintaining the inviolability of property; which provides that none shall be taken *directly* even for public use without indemnification to the owner, and yet *directly* violates the property which individuals have in their opinions, their religion, their persons, and their faculties; nay more, which *indirectly* violates their property, in their actual possessions, in the labor that acquires their daily subsistence, and in the hallowed remnant of time which ought to relieve their fatigues and soothe their cares, the influence [inference?] will have been anticipated, that such a government is not a pattern for the United States.

If the United States mean to obtain or deserve the full praise due to wise and just governments, they will equally respect the rights of property, and the property in rights: they will rival the government that most sacredly guards the former; and by repelling its example in violating the latter, will make themselves a pattern to that and all other governments.

GEORGE WASHINGTON, FAREWELL ADDRESS (1796)

This parting message from America's first president and exemplary statesman is meant to supplement constitutional principle as guidance for his successors.

. . . Of all the dispositions and habits which lead to political prosperity, Religion and morality are indispensable supports. In vain would that man claim the tribute of Patriotism, who should labour to subvert these great Pillars of human happiness, these firmest props of the duties of Men and citizens. The mere Politician, equally with the pious man ought to respect and to cherish them. A volume could not trace all their connections with private and public felicity. Let it simply be asked where is the security for property, for reputation, for life, if the sense of religious obligations desert the oaths, which are the instruments of investigation in Courts of Justice? And let us with caution indulge the supposition, that morality can be maintained without religion. Whatever may be conceded to the influence of refined education on minds of our peculiar structure, reason and experience both forbid us to expect that National morality can prevail in exclusion of religious principle.

'Tis substantially true, that virtue or morality is a necessary spring of popular government. The rule indeed extends with more or less force to every species of free Government. Who that is a sincere friend to it, can look with indifference upon attempts to shake the foundation of the fabric?

Promote then as an object of primary importance, Institutions for the general diffusion of knowledge. In proportion as the structure of a government gives force to public opinion, it is essential that public opinion should be enlightened. . . .

THOMAS JEFFERSON, LETTER TO JOHN ADAMS (1813)

These candid words from one great statesman and thinker to another show Jefferson's faith that democracy can be compatible with human excellence and good government.

. . . For I agree with you that there is a natural aristocracy among men. The grounds of this are virtue and talents. Formerly bodily powers gave place among the aristoi. But since the invention of gunpowder has armed the weak as well as the strong with missile death, bodily strength, like beauty, good humor, politeness and other accomplishments, has become but an auxiliary ground of distinction. There is also an artificial aristocracy founded on wealth and birth, without either virtue or talents; for with these it would belong to the first class. The natural aristocracy I consider as the most precious gift of nature for the instruction, the trusts, and government of society. And indeed it would have been inconsistent in creation to have formed man for the social state, and not to have provided virtue and wisdom enough to manage the concerns of the society. May we not even say that that form of government is the best which provides the most effectually for a pure selection of these natural aristoi in the offices of government? . . .

2

Race and Gender

Most of the selections in this chapter concern the American political community's greatest inconsistency: the presence of slavery and racism in a nation "dedicated to the proposition that all men are created equal." Other selections concern the rights of women, which have also been debated throughout most of the nation's history.

DRED SCOTT v. SANDFORD (1857)

This opinion was put forth in the middle of a national debate over the place of slavery under the Constitution. The central questions focused on the constitutionality of the spread of slavery into newly organized territories. Dred Scott was a slave who sued for his freedom on the grounds that he had spent time in a free state and a free territory and hence was a free man. His claim was that, once the legal bonds of slavery have been broken, they cannot be restored. This claim and his assertion that he was therefore a citizen of the United States with a citizen's right of access to the federal courts imply that the Constitution is fundamentally antislavery in spirit.

CHIEF JUSTICE TANEY delivered the opinion of the Court. . . .

The question is simply this: Can a Negro, whose ancestors were imported into this country, and sold as slaves, become a member of the political community formed and brought into existence by the Constitution of the United States, and as such become entitled to all the rights, and privileges, and immunities, guarantied [*sic*] by that instrument to the citizen? One of which rights is the privilege of suing in a court of the United States in the cases specified in the Constitution.

We think . . . [those Negroes] . . . are not included, and were not intended to be included, under the words "citizens" in the Constitution, and can therefore claim none of the rights and privileges which that instrument provides for and secures to citizens of the United States. On the contrary, they were at that time considered as a subordinate and inferior class of beings, who had been subjugated by the dominant race, and, whether emancipated or not, yet remained subject to their authority, and had no rights or privileges but such as those who held the power and the Government might choose to grant them.

It is not the province of the court to decide upon the justice or injustice, the policy or impolicy, of these laws. The decision of that question belonged to the political or law-making power; to those who formed the sovereignty and framed the Constitution. The duty of the court is, to interpret the instrument they have framed, with the best lights we can obtain on the subject, and to administer it as we find it, according to its true intent and meaning when it was adopted. . . .

The question then arises, whether the provisions of the Constitution, in relation to the personal rights and privileges to which the citizen of a State should be entitled, embraced the Negro African race, at that time in this country, or who might afterwards be imported, who had then or should afterwards be made free in any State; and to put it in the power of a single State to make him a citizen of the United States, and endue him with the full rights of citizenship in every other State without their consent? Does the Constitution of the United States act upon him whenever he shall be made free under the laws of a State, and raised there to the rank of a citizen, and immediately clothe him with all the privileges of a citizen in every other State, and in its own courts?

The court thinks the affirmative of these propositions cannot be maintained. And if it cannot, the plaintiff in error could not be a citizen of the State of Missouri, within the meaning of the Constitution of the United States, and, consequently, was not entitled to sue in its courts. . . .

In the opinion of the court, the legislation and histories of the times, and the language used in the Declaration of Independence, show, that neither the class of persons who had been imported as slaves, nor their descendants, whether they had become free or not, were then acknowledged as a part of the people, nor intended to be included in the general words used in that memorable instrument. . . .

They had for more than a century before been regarded as beings of an inferior order, and altogether unfit to associate with the white race, either in social or political relations; and so far inferior, that they had no rights which the white man was bound to respect; and that the Negro might justly and lawfully be reduced to slavery for his benefit. He was bought and sold, and treated as an ordinary article of merchandise and traffic, whenever a profit could be made by it. This opinion was at that time fixed and universal in the civilized portion of the white race. It was regarded as an axiom in morals as well as in politics, which no one thought of disputing, or supposed to be open to dispute; and men in every grade and position in society daily and habitually acted upon it in their private pursuits, as well as in matters of public concern, without doubting for a moment the correctness of this opinion. . . .

The only two provisions [of the Constitution] which point to them and include them [Article I, Section 9, and Article IV, Section 2], treat them as property, and make it the duty of the Government to protect it; no other power, in relation to this race, is to be found in the Constitution; and as it is a Government of special, delegated, powers, no authority beyond these two provisions can be constitutionally exercised. The Government of the United States had no right to interfere for any other purpose but that of protecting the rights of the owner, leaving it altogether with the several States to deal with this race, whether emancipated or not, as each State may think justice, humanity, and the interests and safety of society, require. The States evidently intended to reserve this power exclusively to themselves.

No one, we presume, supposes that any change in public opinion or feeling, in relation to this unfortunate race, in the civilized nations of Europe or in this country, should induce the court to give to the words of the Constitution a more liberal construction in their favor than they were intended to bear when the instrument was framed and adopted. Such an argument would be altogether inadmissible in any tribunal called on to interpret it. If any of its provisions are deemed unjust, there is a mode prescribed in the instrument itself by which it may be amended; but while it remains unaltered, it must be construed now as it was understood at the time of its adoption. It is not only the same in words, but the same in meaning, and delegates the same powers to the Government, and reserves and secures the same rights and privileges to the citizen; and as long as it continues to exist in its present form, it speaks not only in the same words, but with the same meaning and intent with which it spoke when it came from the hands of its framers, and was voted on and adopted by the people of the United States. Any other rule of construction would abrogate the judicial character of this court, and make it the mere reflex of the popular opinion of the day. . . .

What the construction was at that time, we think can hardly admit of doubt. We have the language of the Declaration of Independence and of the Articles of Confederation, in addition to the plain words of the Constitution itself; we have the legislation of the different States, before, about the time, and since, the Constitution was adopted; we have the legislation of Congress, from the time of its adoption to a recent period; and we have the constant and uniform action of the Executive Department, all concurring together, and leading to the same result. And if anything in relation to the construction of the Constitution can be regarded as settled, it is that which we now give to the word "citizen" and the word "people.". . .

The act of Congress, upon which the plaintiff relies, declares that slavery and involuntary servitude, except as a punishment for crime, shall be forever prohibited in all that part of the territory ceded by France, under the name of Louisiana, which lies north of thirty-six degrees thirty minutes north latitude, and not included within the limits of Missouri. And the . . . inquiry is whether Congress was authorized to pass this law under any of the powers granted to it by the Constitution; for if the authority is not given by that instrument, it is the duty of this court to declare it void and inoperative, and incapable of conferring freedom upon any one who is held as a slave under the laws of any one of the States.

The counsel for the plaintiff has laid much stress upon that article in the Constitution which confers on Congress the power "to dispose of and make all needful rules and regulations respecting the territory or other property belonging to the United States," but, in the judgment of the court, that provision has no bearing on the present controversy, and the power there given, whatever it may be, is confined, and was intended to be confined, to the territory which at that time belonged to, or was claimed by the United States, and was within their boundaries as settled by the treaty with Great Britain, and can have no influence upon a territory afterwards acquired from a foreign Government. It was a special provision for a known and particular territory, and to meet a present emergency, and nothing more.

. . . The powers of the Government and the rights and privileges of the citizen are regulated and plainly defined by the Constitution itself. And when the Territory becomes a part of the United States, the Federal Government enters into possession in the character impressed upon it by those who created it. It enters upon it with its powers over the citizen strictly defined, and limited by the Constitution, from which it derives its own existence, and by virtue of which alone it continues to exist and act as a Government and sovereignty. It has no power of any kind beyond it; and it cannot, when it enters a Territory of the United States, put off its character and assume discretionary or despotic powers which the Constitution has denied to it. It cannot create for itself a new character separated from the citizens of the United States, and the duties it owes them under the provisions of the Constitution. The Territory being a part of the United States, the Government and the citizen both enter it under the authority of the Constitution, with their respective rights defined and marked out; and the Federal Government can exercise no power over his person or property, beyond what that instrument confers, nor lawfully deny any right which it has reserved. . . .

. . . [A]n Act of Congress which deprives a citizen of the United States of his liberty or property, merely because he came himself or brought his property into a particular Territory of the United States, and who had committed no offense against the laws, could hardly be dignified with the name of due process of law.

The powers over person and property of which we speak are not only not granted to Congress, but are in express terms denied, and they are forbidden to exercise them. And this prohibition is not confined to the States, but the words are general, and extend to the whole territory over which the Constitution gives it power to legislate, including those portions of it remaining under Territorial Government, as well as that covered by States. It is a total absence of power everywhere within the dominion of the United States, and places the citizens of a Territory, so far as these rights are concerned, on the same footing with citizens of the States and guards them as firmly and plainly against any inroads which the General Government might attempt, under the plea of implied or incidental powers. And if Congress itself cannot do this—if it is beyond the powers conferred on the Federal Government—it will be admitted, we presume, that it could not authorize a Territorial Government to exercise them. It would confer no power on any local Government, established by its authority, to violate provisions of the Constitution. . . .

No laws or usages of other nations, or reasoning of statesmen or jurists upon the relations of master and slave, can enlarge the powers of the Government, or take from the citizens the rights they have reserved. And if the Constitution recognizes the right of property of the master in a slave, and makes no distinction between that description of property and other property owned by a citizen, no tribunal, acting under the authority of the United States, whether it be legislative, executive, or judicial, has a right to draw such a distinction, or deny to it the benefit of the provisions and guarantees which have been provided for the protection of a private property against the encroachments of the Government. . . .

Upon these considerations, it is the opinion of the court that the act of Congress which prohibited a citizen from holding and owning property of this kind in the territory of the United States north of the line therein mentioned, is not warranted by the Constitution, and is therefore void; and that neither Dred Scott himself, nor any of his family, were made free by being carried into this territory; even if they had been carried there by the owner, with the intention of becoming a permanent resident.

SECTIONS OF THE U.S. CONSTITUTION
CONCERNING SLAVERY

There are only three sections of the original Constitution that concern slavery. Thoughtful reflection on their language and structure calls into question Chief Justice Taney's Dred Scott *interpretation of the Framers' intent.*

Article I, Section 2 (3)

Representatives and direct taxes shall be apportioned among the several states which may be included within this Union, according to their respective numbers, which shall be determined by adding to the whole numbers of free persons, including those bound to service for a term of years, and excluding Indians not taxed, three-fifths of all other persons. . . .

Article I, Section 9 (1)

The migration or importation of such persons as any of the states now existing shall think proper to admit, shall not be prohibited by the Congress prior to the year one thousand eight hundred and eight, but a tax or duty may be imposed on such importation, not exceeding ten dollars for each person.

Article IV, Section 2 (3)

No person held to service or labour in one state, under the laws thereof, escaping into another, shall, in consequence of any law or regulation therein, be discharged from such service or labour, but shall be delivered up on claim of the party to whom such service or labour may be due.

THOMAS JEFFERSON, DRAFT OF THE
DECLARATION OF INDEPENDENCE (1776)

This section of the Declaration was deleted to comply with the objection of the delegates to the Continental Congress from South Carolina and Georgia.

He has waged cruel war against human nature itself, violating its most sacred rights of life and liberty in the persons of a distant people who never offended him, captivating and carrying them into slavery in another hemisphere or to incur miserable death in their transportation thither. This piratical warfare, the opprobrium of infidel powers, is the warfare of the *Christian* king of Great Britain. Determined to keep open a market where *Men* should be bought and sold, he has prostituted his negative for suppressing every legislative attempt to prohibit or to restrain this execrable commerce. And that this assemblage of horrors might want no fact of distinguished die, he is now exciting those very people to rise in arms among us, and to purchase that liberty of which he has deprived them, by murdering the people on whom he also obtruded them; thus paying off former crimes committed against the *Liberties* of one people, with crimes which he urges them to commit against the *lives* of another.

THOMAS JEFFERSON, *NOTES ON THE STATE OF VIRGINIA* (1784)

Jefferson, author of the Declaration of Independence, wrote only one book, Notes on the State of Virginia. *It is organized as a series of responses to questions about Virginia that had been raised by a French theorist. Jefferson's response to Query XVIII, on Virginia's "customs and manners," is a forceful statement regarding the pernicious effects of slavery on Virginia's masters.*

It is difficult to determine on the standard by which the manners of a nation may be tried, whether catholic, or *particular.* It is more difficult for a native to bring to that standard the manners of his own nation, familiarized to him by habit. There must doubtless be an unhappy influence on the manners of our people produced by the existence of slavery among us. The whole commerce between master and slave is a perpetual exercise of the most boisterous passions, the most unremitting despotism on the one part, and degrading submissions on the other. Our children see this, and learn to imitate it; for man is an imitative animal. This quality is the germ of all education in him. From his cradle to his grave he is learning to do what he sees others do. If a parent could find no motive either in his philanthropy or his self-love, for restraining the intemperance of passion towards his slave, it should always be a sufficient one that his child is present. But generally it is not sufficient. The parent storms, the child looks on, catches the lineaments of wrath, puts on the same airs in the circle of smaller slaves, gives a loose to the worst of passions, and thus nursed, educated, and daily exercised in tyranny, cannot but be stamped by it with odious peculiarities. The man must be a prodigy who can retain his manners and morals undepraved by such circumstances. And with what execration should the statesman be loaded, who permitting one half the citizens thus to trample on the rights of the other, transforms those into despots, and these into enemies, destroys the morals of the one part, and the *amor patriae* of the other. For if a slave can have a country in this world, it must be any other in preference to that in which he is born to live and labor for another; in which he must lock up the faculties of his nature, contribute as far as depends on his individual endeavors to the evanishment of the human race, or entail his own miserable condition on the endless generations proceeding from him. With the morals of the people, their industry also is destroyed. For in a warm climate, no man will labor for himself who can make another labor for him. This is so true, that of the proprietors of slaves a very small proportion indeed are ever seen to labor. And can the liberties of a nation be thought secure when we have removed their only firm basis, a conviction in the minds of the people that these liberties are of the gift of God? That they are not to be violated but with his wrath? Indeed I tremble for my country when I reflect that God is just; that his justice cannot sleep forever: that considering numbers, nature and natural means only, a revolution of the wheel of fortune, an exchange of situation is among possible events: that it may become probable by supernatural interference! The Almighty has no attribute which can take side with us in such a contest.—But it is impossible to be temperate and to pursue this subject through the various considerations of policy, of morals, of history natural and civil. We must be contented to hope they will force their way into every one's mind. I think a change already perceptible, since the origin of the present revolution. The spirit of the master is abating, that of the slave rising from the dust, his condition mollifying, the way I hope preparing, under the auspices of heaven, for a total emancipation, and that this is disposed, in the order of events, to be with the consent of the masters, rather than by their extirpation.

ABRAHAM LINCOLN, SPEECH ON REPEAL
OF THE MISSOURI COMPROMISE (1854)

This is a response to Senator Stephen Douglas's application of the principle of "popular sovereignty" in his bill concerning Nebraska. Popular sovereignty allowed the citizens of territories to decide for themselves whether or not to have slavery. Nebraska was part of the Louisiana Territory north of the 36th parallel, where slavery had been prohibited by the Missouri Compromise of 1820.

This is the *repeal* of the Missouri Compromise. . . .

I think, and I shall try to show, that it is wrong; wrong in its direct effect, letting slavery into Kansas and Nebraska—and wrong in the prospective principle, allowing it to spread to every other part of the wide world, where men can be found inclined to take it.

This *declared* indifference, but as I must think, covert *real* zeal for the spread of slavery, I can not but hate. I hate it because of the monstrous injustice of slavery itself. I hate it because it deprives our republican example of its just influence in the world—enables the enemies of free institutions, with plausibility, to taunt us as hypocrites—causes the real friends of freedom to doubt our sincerity, and especially because it forces so many really good men amongst ourselves into an open war with the very fundamental principles of civil liberty—criticizing the Declaration of Independence, and insisting that there is no right principle of action but *self-interest*.

Before proceeding, let me say I think I have no prejudice against the Southern people. They are just what we would be in their situation. If slavery did not now exist amongst them, they would not introduce it. This I believe of the masses north and south. Doubtless there are individuals, on both sides, who would not hold slaves under any circumstances; and others who would gladly introduce slavery anew, if it were out of existence. We know that some southern men do free their slaves, go north, and become tip-top abolitionists; while some northern ones go south, and become most cruel slave-masters.

When southern people tell us they are no more responsible for the origin of slavery, than we, I acknowledge the fact. When it is said that the institution exists; and that it is very difficult to get rid of it, in any satisfactory way, I can understand and appreciate the saying. I surely will not blame them for not doing what I should not know how to do myself. If all earthly power were given me, I should not know what to do, as to the existing institution. My first impulse would be to free all slaves, and send them to Liberia,—to their own native land. But a moment's reflection would convince me, that whoever of high hope, (as I think there is) there may be in this, in the long run, its sudden execution is impossible. If they were all landed there in a day, they would all perish in the next ten days; and there are not surplus shipping and surplus money enough in the world to carry them therein many times ten days. What then? Free them all, and keep them among us as underlings? Is it quite certain that this betters their condition? I think I would not hold one in slavery, at any rate; yet the point is not clear enough for me to denounce people upon. What next? Free them, and make them politically and socially, our equals? My own feelings will not admit of this; and if mine would, we well know that those of the great mass of white people will not. Whether this feeling accords with justice and sound judgment, is not the sole question, if indeed, it is any part of it. A universal feeling, whether well or ill-founded, can not be safely disregarded. We can not, then, make them equals. It does seem to me that systems of gradual emancipation might be adopted; but for their tardiness in this, I will not undertake to judge our brethren of the south.

When they remind us of their constitutional rights, I acknowledge them, not grudgingly, but fully, and fairly; and I would give them any legislation for the reclaiming of their fugitives, which should not, in its stringency, be more likely to carry a free man into slavery, than our ordinary criminal laws are to hang an innocent one.

But all this, to my judgment, furnishes no more excuse for permitting slavery to go into our free territory, than it would be reviving the African slave trade by law. The law which forbids the bringing of slaves *from* Africa, and that which as so long forbid the taking of them *to* Nebraska, can hardly be distinguished on any moral principle. . . .

Equal justice to the south, it is said, requires us to consent to the extending of slavery to new countries. That is to say, inasmuch as you do not object to my taking my hog to Nebraska, therefore, I must not object to you taking your slave. Now, I admit this is perfectly logical, if there is no difference between hogs and negroes. But while you thus require me to deny the humanity of the negro, I wish to ask whether you of the south yourselves, have ever been willing to do as much? It is kindly provided that of all those who come into the world, only a small percentage are natural tyrants. That percentage is no larger in the slave States than in the free. The great majority, south as well as north, have human sympathies, of which they can no more divest themselves than they can of their sensibility to physical pain. These sympathies in the bosoms of the southern people, manifest in many ways, their sense of the wrong of slavery, and their consciousness that, after all, there is humanity in the negro. If they deny this, let me address them a few plain questions. In 1820 you joined the north, almost unanimously, in declaring the African slave trade piracy, and in annexing to it the punishment of death. Why did you do this? If you did not feel that it was wrong, why did you join in providing that men should be hung for it? The practice was no more than bringing wild negroes from Africa, to sell to such as would buy them. But you never thought of hanging men for catching and selling wild horses, wild buffaloes or wild bears.

Again, you have amongst you, a sneaking individual, of the class of native tyrants, know as the "SLAVE-DEALER." He watches your necessities, and crawls up to buy your slave, at a speculating price. If you cannot help it, you sell to him; but if you can help it, you drive him from your door. You despise him utterly. You do not recognize him as friend, or even as an honest man. Your children must not play with his; they may frolic freely with the little negroes, but not with the "slave-dealer's" children. If you are obliged to deal with him, you try to get through the job without so much as touching him. It is common with you to join hands with the men you meet; but with the slave dealer you avoid the ceremony—instinctively shrinking from the snaky contact. If he grows rich and retires from business, you still remember him, and still keep up the ban of non-intercourse upon him and his family. Now why is this? You do not so treat the man who deals in corn, cattle or tobacco. . . .

But one great argument in the support of the repeal of the Missouri Compromise is still to come. That argument is "the sacred right to self government." It seems our distinguished Senator has found great difficulty in getting his antagonists, even in the Senate to meet him fairly on his argument—some poet has said

"Fools rush in where angels fear to tread."

At the hazard of being thought one of the fools of this quotation, I meet that argument—I rush in, I take that bull by the horns.

I trust I understand, and trust estimate, the right of self-government. My faith in the proposition that each man should do precisely as he pleases with all which is exclusively his own, lies at the foundation of the sense of justice there is in me. I extend the principles to communities of men, as well as to individuals. . . .

The doctrine of self-government is right—absolutely and eternally right—but it has no just application, as here attempted. Or perhaps I should rather say that whether it has such just application depends upon whether a negro is *not or is* a man. If he is not a man, why in that case, he who is a man may, as a matter of self-government, do just as he pleases with him. But if the negro is a man, is it not to that extent, a total destruction of self-government, to say that he too shall not govern *himself*? When the white man governs himself that is self-government; but when he governs himself, he also governs another man, that is more than self-government—that is despotism. If the negro is a man, why then my ancient faith teaches me that "all men are created equal;" and that there can be no moral rights in connection with one man's making a slave of another.

Judge Douglas frequently with bitter irony and sarcasm, paraphrases our argument by saying "The white people of Nebraska are good enough to govern themselves, *but they are not good enough to govern a few miserable negroes!*"

Well I doubt not that the people of Nebraska are, and will continue to be as good as the average of people elsewhere. I do not say the contrary. What I do say is, that no man is good enough to govern another man, *without the other's consent.* I say this is the leading principle—the sheet anchor of American republicanism. Our Declaration of Independence says:

> We hold these truths to be self evident; that all men are created equal; that they are endowed by their Creator with certain inalienable rights; that among these are life, liberty and the pursuit of happiness. That to secure these rights, governments are instituted among men, DERIVING THEIR JUST POWERS FROM THE CONSENT OF THE GOVERNED.

I have quoted so much at this time merely to show that according to our ancient faith, the just powers of governments are derived from the consent of the governed.

Slavery is founded in the selfishness of man's nature—opposition to it, is in his love of justice. These principles are an eternal antagonism and when brought into collision so fiercely, as slavery extension brings them, shocks, and throes, and convulsions must ceaselessly follow. Repeal the Missouri Compromise—repeal all compromises—repeal the Declaration of Independence—repeal all past history, you still can not repeal human nature. It still will be the abundance of man's heart that slavery extension is wrong; and out of the abundance of his heart, his mouth will continue to speak. . . .

I particularly object to the NEW position which the avowed principle of this Nebraska law gives to slavery in the body politic. I object to it because it assumes that there CAN be MORAL RIGHT in the enslaving of one man by another. I object to it as a dangerous dalliance for a few free people—a sad evidence that, feeling prosperity we forget right—that liberty, as a principle, we have ceased to revere. I object to it because the fathers of the republic eschewed, and rejected it. The argument of "Necessity" was the only argument they ever admitted in favor of slavery; and so far only as it carried them, did they ever go. They found the institution exist-ing among us, which they could not help; and they cast blame upon the British King for having permitted its introduction. BEFORE the constitution, they prohibited its introduction into the northwestern Territory—the only country we owned, then free from it. AT the framing and adoption of the Constitution, they forbore to so much as mention the word "slave" or "slavery" in the whole instrument. In the provision for the recovery of fugitives, the slave is spoke of as a "PERSON HELD TO SERVICE OR LABOR." In that prohib-iting the abolition of the African slave trade for twenty years, that trade is spoken of as "The migration or importation of such per-sons as any of the States NOW EXISTING, shall think proper to admit," &c. These are the only provisions alluding to slavery. Thus, the thing is hid away, in the constitution, just as an afflicted man hides away a wen or a cancer, which he dares not cut out at once, lest he bleed to death; with the promise, nevertheless, that the cut-ting may begin at the end of a given time. Less than this our fathers COULD not do, and more they would not do. But this is not all. The earliest Congress, under the constitution, took the same view of slavery. They hedged and hemmed it into the narrowest limits of necessity. . . .

Our republican robe is soiled, and trailed in the dust. Let us re-purify it. Let us turn and wash it white, in the spirit, if not the blood, of the Revolution. Let us turn slavery from its claims of "moral right" back upon its existing legal rights, and its arguments of "ne-cessity." Let us return it to the position our fathers gave it; and there let it rest in peace. Let us re-adopt the Declaration of Inde-pendence, and with it, the practices, and policy, which harmonize with it. Let north and south—let all Americans—let all lovers of liberty everywhere—join in the great and good work. If we do this, we shall not only have saved the Union; but we shall have so saved it, as to make, and to keep it, forever worthy of the saving. We shall have so saved it, that the succeeding millions of free happy people, the world over, shall rise up, and call us blessed, to the latest generations. . . .

FREDERICK DOUGLASS, ADDRESS FOR THE PROMOTION OF COLORED ENLISTMENT (1864)

Frederick Douglass was born a slave on the Eastern Shore of Maryland. He taught himself to read and write as a child,

escaped to the North in 1838 at the age of 21, and came to
prominence as a spokesman for free blacks in the abolitionist
movement. Later he broke with the abolitionists because he
rejected their moralistic disavowal of political activity within
the framework of the Constitution.

I hold that the Federal Government was never, in its essence, anything but an anti-slavery government. Abolish slavery tomorrow, and not a sentence or syllable of the Constitution need be altered. It was purposely so framed as to give no claim, no sanction to the claim, of property in man. If in its origin slavery had any relation to the government, it was only as the scaffolding to the magnificent structure, to be removed as soon as the building was completed.

ALEXANDER STEPHENS, THE "CORNER STONE" SPEECH (1861)

Stephens was vice president of the Confederate States of America. This defense of his new government acknowledges the truth of Frederick Douglass's and Abraham Lincoln's views on the Constitution of 1787.

The prevailing ideas entertained by [Jefferson] and most of the leading statesmen at the time of the formation of the old Constitution, were that the enslavement of the African was in violation of the laws of nature: that it was wrong in principle, socially, morally, and politically. It was an evil they knew not well how to deal with, but the general opinion of the men of that day was, that somehow or other, in the order of Providence, the institution would be evanescent and pass away.

Those ideas were fundamentally wrong. They rested upon the assumption of the equality of the races. This was an error. It was a sandy foundation, and the idea of a government built upon it; when the "storm came and the wind blew, it fell." Our new government is founded upon exactly the opposite idea; its foundations are laid, its corner stone rests upon the great truth that the negro is not the equal to the white man. That slavery—the subordination to the superior race, is his natural and normal condition. This our new Government [the Confederate States of America] is the first in the history of the world, based upon this great physical and moral truth. This truth has been slow in the process of its development, like all other truths in the various departments of science. . . .

FREDERICK DOUGLASS, ORATION IN MEMORY OF ABRAHAM LINCOLN (1876)

Douglass had a nuanced, critical appreciation of Lincoln's intentions and accomplishments from the perspective of a black American.

I have said that President Lincoln was a white man, and shared the prejudices common to his countrymen towards the colored race. Looking back to his times and to the condition of his country, we are compelled to admit that this unfriendly feeling on his part may be safely set down as one element of his wonderful success in organizing the loyal American people for the tremendous conflict before them, and bring them safely through the conflict. His great mission was to accomplish two things: first, to save his country from dismemberment and ruin; and, second, to free his country from the great crime of slavery. To do one or the other, or both, he must have the earnest sympathy and the powerful cooperation of his loyal fellow countrymen. Without this primary and essential condition to success his effort must have been vain and utterly fruitless. Had he put the abolition of slavery before the salvation of the Union, he would have inevitably driven from him a powerful class of the American people and rendered resistance to rebellion impossible. Viewed from the genuine abolition ground, Mr. Lincoln seemed tardy, cold, dull and indifferent; but measuring him by the sentiment of his country, a sentiment he has bound as a statesman to consult, he was swift, zealous, radical, and determined.

Though Mr. Lincoln shared the prejudices of his white fellow countrymen against the negro, it is hardly necessary to say that in his heart of hearts he loathed and hated slavery. The man who could say, "Fondly do we hope, fervently do we pray, that his mighty scourge of war shall soon pass away, yet if God will it continue till all the wealth piled by two hundred years of bondage shall have been wasted, and each drop of blood drawn by the lash shall have been paid for by one drawn by the sword, the judgments of the

Lord are true and righteous altogether," gives all needed proof of his feelings on the subject of slavery. He was willing, while the South was loyal, that it should have its pound of flesh, because he thought it was so nominated in the bond; but farther than this no earthly power could make him go. . . .

PLESSY v. FERGUSON (1896)

This case involves the constitutionality of a Louisiana law that required the segregation of the races by "railway companies carrying passengers in their coaches."

JUSTICE BROWN delivered the opinion of the Court. . . .

So far, then, as a conflict with the Fourteenth Amendment is concerned the case reduces itself to the question whether the statute of Louisiana is a reasonable regulation, and with respect to this there must necessarily be a large discretion on the part of the legislature. In determining the question of reasonableness it is at liberty to act with reference to the established usages, customs and traditions of the people, and with a view to the promotion of their comfort, and the preservation of the public peace and good order. Gauged by this standard, we cannot say that a law which authorizes or even requires the separation of the two races in public conveyances is unreasonable, or more obnoxious to the Fourteenth Amendment than the acts of Congress requiring separate schools for colored children in the District of Columbia, the constitutionality of which does not seem to have been questioned, or the corresponding acts of state legislatures.

We consider the underlying fallacy of the plaintiff's argument to consist in the assumption that the enforced separation of the two races stamps the colored race with a badge of inferiority. If this be so, it is not by reason of anything found in the act, but solely because the colored race chooses to put that construction upon it. The argument necessarily assumes that if, as has been more than once the case, and is not unlikely to be so again, the colored race should become the dominant power in the state legislature, and should enact a law in precisely similar terms, it would thereby relegate the white race to an inferior position. We imagine that the white race, at least, would not acquiesce in this assumption. The argument also assumes, that social prejudices may be overcome by legislation, and that equal rights cannot be secured to the negro except by an enforced commingling of the two races. We cannot accept this proposition. If the two races are to meet upon terms of social equality, it must be the result of natural affinities, a mutual appreciation of each other's merits and a voluntary consent of individuals. . . .

Legislation is powerless to eradicate racial instincts or to abolish distinctions based upon physical difficulties, and the attempt to do so can only result in accentuating the differences of the present situation. If the civil and political rights of both races be equal one cannot be inferior to the other civilly or politically. If one race be inferior to the other socially, the Constitution of the United States cannot put them upon the same plane. . . .

JUSTICE HARLAN, dissenting. . . .

The white race deems itself to be the dominant race in this country. And so it is, in prestige, in achievements, in education, in wealth and in power. So, I doubt not, it will continue to be for all times, if it remains true to its great heritage and holds fast to the principles of constitutional liberty. But in view of the Constitution, in the eye of the law, there is in this country no superior, dominant, ruling class of citizens. There is no caste here. Our Constitution is colorblind, and neither knows nor tolerates classes among citizens. In respect of civil rights, all citizens are equal before the law. The humblest is the peer of the most powerful. The law regards man as man, and takes no account of his surroundings or of his color when his civil rights as guaranteed by the supreme law of the land are involved. It is, therefore, to be regretted that this high tribunal, the final expositor of the fundamental law of the land, has reached the conclusion that it is competent for a state to regulate the enjoyment by citizens of their civil rights solely upon the basis of race. . . .

BROWN v. BOARD OF EDUCATION (1954)

This opinion, in which the chief justice speaks for a unanimous Court, supports a decision declaring segregation unconstitutional in public education.

CHIEF JUSTICE WARREN delivered the opinion of the Court.
. . .

These cases come to us from the States of Kansas, South Carolina, Virginia, and Delaware. They are premised on different facts and different local conditions, but a common legal question justifies their consideration together in this consolidated opinion.

In each of the cases, minors of the Negro race, through their legal representatives, seek the aid of the courts in obtaining admission to the public schools of their community on a nonsegregated basis. In each instance, they had been denied admission to schools attended by white children under laws requiring or permitting segregation according to race.

This segregation was alleged to deprive the plaintiffs of the equal protection of the laws under the Fourteenth Amendment. In each of the cases other than the Delaware case, a three-judge Federal District Court denied relief to the plaintiffs on the so-called "separate but equal" doctrine, announced by this court in *Plessy v. Ferguson*.
. . .

Under that doctrine, equality of treatment is accorded when the races are provided substantially equal facilities, even though these facilities be separate. In the Delaware case, the Supreme Court of Delaware adhered to that doctrine, but ordered that the plaintiffs be admitted to the white schools because of their superiority to the Negro schools.

The plaintiffs contend that segregated public schools are not "equal" and cannot be made "equal," and that, hence, they are deprived of the equal protection of the laws. Because of the obvious importance of the question presented, the Court took jurisdiction. Argument was heard in the 1952 term, and reargument was heard this term on certain questions propounded by the Court.

Reargument was largely devoted to the circumstances surrounding the adoption of the Fourteenth Amendment in 1868. It covered, exhaustively, consideration of the Amendment in Congress, ratification by the states, then existing practices in racial segregation, and the views of proponents and opponents of the Amendment.

This discussion and our own investigation convince us that, although these sources cast some light, it is not enough to resolve the problem with which we are faced.

At best, they are inconclusive. The most avid proponents of the postwar Amendments undoubtedly intended them to remove all legal distinctions among "all persons born or naturalized in the United States."

Their opponents, just as certainly, were antagonistic to both the letter and the spirit of the Amendments and wished them to have the most limited effect. What others in Congress and the State legislature had in mind cannot be determined with any degree of certainty.

An additional reason for the illusive nature of the Amendment's history, with respect to segregated schools, is the status of public education at that time. In the South; the movement toward free common schools, supported by general taxation, had not yet taken hold. Education of white children was largely in the hands of private groups. Education of Negroes was almost nonexistent, and practically all of the race was illiterate. In fact, any education of Negroes was forbidden by law in some states.

Today, in contrast, many Negroes have achieved outstanding success in the arts and sciences as well as in the business and professional world. It is true that public school education at the time of the Amendment had advanced further in the North, but the effect of the Amendment on Northern States was generally ignored by the Congressional debates.

Even in the North, the conditions of public education did not approximate those existing today. The curriculum was usually rudimentary; ungraded schools were common in rural areas; the school term was but three months a year in many states; and compulsory school attendance was virtually unknown.

As a consequence, it is not surprising that there should be so little in the history of the Fourteenth Amendment relating to its intended effect on public education.

In the first cases in this court, construing the Fourteenth Amendment, decided shortly after its adoption, the court interpreted it as proscribing all state imposed discriminations against the Negro race.

The doctrine of "separate but equal" did not make its appearance in this court until 1896 in the case of *Plessy v. Ferguson* . . . involving not education but transportation.

[A footnote explains that "the doctrine apparently originated in *Roberts v. City of Boston,* 59 Mass. 198, 206 (1849) upholding school segregation against attack as being violative of a state constitutional guarantee of equality. Segregation in Boston public schools was eliminated in 1855. . . . But elsewhere in the north segregation in public education has persisted until recent years."]

American courts have since labored with the doctrine for over half a century. In this court, there have been six cases involving the "separate but equal" doctrine in the field of public education.

In *Cumming v. County Board of Education,* 175 U.S. 528, and *Gong Lum v. Rice,* 275 U.S. 78, the validity of the doctrine itself was not challenged. In most recent cases, all on the graduate school level, inequality was found in that specific benefits enjoyed by white students were denied to Negro students of the same educational qualifications. *Missouri ex rel. Gaines v. Canada,* 305 U.S. 337; *Sipuel v. Oklahoma,* 332 U.S. 631; *Sweatt v. Painter,* 339 U.S. 629; *McLaurin v. Oklahoma State Regents,* 339 U.S. 637.

In none of these cases was it necessary to reexamine the doctrine to grant relief to the Negro plaintiff. And in *Sweatt v. Painter* . . . the court expressly reserved decision on the question whether *Plessy v. Ferguson* should be held inapplicable to public education.

In the instant cases, that question is directly presented. Here, unlike *Sweatt v. Painter,* there are findings below that the Negro and white schools involved have been equalized, or are being equalized, with respect to buildings, curricula, qualifications and salaries of teachers, and other "tangible" factors.

Our decision, therefore, cannot turn on merely a comparison of these tangible factors in the Negro and white schools involved in each of the cases. We must look instead to the effect of segregation itself on public education.

In approaching this problem, we cannot turn the clock back to 1868, when the Amendment was adopted, or even to 1896, when *Plessy v. Ferguson* was written. We must consider public education in the light of its full development and its present place in American life throughout the nation. Only in this way can it be determined if segregation in public schools deprives these plaintiffs of the equal protection of the laws.

Today, education is perhaps the most important function of state and local governments. Compulsory school attendance laws and the great expenditures for education both demonstrate our recognition of the importance of education to our democratic society. It is required in the performance of our most basic public responsibilities, even service in the armed forces. It is the very foundation of good citizenship.

Today, it is a principal instrument in awakening the child to cultural values, in preparing him for later professional training, and in helping him to adjust normally to his environment.

In these days, it is doubtful that any child may reasonably be expected to succeed in life if he is denied the opportunity of an education. Such an opportunity, where the state has undertaken to provide it, is a right which must be made available to all on equal terms.

We come then to the question presented: Does segregation of children in public schools solely on the basis of race, even though the physical facilities and other "tangible" factors may be equal, deprive the children of the minority group of equal educational opportunities? We believe that it does.

In *Sweatt v. Painter* . . . in finding that a segregated law school for Negroes could not provide them equal educational opportunities, this court relied in large part on "those qualities which are incapable of objective measurement but which make for greatness in a law school."

In *McLaurin v. Oklahoma State Regents* . . . the court, in requiring that a Negro admitted to a white graduate school be treated like all other students, again resorted to intangible considerations: ". . . his ability to study, engage in discussions and exchange views with other students, and, in general, to learn his profession" [ellipsis in *Brown*].

Such considerations apply with added force to children in grade and high schools. To separate them from others of similar age and qualifications solely because of their race generates a feeling of inferiority as to their status in the community that may affect their hearts and minds in a way unlikely ever to be undone.

The effect of this separation on their educational opportunities was well stated by a finding in the Kansas case by a court which nevertheless felt compelled to rule against the Negro plaintiffs:

Segregation of white and colored children in public schools has a detrimental effect upon the colored children. The impact is greater when it has the sanction of the law; for the policy of separating the races is usually interpreted as denoting the inferiority of the Negro group.

A sense of inferiority affects the motivation of a child to learn. Segregation with the sanction of law, therefore, has a tendency to retard the educational and mental development of Negro children and to deprive them of some of the benefits they would receive in a racially integrated school system.

Whatever may have been the extent of psychological knowledge at the time of *Plessy v. Ferguson,* this finding is amply supported by modern authority. [Here a footnote lists a number of recent works in social science.] Any language in *Plessy v. Ferguson* contrary to this finding is rejected.

We conclude that in the field of public education the doctrine of "separate but equal" has no place. Separate educational facilities are inherently unequal. Therefore, we hold that the plaintiffs and others similarly situated for whom the actions have been brought are, by reason of the segregation complained of, deprived of the equal protection of the laws guaranteed by the Fourteenth Amendment. This disposition makes unnecessary any discussion whether such segregation also violates the Due Process Clause of the Fourteenth Amendment. . . .

MARTIN LUTHER KING JR., LETTER FROM A BIRMINGHAM JAIL (1963)

Martin Luther King was the most thoughtful and influential spokesperson for American blacks during the civil rights movement of the late 1950s and the 1960s.

You may well ask: "Why direct action? Why sit-ins, marches and so forth? Isn't negotiation a better path?" You are quite right in calling for negotiation. Indeed, this is the very purpose of direct action. Nonviolent direct action seeks to create such a crisis and foster such a tension that a community which has constantly refused to negotiate is forced to confront the issue. It seeks so to dramatize the issue that it can no longer be ignored. My citing the creation of tension as part of the work of the nonviolent-resister may sound rather shocking. But I must confess that I am not afraid of the word "tension." I have earnestly opposed violent tension, but there is a type of constructive, nonviolent tension which is necessary for growth. Just as Socrates felt that it was necessary to create a tension in the mind so that individuals could rise from the bondage of myths and half-truths to the unfettered realm of creative analysis and objective appraisal, so must we see the need for nonviolent gadflies to create the kind of tension in society that will help men rise from the dark depths of prejudice and racism to the majestic heights of understanding and brotherhood.

The purpose of our direct-action program is to create a situation so crisis-packed that it will inevitably open the door to negotiation. I therefore concur with you in your call for negotiation. Too long has our beloved Southland been bogged down in a tragic effort to live in monologue rather than dialogue.

One of the basic points in your statement is that the action I and my associates have taken in Birmingham is untimely. Some have asked: "Why didn't you give the new city administration time to act?" The only answer that I can give to this query is that the new Birmingham administration must be prodded about as much as the outgoing one, before it will act. We are sadly mistaken if we feel that the election of Albert Boutwell as mayor will bring the millennium to Birmingham. While Mr. Boutwell is a much more gentle person that Mr. Connor, they are both segregationists, dedicated to maintenance of the status quo. I have hope that Mr. Boutwell will be reasonable enough to see the futility of massive resistance to desegregation. But he will not see this without pressure from devotees of civil rights. My friends, I must say to you that we have not made a single gain in civil rights without determined legal and nonviolent pressure. Lamentably, it is an historical fact that privileged groups seldom give up their privileges voluntarily. Individuals may see the moral light and voluntarily give up their unjust posture; but, as Reinhold Niebuhr has reminded us, groups tend to be more immoral than individuals.

We know through painful experience that freedom is never voluntarily given by the oppressor; it must be demanded by the oppressed. Frankly, I have yet to engage in a direct-action campaign that was "well timed" in the view of those who have not suffered unduly from the disease of segregation. For years now I have heard the word "Wait!" It rings in the ear of every Negro with piercing familiarity. This "Wait" has almost always meant "Never." We must come to see, with one of our distinguished jurists, that "justice too long delayed is justice denied."

We have waited for more than 340 years for our constitutional and God-given rights. The nations of Asia and Africa are moving with jetlike speed toward gaining political independence, but we still creep at horse-and-buggy pace toward gaining a cup of coffee at a lunch counter. Perhaps it is easy for those who have never felt the stinging darts of segregation to say, "Wait." But when you have seen vicious mobs lynch your mothers and fathers at will and drown your sisters and brothers at whim; when you have seen hate-filled policemen curse, kick and even kill your black brothers and sisters; when you see the vast majority of your twenty million Negro brothers smothering in an air-tight cage of poverty in the midst of an affluent society; when you suddenly find your tongue twisted and your speech stammering as you seek to explain to your six-year-old daughter why she can't go to the public amusement park that has just been advertised on television, and see tears welling up in her eyes when she is told that Funtown is closed to colored children, and see ominous clouds of inferiority beginning to form in her little mental sky, and see her beginning to distort her personality by developing an unconscious bitterness toward white people; when you have to concoct an answer for a five-year-old son who is asking: "Daddy, why do white people treat colored people so mean?"; when you take a cross-country drive and find it necessary to sleep night after night in the uncomfortable corners of your automobile because no motel will accept you; when you are humiliated day in and day out by nagging signs reading "white" and "colored," when your first name becomes "nigger," your middle name becomes "boy" (however old you are) and your last name becomes "John," and your wife and mother are never given the respected title "Mrs."; when you are harried by day and haunted by night by the fact that you are a Negro, living constantly at tiptoe stance, never quite knowing what to expect next, and are plagued with inner fears and outer resentments; when you are forever fighting a degenerating sense of "nobodiness"—then you will understand why we find it difficult to wait. There comes a time when the cup of endurance runs over, and men are no longer willing to be plunged into the abyss of despair. I hope, sirs, you can understand our legitimate and unavoidable impatience.

You express a great deal of anxiety over our willingness to break laws. This is certainly a legitimate concern. Since we so diligently urge people to obey the Supreme Court's decision of 1954 outlawing segregation in the public schools, at first glance it may seem rather paradoxical for us consciously to break laws. One may well ask: "How can you advocate breaking some laws and obeying others?" The answer lies in the fact that there are two types of laws: just and unjust. I would be the first to advocate obeying just laws. One has not only a legal but a moral responsibility to obey just laws. Conversely, one has a moral responsibility to disobey unjust laws. I would agree with St. Augustine that "an unjust law is no law at all."

Now, what is the difference between the two? How does one determine whether a law is just or unjust? A just law is a manmade code that squares with the moral law or the law of God. An unjust law is a code that is out of harmony with the moral law. To put it in the terms of St. Thomas Aquinas: An unjust law is a human law that is not rooted in eternal law and natural law. Any law that uplifts human personality is just. Any law that degrades human personality is unjust. All segregation statutes are unjust because segregation distorts the soul and damages the personality. It gives the segregator a false sense of superiority and the segregated a false sense of inferiority. Segregation, to use the terminology of the Jewish philosopher Martin Buber, substitutes an "I—it" relationship for an "I—thou" relationship and ends up relegating persons to the status of things. Hence segregation is not only politically, economically and sociologically unsound, it is morally wrong and sinful. Paul Tillich has said that sin is separation. Is not segregation an existential expression of man's tragic separation, his awful estrangement, his terrible sinfulness? Thus it is that I can urge men to obey the 1954 decision of the Supreme Court, for it is morally right; and I can urge them to disobey segregation ordinances, for they are morally wrong.

Let us consider a more concrete example of just and unjust laws. An unjust law is a code that a numerical or power majority group compels a minority group to obey but does not make binding on itself.

This is difference made legal. By the same token, a just law is a code that a majority compels a minority to follow and that it is willing to follow itself. This is sameness made legal.

Let me give another explanation. A law is unjust if it is inflicted on a minority that, as a result of being denied the right to vote, had no part in enacting or devising the law. Who can say that the legislature of Alabama which set up that state's segregation laws was democratically elected? Throughout Alabama all sorts of devious methods are used to prevent Negroes from becoming registered voters, and there are some counties in which, even though Negroes constitute a majority of the population, not a single Negro is registered. Can any law enacted under such circumstances be considered democratically structured?

Sometimes a law is just on its face and unjust in its application. For instance, I have been arrested on a charge of parading without a permit. Now, there is nothing wrong in having an ordinance which requires a permit for a parade. But such an ordinance becomes unjust when it is used to maintain segregation and to deny citizens the First-Amendment privilege of peaceful assembly and protest.

I hope you are able to see the distinction I am trying to point out. In no sense do I advocate evading or defying the law, as would the rabid segregationist. That would lead to anarchy. One who breaks an unjust law must do so openly, lovingly, and with a willingness to accept the penalty. I submit that an individual who breaks a law that conscience tells him is unjust, and who willingly accepts the penalty of imprisonment in order to arouse the conscience of the community over its injustice, is in reality expressing the highest respect for law.

Of course, there is nothing new about this kind of civil disobedience. It was evidenced sublimely in the refusal of Shadrach, Meshach and Abednego to obey the laws of Nebuchadnezzar, on the ground that a higher moral law was at stake. It was practiced superbly by the early Christians, who were willing to face hungry lions and the excruciating pain of chopping blocks rather than submit to certain unjust laws of the Roman Empire. To a degree, academic freedom is a reality today because Socrates practiced civil disobedience. In our own nation, the Boston Tea Party represented a massive act of civil disobedience.

We should never forget that everything Adolf Hitler did in Germany was "legal" and everything the Hungarian freedom fighters did in Hungary was "illegal." It was "illegal" to aid and comfort a Jew in Hitler's Germany. Even so, I am sure that, had I lived in Germany at the time, I would have aided and comforted my Jewish brothers. If today I lived in a Communist country where certain principles dear to the Christian faith are suppressed, I would openly advocate disobeying that country's antireligious laws.

I must make two honest confessions to you, my Christian and Jewish brothers. First, I must confess that over the past few years I have been gravely disappointed with the white moderate. I have almost reached the regrettable conclusion that the Negro's great stumbling block in his stride toward freedom is not the White

Citizen's Counciler or the Ku Klux Klanner, but the white moderate, who is more devoted to "order" than to justice; who prefers a negative peace which is the absence of tension to a positive peace which is the presence of justice; who constantly says: "I agree with you in the goal you seek, but I cannot agree with your methods of direct action"; who paternalistically believes he can set the timetable for another man's freedom; who lives by a mythical concept of time and who constantly advises the Negro to wait for a "more convenient season." Shallow understanding from people of good will is more frustrating than absolute misunderstanding from people of ill will. Luke-warm acceptance is much more bewildering than outright rejection.

I had hoped that the white moderate would understand that law and order exist for the purpose of establishing justice and that when they fail in this purpose they become the dangerously structured dams that block the flow of social progress. I had hoped that the white moderate would understand that the present tension in the South is a necessary phase of the transition from an obnoxious negative peace, in which the Negro passively accepted his unjust plight, to a substantive and positive peace, in which all men will respect the dignity and worth of human personality. Actually, we who engage in nonviolent direct action are not the creators of tension. We merely bring to the surface the hidden tension that is already alive. We bring it out in the open, where it can be seen and dealt with. Like a boil that can never be cured so long as it is covered up but must be opened with all its ugliness to the natural medicines of air and light, injustice must be exposed, with all the tension its exposure creates, to the light of human conscience and the air of national opinion before it can be cured.

FULLILOVE v. KLUTZNICK (1980)

This is an important decision on the constitutionality of affirmative action programs. Its particular concern is the "minority business enterprise" (MBE) provision of the Public Works Employment Act of 1977, which requires that, in the absence of an administrative waiver, at least 10 percent of federal funds granted for local public work projects must be used to procure services or supplies from business owned by citizens "who

are Negroes, Spanish-speaking, Orientals, Indians, Eskimos, and
Aleuts." Contracts may be granted to minority business enter-
prises that are not the lowest bidders.

CHIEF JUSTICE BURGER announced the judgment of the Court
and delivered an opinion in which JUSTICE WHITE and JUSTICE
POWELL joined. . . .

We now turn to the question whether, as a means to accomplish
these plainly constitutional objectives, Congress may use racial and
ethnic criteria, in this limited way, as a condition attached to a federal grant. We are mindful that "(i)n no matter should we pay more
deference to the opinion of Congress than in its choice of instru-
mentalities to perform a function that is within its power." *National*
Mutual Insurance Co. v. Tidewater Transfer Co., 337 U.S. 582, 603
(1949) (opinion of Jackson, J.). However, Congress may employ
racial or ethnic classifications in exercising its Spending or other
legislative Powers only if those classifications do not violate the
equal protection component of the Due Process Clause of the Fifth
Amendment. We recognize the need for careful judicial evaluation
to assure that any congressional program that employs racial or ethnic criteria to accomplish the objective of remedying the present
effects of past discrimination is narrowly tailored to the achievement of that goal. . . .

As a threshold matter, we reject the contention that in the remedial context the Congress must act in a wholly "color-blind" fashion.
In *Swann v. Charlotte-Mecklenberg Board of Education,* 402 U.S.
1, 18-21 (1971), we rejected this argument in considering a court-
formulated school desegregation remedy on the basis that
examination of the racial composition of student bodies was an
unavoidable starting point and that racially based attendance assignments were permissible so long as no absolute racial balance of each
school was required. In *McDaniel v. Barresi,* 402 U.S. 39, 41 (1971),
citing *Swann,* we observed that "[i]n this remedial process, steps
will almost invariably require that students be assigned 'differently
because of their race.'. . . Any other approach would freeze the
status quo that is the very target of all desegregation processes"
[ellipsis in *Fullilove*]. [Citations omitted.] And in *North Carolina*
Board of Education v. Swann, 402 U.S. 43 (1971), we invalidated a

state law that absolutely forbade assignment of any student on account of race because it foreclosed implementation of desegregation
plans that were designed to remedy constitutional violations. We held
that "[j]ust as the race of students must be considered in determining whether a constitutional violation has occurred, so also must
race be considered in formulating a remedy." 402 U.S., at 46.

In these school desegregation cases we dealt with the authority
of a federal court to formulate a remedy for unconstitutional racial
discrimination. However, the authority of a court to incorporate
racial criteria into a remedial decree also extends to statutory violations. Where federal antidiscrimination laws have been violated,
an equitable remedy may in the appropriate case include a racial or
ethnic factor. . . . In another setting we have held that a state may
employ racial criteria that are reasonably necessary to assure compliance with federal voting rights legislation, even though the state
action does not entail the remedy of a constitutional violation.
United Jewish Organizations of Williamsburgh, Inc. v. Carey, 430
U.S. 144, 147-165 (1977 opinion of White, J., joined by Brennan,
Blackmun, and Stevens, J.J.); *id.,* at 180-187 (Burger, C.J., dissenting on other grounds).

When we have discussed the remedial powers of a federal court,
we have been alert to the limitation that "[t]he power of the federal courts to restructure the operation of local and state government
entities is not plenary. . . . [A] federal court is required to tailor
the scope of the remedy to fit the nature and extent of the . . .
violation" [ellipses in *Fullilove*]. *Dayton Board of Education v.
Brinkman,* 433 U.S. 406, 419-420 [1977] (quoting *Milliken v. Bra-
dley,* 418 U.S. 717, 738 (1974), and *Swann v. Charlotte-Mecklenburg
Board of Education, supra,* 402 U.S., at 16).

Here we deal, as we noted earlier, not with the limited remedial
powers of a federal court, for example, but with the broad remedial powers of Congress. It is fundamental that in no organ of
government, state or federal, does there repose a more comprehensive remedial power than in the Congress, expressly charged by the
Constitution with competence and authority to enforce equal protection guarantees. Congress not only may induce voluntary action
to assure compliance with existing federal statutory or constitutional

antidiscrimination provisions, but also, where Congress has authority to declare certain conduct unlawful, it may, as here, authorize and induce state action to avoid such conduct. *Supra.*

A more specific challenge to the MBE program is the charge that it impermissibly deprives nonminority businesses of access to at least some portion of the government contracting opportunities generated by the Act. It must be conceded that by its objective of remedying the historical impairment of access, the MBE provision can have the effect of awarding some contracts to MBEs which otherwise might be awarded to other businesses, who may themselves be innocent of any prior discriminatory actions. Failure of nonminority firms to receive certain contracts is, of course, an incidental consequence of the program, not part of its objective; similarly, past impairment of minority-firm access to public contracting opportunities may have been an incidental consequence of "business-as-usual" by public contracting agencies and among prime contractors.

It is not a constitutional defect in this program that it may disappoint the expectations of nonminority firms. When effectuating a limited and properly tailored remedy to cure the effects of prior discrimination, such "a sharing of the burden" by innocent parties is not impermissible. *Franks, supra,* at 777; see *Albemarle Paper Co., supra; United Jewish Organizations, supra.* The actual "burden" shouldered by nonminority firms is relatively light in this connection when we consider the scope of this public works program as compared with overall construction contracting opportunities. Moreover, although we may assume that the complaining parties are innocent of any discriminatory conduct, it was within congressional power to act on the assumption that in the past some nonminority businesses may have reaped competitive benefit over the years from the virtual exclusion of minority firms from these contracting opportunities. . . .

JUSTICE MARSHALL, with whom JUSTICE BRENNAN and JUSTICE BLACKMUN join, concurring in the judgment. . . .

. . . [I]t is clear to me that the racial classifications employed in the set-aside provision are substantially related to the achievement of the important and congressionally articulated goal of remedying the present effects of past racial discrimination. The provision, therefore, passes muster under the equal protection standard I adopted in *Bakke*. . . .

Those doors [to positions of influence, affluence, and prestige in the United States] cannot be fully opened without the acceptance of race-conscious remedies. As my Brother Blackmun observed in *Bakke,* "[I]n order to get beyond racism, we must first take account of race. There is no other way." *Id.,* at 407 (separate opinion).

Congress recognized these realities when it enacted the minority set-aside provision at issue in this case. Today, by upholding this race-conscious remedy, the Court accords Congress the authority necessary to undertake the task of moving our society toward a state of meaningful equality of opportunity, not an abstract version of equality in which the effects of past discrimination would be forever frozen into our social fabric. I applaud this result. Accordingly, I concur in the judgment of the Court.

JUSTICE STEWART, with whom JUSTICE REHNQUIST joins, dissenting. . . .

"Our Constitution is color-blind, and neither knows nor tolerates classes among citizens. . . . The law regards man as man, and takes no account of his surroundings or of his color . . ." [ellipses in *Fullilove*]. Those words were written by a Member of this Court 84 years ago. *Plessy v. Ferguson* 163 U.S. 537, 559 [1896] (Harlan, J., dissenting). His colleagues disagreed with him, and held that a statute that required the separation of people on the basis of their race was constitutionally valid because it was a "reasonable" exercise of legislative power and had been "enacted in good faith for the promotion [of] the public good . . ." [ellipsis in *Fullilove*]. *Id.,* at 550. Today, the Court upholds a statute that accords a preference to citizens who are "Negroes, Spanish-speaking, Orientals, Indians, Eskimos, and Aleuts," for much the same reasons. I think today's decision is wrong for the same reason that *Plessy v. Ferguson* was wrong, and I respectfully dissent.

JUSTICE STEVENS, dissenting. . . .

The ultimate goal must be to eliminate entirely from governmental decisionmaking such irrelevant factors as a human being's race. The removal of barriers to access to political and economic processes serves that goal. But the creation of new barriers can only frustrate true progress. For as Mr. Justice Powell and Mr. Justice Douglas have perceptively observed, such protective barriers reinforce habitual ways of thinking in terms of classes instead of individuals. Preferences based on characteristics acquired at birth foster intolerance and antagonism against the entire membership of the favored classes. For this reason, I am firmly convinced that this "temporary measure" will disserve the goal of equal opportunity. . . .

. . . [R]ather than take the substantive position expressed in Mr. Justice Stewart's dissenting opinion, I would hold this statute unconstitutional on a narrower ground. It cannot fairly be characterized as a "narrowly tailored" racial classification because it simply raises too many serious questions that Congress failed to answer or even to address in a responsible way. The risk that habitual attitudes toward classes of persons, rather than analysis of the relevant characteristics of the class, will serve as a basis for a legislative classification if present when benefits are distributed as well as when burdens are imposed. In the past, traditional attitudes too often provided the only explanation for discrimination against women, aliens, illegitimates, and black citizens. Today there is a danger that awareness of past injustice will lead to automatic acceptance of new classifications that are not in fact justified by attributes characteristic of the class as a whole.

When Congress creates a special preference, or a special disability, for a class of persons, it should identify the characteristic that justifies the special treatment. When the classification is defined in racial terms, I believe that such particular identification is imperative.

CITY OF RICHMOND v. CROSON (1989)

The City of Richmond, Virginia, adopted a Minority Business Utilization Plan requiring prime contractors awarded city construction contracts to subcontract at least 30 percent of the total dollar amount of each contract to one or more Minority

*Business Enterprises (MBEs), which the city defined to include
a business from anywhere in the country at least 51 percent of
which is owned and controlled by black, Spanish-speaking,
Oriental, Indian, Eskimo, or Aleut citizens. Although Richmond
declared that the plan was "remedial" in nature, the city
adopted it after a public hearing at which no direct evidence
was presented that the city had discriminated on the basis of
race in awarding contracts or that its prime contractors had
discriminated against minority subcontractors.*

JUSTICE O'CONNOR delivered the opinion of the Court. . . .

In this case, we confront once again the tension between the
Fourteenth Amendment's guarantee of equal treatment to all citizens, and the use of race-based measures to ameliorate the effects
of past discrimination on the opportunities enjoyed by members of
minority groups in our society. In *Fullilove v. Klutznick*, we held
that a congressional program requiring that 10% of certain federal
construction grants be awarded to minority contractors did not violate the equal protection principles embodied in the Due Process
Clause of the Fifth Amendment. Relying largely on our decision in
Fullilove, some lower federal courts have applied a similar standard of review in assessing the constitutionality of state and local
minority set-aside provision under the Equal Protection Clause of
the Fourteenth Amendment. . . .

The principal opinion in *Fullilove*, written by Chief Justice Burger,
did not employ "strict scrutiny" or any other traditional standard of
equal protection review. The Chief Justice noted at the outset that
although racial classifications call for close examination, the Court
was at the same time, "bound to approach [its] task with appropriate deference to the Congress, a co-equal branch charged by the
Constitution with the power to 'provide for the . . . general Welfare of the United States' and 'to enforce by appropriate legislation,'
the equal protection guarantees of the Fourteenth Amendment." . . .
The principal opinion asked two questions: first, were the objectives of the legislation with the power of Congress? Second, was
the limited use of racial and ethnic criteria a permissible means for
Congress to carry out its objectives within the constraints of the
Due Process Clause? . . .

The Chief Justice . . . turned to the constraints on Congress' power to employ race-conscious remedial relief. His opinion stressed two factors in upholding the MBE set-aside. First was the unique remedial powers of Congress under Section 5 of the Fourteenth Amendment:

"Here we deal . . . not with the limited remedial powers of a federal court, for example, but with the broad remedial powers of Congress. It is fundamental that *in no organ of government, state or federal, does there repose a more comprehensive remedial power than in the Congress, expressly charged by the Constitution with the competence and authority to enforce equal protection guarantees.".* . .

Because of these unique powers, the Chief Justice concluded that "Congress not only may induce voluntary action to assure compliance with existing federal statutory or constitutional antidiscrimination provisions, but also, where Congress has authority to *declare certain conduct unlawful*, it may, as here, authorize and induce state action to avoid such conduct."

The second factor emphasized by the principal opinion in *Fullilove* was the flexible nature of the 10% set-aside. Two "congressional assumptions" underlay the MBE program: first, that the effects of past discrimination had impaired the competitive position of minority businesses, and second that "adjustment for the effects of past discrimination" would assure that at least 10% of funds from the federal grant program would flow to minority businesses. The Chief Justice noted that both of these "assumptions" could be "rebutted" by a grantee seeking a waiver of the 10% requirement. . . . Thus a waiver could be sought where minority businesses were not available to fill the 10% requirement or, more importantly, where an MBE attempted "to exploit the remedial aspects of the program by charging an unreasonable price, i.e. a price not attributable to the present effects of prior discrimination.". . . The Chief Justice indicated that without this fine tuning to remedial purpose, the statute would not have "pass[ed] muster.". . .

Appellant and its supporting *amici* rely heavily on *Fullilove* for the proposition that a city council, like Congress, need not make specific findings of discrimination to engage in race-conscious relief. Thus, appellant argues "[i]t would be a perversion of federalism to hold that the federal government has a compelling interest in remedying the effects of racial discrimination in its own public works program, but a city government does not."

What appellant ignores is that Congress, unlike any State or political subdivision, has a specific constitutional mandate to enforce the dictates of the Fourteenth Amendment. The power to "enforce" may at times also include the power to define situations which *Congress* determines threaten principles of equality and to adopt prophylactic rules to deal with those situations. . . .

That Congress may identify and redress the effects of society-wide discrimination does not mean that, *a fortiori*, the States and their political subdivisions are free to decide that such remedies are appropriate. . . .

It would seem equally clear, however, that a state or local subdivision (if delegated the authority from the State) has the authority to eradicate the effects of private discrimination within its own legislative jurisdiction. This authority must, of course, be exercised within the constraints of Section 1 of the Fourteenth Amendment. . . .

The Equal Protection Clause of the Fourteenth Amendment provides that "[N]o State shall . . . deny to *any person* within its jurisdiction the equal protection of the laws" (emphasis added). As this Court has noted in the past, the "rights created by the first section of the Fourteenth Amendment are, by its terms, guaranteed to the individual. The rights established are personal rights." *Shelley v. Kraemer* . . . (1948). The Richmond Plan denies certain citizens the opportunity to compete for a fixed percentage of public contracts based solely upon their race. To whatever racial group these citizens belong, the "personal rights" to be treated with equal dignity and respect are implicated by a rigid rule erecting race as the sole criterion in an aspect of public decisionmaking.

Absent searching judicial inquiring into the justification for such race-based measures, there is simply no way of determining what classifications are "benign" or "remedial" and what classifications are in fact motivated by illegitimate notions of racial inferiority or simple racial politics. . . .

Classifications based on race carry a danger of stigmatic harm. Unless they are strictly reserved for remedial settings, they may in fact promote notions of racial inferiority and lead to a politics of racial hostility. . . . We thus reaffirm the view expressed by the plurality in *Wygant* that the standard of review under the Equal Protection Clause is not dependent on the race of those burdened or benefited by a particular classification. . . .

Even were we to accept a reading of the guarantee of equal protection under which the level of scrutiny varies according to the ability of different groups to defend their interests in the representative process, heightened scrutiny would still be appropriate in the circumstances of this case. One of the central arguments for applying a less exacting standard to "benign" racial classifications is that such measures essentially involve a choice made by dominant racial groups to disadvantage themselves. If one aspect of the judiciary's role under the Equal Protection Clause is to protect "discrete and insular minorities" from majoritarian prejudice or indifference, . . . some maintain that these concerns are not implicated when the "white majority" places burdens upon itself.

In this case, blacks comprise approximately 50% of the population of the City of Richmond. Five of the nine seats on the City Council are held by blacks. The concern that a political majority will more easily act to the disadvantage of a minority based on unwarranted assumptions or incomplete facts would seem to militate for, not against, the application of heightened judicial scrutiny in this case. . . .

While there is no doubt that the sorry history of both private and public discrimination in this country has contributed to a lack of opportunities for black entrepreneurs, this observation, standing alone, cannot justify a rigid racial quota in the awarding of public contracts in Richmond, Virginia. Like the claim that discrimination in primary and secondary schooling justifies a rigid racial preference in medical school admissions, an amorphous claim that there has been past discrimination in a particular industry cannot justify the use of an unyielding racial quota. . . .

Because the city of Richmond has failed to identify the need for remedial action in the awarding of its public construction contracts, its treatment of its citizens on a racial basis violates the dictates of the Equal Protection Clause. Accordingly, the judgment of the Court of Appeals for the Fourth Circuit is

Affirmed.

JUSTICE SCALIA, concurring in the judgment. . . .

I agree with much of the Court's opinion, and, in particular, with its conclusion that strict scrutiny must be applied to all governmental classification by race, whether or not its asserted purpose is "remedial" or "benign." . . . I do not agree, however, with the Court's dicta suggesting that, despite the Fourteenth Amendment, state and local governments may in some circumstances discriminate on the basis of race in order (in a broad sense) "to ameliorate the effects of past discrimination." The difficulty of overcoming the effects of past discrimination is nothing compared with the difficulty of eradicating from our society the source of those effects, which is the tendency—fatal to a nation such as ours—to classify and judge men and women on the basis of their country of origin or the color of their skin. . . .

We have in some contexts approved the use of racial classifications by the Federal Government to remedy the effects of past discrimination. I do not believe that we must or should extend these holdings to the States. . . .

A sound distinction between federal and state (or local) action based on race rests not only upon the substance of the Civil War Amendments, but upon social reality and governmental theory. It is a simple fact that what Justice Stewart described in *Fullilove* as "the dispassionate objectivity [and] the flexibility that are needed to mold a race-conscious remedy around the single objective of eliminating the effects of past or present discrimination" . . . are substantially less likely to exist at the state or local level. The struggle for racial justice has historically been a struggle by the national society against oppression in the individual States. . . .

JUSTICE STEVENS, concurring in part and dissenting in part. . . .

The ordinance is . . . vulnerable because of its failure to identify the characteristics of the disadvantaged class of white contractors that justify the disparate treatment. . . . The composition of the disadvantaged class of white contractors presumably includes some who have been guilty of unlawful discrimination, some who practiced discrimination before it was forbidden by law, and some who have never discriminated against anyone on the basis of race. Imposing a common burden on such a disparate class merely because each member of the class is of the same race stems from reliance on the stereotype rather than fact or reason.

JUSTICE MARSHALL, with whom JUSTICE BRENNAN and JUSTICE BLACKMUN join, dissenting. . . .

It is a welcome symbol of racial progress when the former capital of the Confederacy acts forthrightly to confront the effects of racial discrimination in its midst. In my view, nothing in the Constitution can be construed to prevent Richmond, Virginia from allocating a portion of its contracting dollars for businesses owned or controlled by members of minority groups. Indeed, Richmond's set-aside program is indistinguishable in all meaningful respects from—and in fact was patterned upon—the federal set-aside plan which this Court upheld in *Fullilove v. Klutznick.* . . .

. . . [T]oday's decision marks a deliberate and giant step backward in this Court's affirmative action jurisprudence. Cynical of one municipality's attempt to redress the effects of past racial discrimination in a particular industry, the majority launches a grapeshot attack on race-conscious remedies in general. The majority's unnecessary pronouncements will inevitably discourage or prevent governmental entities, particularly States and localities, from acting to rectify the scourge of past discrimination. . . .

Today, for the first time, a majority of this Court has adopted strict scrutiny as its standard of Equal Protection Clause review of race-conscious remedial measures. . . . This is an unwelcome development. A profound difference separates governmental actions that themselves are racist, and governmental actions that seek to remedy the effects of prior racism or to prevent neutral governmental activity from perpetuating the effects of such racism. . . .

In concluding that remedial classifications warrant no different standard of review under the Constitution than the most brute and repugnant forms of state-sponsored racism, a majority of this Court signals that it regards racial discrimination as largely a phenomenon of the past, and that government bodies need no longer preoccupy themselves with rectifying racial injustice. . . .

While I agree that the numerical and political supremacy of a given racial group is a factor bearing upon the level of scrutiny to be applied, this Court has never held that numerical inferiority, standing alone, makes a racial group "suspect" and thus entitled to strict scrutiny review. . . .

ABIGAIL ADAMS, LETTER TO JOHN ADAMS (1776)

This remarkable letter from Abigail Adams to her husband on the eve of the American Revolution is a plea to the husband-Founders to "Remember the Ladies" in their fight against tyranny.

. . . I long to hear that you have declared an independency—and by the way in the new Code of Laws which I suppose it will be necessary for you to make I desire you would Remember the Ladies, and be more generous and favourable to them than your ancestors. Do not put such unlimited power into the hands of the Husbands. Remember all Men would be tyrants if they could. If particular care and attention is not paid to the Ladies we are determined to foment a Rebellion, and will not hold ourselves bound by any Laws in which we have no voice, or Representation.

That your Sex are Naturally Tyrannical is a Truth so thoroughly established as to admit of no dispute, but such of you as wish to be happy willingly give up the harsh title of Master for the more tender and endearing one of Friend. Why then, not put it out of the power of the vicious and the Lawless to sue us with cruelty and indignity with impunity. Men of Sense in all Ages abhor those customs which treat us only as the vassals of your Sex. Regard us then as Beings placed by providence under your protection and in imitation of the Supreme Being make use of that power only for our happiness.

JOHN ADAMS, LETTER TO ABIGAIL ADAMS (1776)

John's reply to Abigail might be taken as evidence of the Founder's indifference to the legal rights of women.

. . . As to your extraordinary Code of Laws, I cannot but laugh. We have been told that our Struggle has loosened the bands of Government every where. That Children and Apprentices were disobedient—that schools and Colleges were grown turbulent—that Indians slighted their Guardians and Negroes grew insolent to their Masters. But your Letter was the first Intimation that another Tribe more numerous and powerful than all the rest were grown discontented.—This is rather too coarse a Compliment but you are so saucy, I won't blot it out.

Depend upon it, We know better than to repeal our Masculine systems. Although they are in full Force, you know they are little more than Theory. We dare not exert our Power in its full Latitude. We are obliged to go fair, and softly, and in Practice you know We are the subjects. We have only the Name of Masters, rather than give up this, which would completely subject Us to the Despotism of the Petticoat, I hope General Washington, and all our brave Heroes would fight. . . .

FREDERICK DOUGLASS, WOMAN'S SUFFRAGE MOVEMENT (1870)

Several months after blacks gained the right to vote with the ratification of the Fifteenth Amendment, Douglass issued a call in his journal, The New National Era, *for female suffrage. For him, the rights of blacks and those of women are part of "the same system of truths."*

The simplest truths often meet the sternest resistance, and are slowest in getting general acceptance. There are none so blind as those who will not see, is an old proverb. Usage and prejudice, like forts built of sand, often defy the power of shot and shell, and play havoc with their besiegers. No simpler proposition, no truth more self-evident or more native to the human soul, was ever presented to human reason or consciousness than was that which formed our late anti-slavery movement. It only affirmed that every man is, and of right ought to be, the owner of his own body; and that no man can rightfully claim another man as his property. And yet what a tempest and whirlwind of human wrath, what clouds of ethical and theological dust, this simple proposition created. Families, churches, societies, parties, and States were riven by it, and at last the sword was called in to decide the questions which it raised. What was true of this simple truth was also true as to the people's right to a voice in their own Government, and the right of each man to form for himself his own religious opinions. All Europe ran blood before humanity and reason won this sacred right from priestcraft, bigotry and superstition. What today seems simple, obvious and undeniable, men looking through old customs, usages, and prejudices in other days denied altogether. Our friends of the woman's suffrage movement should bear this fact in mind, and share the patience of truth while they advocate the truth. It is painful to encounter stupidity as well as malice; but such is the fate of all who attempt to reform an abuse, to urge on humanity to nobler heights, and illumine the world with a new truth.

Now we know of no truth more easily made appreciable to human thought than the right of woman to vote, or in other words, to have a voice in the Government under which she lives and to which she owes allegiance. The very admission that woman owes allegiance, implies her right to vote. No man or woman who is not consulted can contract an obligation, or have an obligation created for him or her as the case may be. We can owe nothing by the mere act of another. Woman is not a consenting party to this Government. She has never been consulted. Ours is a Government of men, by men, each agreeing with all and all agreeing with each in respect to certain propositions, and women are wholly excluded. So far as respects its relation to woman, our Government is in its essence, a simple usurpation, a Government of force, and not of reason. We legislate for woman, and protect her, precisely as we legislate for and protect animals, asking the consent of neither.

It is nothing against this conclusion that our legislation has for the most part been eminently just and humane. A despotism is no less a despotism because the reigning despot may be a wise and good man. The principle is unaffected by the character of the man who for the moment may represent it. He may be kind or cruel, benevolent or selfish, in any case he rules according to his own sovereign will—and precisely such is the theoretical relation of our American Government toward woman. It simply takes her money without asking her consent and spends the same without in any wise consulting her wishes. It tells her that there is a code of laws which men have made, which she must obey or she must suffer the consequences. She is absolutely in the hands of her political masters: and though these may be kind and tender hearted, (the same was true of individual slave masters, as before stated,) this in no way mitigates the harshness of the principle—and it is against the principle we understand the woman's suffrage movement to be directed. It is intended to claim for woman a place by the side of man, as an equal subject to the solemn requirements of reason and law.

To ourselves, the great truth underlying this woman's movement is just as simple, obvious, and indisputable as either of the great truths referred to at the beginning of this article. It is a part of the same system of truths. Its sources are individuality, rationality, and sense of accountability.

If woman is admitted to be a moral and intellectual being, possessing a sense of good and evil, and a power of choice between them, her case is already half gained. Our natural powers are the foundation of our natural rights; and it is a consciousness of powers which suggests the exercise of rights. Man can only exercise the powers he possesses, and he can only conceive of rights in presence of powers. The fact that a woman has the power to say "I choose this rather than that" is sufficient proof that there is no natural reason against the exercise of that power. The power that makes her a moral and an accountable being gives her a natural right to choose the legislators who are to frame the laws under which she is to live, and the requirements of which she is bound to obey. By every fact and by every argument which man can wield in defence of his natural right to participate in government, the right of woman so to participate is equally defended and rendered unassailable.

Thus far all is clear and entirely consistent. Woman's natural abilities and possibilities, not less than man's, constitute the measure of her rights in all directions and relations, including her right to participate in shaping the policy and controlling the action of the Government under which she lives, and to which she is assumed to owe obedience. Unless it can be shown that woman is morally, physically and intellectually incapable of performing the act of voting, there can be no natural prohibition of such action on her part. Usage, custom, and deeply rooted prejudices are against woman's freedom. They have been against man's freedom, national freedom, religious freedom, but these will all subside in the case of woman as well as elsewhere. The thought has already been conceived; the word has been spoken; the debate has begun; earnest men and women are choosing sides. Error may be safely tolerated while truth is left free to combat it, and nobody need fear the result. The truth can hurt nothing which ought not to be hurt, and it alone can make men and women free.

ROSTKER v. GOLDBERG (1981)

The Military Selective Service Act (MSSA) authorized the president to require the registration for possible military service of males, but not females. Registration is for conscription, and only males are eligible for the draft. Registration for the draft was discontinued by a presidential proclamation in 1975. President Jimmy Carter decided in 1980 that it was necessary to reactivate the registration process and requested Congress to allocate funds for that purpose. He also recommended that Congress amend the MSSA to permit the registration and conscription of women. Although Congress agreed to reactivate the registration process, it declined to amend the MSSA to permit the registration of women and allocated funds only to register males. Thereafter, the president ordered the registration of

specified groups of young men. A lawsuit was brought against
Selective Service Director Bernard Rostker, by several men,
challenging the act's constitutionality.

JUSTICE REHNQUIST delivered the opinion of the Court. . . .

Whenever called upon to judge the constitutionality of an Act of
Congress—"the gravest and most delicate duty that this Court is
called upon to perform" . . . the Court accords "great weight to the
decisions of Congress." . . .

This is not, however, merely a case involving the customary deference accorded congressional decisions. The case arises in the
context of Congress' authority over national defense and military
affairs, perhaps in no other area has the Court accorded Congress
greater deference in rejecting the registration of women. . . .

Not only is the scope of Congress' constitutional power in this
area broad, but the lack of competence on the part of the courts is
marked. . . .

Congress determined that any future draft, which would be facilitated by the registration scheme, would be characterized by a
need for combat troops. . . .

Women as a group, however, unlike men as a group, are not eligible for combat. The restrictions on the participation of women in
combat in the Navy and Air Force are statutory. . . .

The Army and Marine Corps preclude the use of women in combat as a matter of established policy. . . .

Congress specifically recognized and endorsed the exclusion of
women from combat in exempting women from registration. In the
words of the Senate Report: "The principle that women should not
intentionally and routinely engage in combat is fundamental, and
enjoys wide support among our people.". . .

The existence of the combat restrictions clearly indicates the basis for Congress' decision to exempt women from registration. The purpose of registration was to prepare for a draft of combat troops. . . .

JUSTICE MARSHALL, with whom JUSTICE BRENNAN joins, dissenting. . . .

The Court today places its imprimatur on one of the most potent remaining public expressions of "ancient canards about the proper role of women.". . . It upholds a statute that requires males but not females to register for the draft, and which thereby categorically excludes women from a fundamental civic obligation. Because I believe the Court's decision is inconsistent with the Constitution's guarantee of equal protection of the laws, I dissent.

. . . The Court essentially reasons that the gender classification employed by the MSSA is constitutionally permissible because non-discrimination is not necessary to achieve the purpose of registration to prepare for a draft of combat troops. In other words, the majority concludes that women may be excluded from registration because they will not be needed in the event of a draft.

. . . [T]he question is whether the gender-based classification is itself substantially related to the achievement of the asserted governmental interest. Thus, the Government's task in this case is to demonstrate that excluding women from registration substantially furthers the goal of preparing for a draft of combat troops. Or to put it another way, the Government must show that registering women would substantially impede its efforts to prepare for such draft. Under our precedents, the Government cannot meet this burden without showing that a gender neutral statute would be a less effective means of attaining this end. . . . In this case, the Government makes no claim that preparing for a draft of combat troops cannot be accomplished just as effectively by registering both men and women but drafting only men if only men turn out to be needed. Nor can the Government argue that this alternative entails the additional cost and administrative inconvenience of registering women. This Court has repeatedly stated that the administrative convenience of employing a gender classification is not an adequate constitutional justification. . . .

PAT SCHROEDER, GREAT EXPECTATIONS:
ABIGAIL ADAMS TO THE WHITE HOUSE (1984)

Congresswoman Schroeder, a Democrat from Colorado, gives her view of the progress of feminism in America. She includes controversial observations on "comparable worth" and the effect of the perspective of women on political life.

Political and economic currents rarely move straight ahead, like a train on a track. They meander, double back and cross over before finally building up enough pressure to force permanent changes in the political landscape.

The 200th anniversary of feminism in America was celebrated in 1976 without much particular fanfare when we honored Abigail Adams as the first American feminist. Abigail Adams was the Tom Paine of the colonial women's movement. She lobbied George Washington and Thomas Jefferson to emancipate women in the Constitution. Here is what she told them:

If particular care and attention are not paid to the ladies we are determined to foment a rebellion and will not hold ourselves bound to obey any law in which we have no voice or representation.

The Abigail Adams rebellion has been some time fomenting. Her plea went unheeded and the Constitution ignored "the ladies."

Women did not issue their declaration of independence until almost 75 years later, at the famed Seneca Falls convention in 1848. In the decades following Seneca Falls, feminist activism swept America, entwined with a host of other social causes, such as the abolition of slavery, prohibition and restrictions on child labor.

Women gained property, occupational, educational and political rights, and in 1920 won the long-sought right to vote. They had great expectations for a strong women's party or, at the least, an immediate and significant feminist impact on American politics.

But the movement ran out of political steam. Many women thought the battle was won and their interests turned elsewhere. The

Depression hit, followed by World War II, the Cold War and the Korean War.

After World War II, the GI Bill sent thousands of mostly male veterans off to college. The marriage rate increased, followed by a baby boom. The average marriage age for women dropped clear past 20 and down into the teens.

In the 1950s, the Model Woman was cheerfully waxing the kitchen floor in a white clapboard house in suburbia. All was well, or so it seemed.

In 1960, *Redbook* magazine featured an article, "Why Do Young Mothers Feel Trapped," and asked their readers to write in with their stories. Over 24,000 mothers did. All was not well.

Betty Friedan's book, *The Feminine Mystique*, came out in 1963 and sold two million copies over the next 20 years. The mystique was "the problem that had no name"—the problem that had prompted 24,000 letters from *Redbook* readers.

Friedan focused attention on the identity crisis many women experienced, the lack of fulfillment, the mystery that being a woman was enough, and she gave it a name.

Ten years later, in a 1973 epilogue to her now famous book, Friedan explained that the solution was "suggesting new patterns, a way out of the conflicts, whereby women could use their abilities fully in society to find their own . . . human identity, sharing its action, decisions and challenges without at the same time renouncing home, children, love, their own sexuality."

Although attention focused on the sensational aspects of the "new feminism," the movement was not as shrill or polarizing as the rhetoric may have sounded.

Unfortunately, as we all know, sensationalism sells newspapers.

George Bernard Shaw said that "Newspapers are unable to discriminate between a bicycle accident and the collapse of civilization." To which Fred Allen added, "Television is called a medium because so little of it is rare or well done."

In her new book, *The Second Stage*, published [in 1983], Friedan described the spirit of the next, logical phase in the women's movement:

> There is no going back. The women's movement was necessary. But the liberation that began with the women's movement isn't finished. How do we transcend the polarization between women and women and between women and men, to achieve the new human wholeness that is the promise of feminism, and get on with solving the concrete practical, everyday problems of living, working and loving as equal persons? That is the personal and political business of the second stage.

What were the changes in society that moved us this far, and where are we headed?

Over the past several generations, while political feminism rose and fell, there were major social and economic changes going on in America.

Some, like the migration of Americans from rural to urban areas, are well known.

Others are less known, or are seen as recent trends. In fact, however, they have been building for decades.

For example, female participation in the salaried work force has been steadily increasing for the past century. It is not just a post-World War II phenomenon.

In 1890, only 5 percent of married women and 20 percent of all women were in the salaried work force. By 1910, 10 percent of the married and 25 percent of all women held jobs outside the home. The rates dropped in the 1920s, and began to climb again during the Depression and war years.

More significantly, the work participation difference between married and unmarried women all but disappeared. By 1980, half of all women in America were in the work force.

"My wife doesn't work," the former boast of many American men, was wrong on two counts. She either worked at home, in an unsalaried job, or she worked outside the home in a salaried job. In many cases, she did both.

Look at education: over the past century, the number of under-graduate degrees awarded to women climbed slowly but inexorably. In 1870, 15 percent went to women; by 1930 that number had risen to 40 percent. The GI Bill era reversed that trend, but only tempo-rarily. By 1970, the gap was narrowing again. In 1980, women received 49 percent of all undergraduate degrees.

And female students were now majoring in traditionally male fields such as engineering (up 830 percent between 1972 and 1982); agriculture (up 429 percent); business (up 247 percent); architec-ture (up 130 percent); and computer sciences (up 123 percent).

Similar changes were occurring in the professions: between 1972 and 1982, women receiving degrees in law quadrupled from 7 per-cent to 30 percent; medicine more than doubled from 9 percent to 23 percent; dentistry went up sharply, from 1 percent to 14 per-cent; and veterinary science almost quadrupled from 9 percent to 33 percent.

The percentage of doctorate degrees awarded to women in the last 10 years has almost doubled—from 16 percent up to 30 per-cent. . . .

A history lesson. Just over twenty years ago, in 1963, Congress passed the Equal Pay Act requiring businesses to pay equal wages for equal work. If you think that was a simple move, you're wrong. The fight to pass that law went on for years. Employer organiza-tions argued it would cost them too much money and was improper government interference.

The equal pay fight was just beginning. The simple fact remains that occupations filled with women—nursing, teaching, and secre-tarial—are generally low paying.

Comparable worth does not mean pay men less, nor does it mean pay women more. It means pay PEOPLE what they are worth. In many cases it will mean paying women more—I'm sure we can live with that.

Now the naysayers argue that there are no standards—no one can determine what a job is worth.

If you will permit me a farm term, that's hog wash. Every business, company, union and government agency has standards to set wages and salaries. Large corporations even have rules to decide the size of your office, the carpet on the floor, and the size desk you get.

No, the problem is not a lack of standards. The problem is that there are standards and the standards are wrong.

When a nurse or high school math teacher with a college education is paid less than a liquor store clerk with a high school education, there is something wrong with our wage standards, not to mention our values.

One of the naysayers, Phyllis Schlafly, was in Colorado recently. She said that liquor store clerks should be paid more than nurses because they lift heavy boxes; and tree trimmers should be paid more than teachers because they work outdoors.

Fine, let's pay nurses the same as surgeons, because they both work indoors. And the secretaries the same as lawyers because neither lift heavy boxes. Furthermore, the kids who deliver our newspapers should be paid six figure salaries because they drag around heavy bundles and brave the elements.

The real cause of the wage disparity is that most women's jobs— 80 percent of all women are in 25 job categories like nursing, teaching, service and office jobs—are not highly valued. Can someone explain to me why cutting a lawn is more valuable to society than teaching kindergarten?

Paradoxically, as we see more women in the work force and more women getting more education, we are also seeing the feminization of poverty.

The startling rise in the number of female heads of household and poor elderly women has feminized poverty. Divorce is a pivotal factor. Although there are indications that the divorce rate may have plateaued in recent years, between 1920 and 1980 it more than tripled.

And if it has leveled off, it's a rather high plateau—more than 50 percent of marriages contracted today will end in divorce, separation or desertion. The economic effect of divorce on women, especially those with children, is nothing short of disastrous.

Less than half the women who retain custody of the children receive full, court-ordered child support. Almost one quarter receive nothing.

A California study of 3,000 divorced couples found that one year after divorce, the woman's income had dropped 73 percent while the man's had increased 43 percent! It is little wonder, if present trends continue, that by the year 2000, the poor in America will be almost entirely women and children.

The anti-ERA lobby talks a lot about women needing to be "protected." But that's exactly the point of the ERA: inequality is no protection. Whatever the standard—wages, pensions, child support, survivor's benefits—women come up short.

It is no wonder that the ERA has become an economic issue. The gender gap, the difference between how men and women tend to vote, is largely based on economic issues. Inequality is an economic issue.

Most public opinion polls show that men and women agree on what are called "women's issues" like ERA, day care, etc. The disagreements are on economic and peace issues. The margin in the gender gap pools range from 5 percent to 15 percent—a large margin considering that women make up 53 percent of the voters.

These trends are reshaping American politics because our political system accommodates itself to shifting currents. Women have adjusted to the new interest by male politicians in women's issues, and men have adjusted to the increased role of women and women's concerns in politics.

. . . [T]he new feminist awareness in politics makes it more likely that the presidential and vice-presidential nominees, male or female, will be committed to social, political and economic equality for women.

That commitment, by the way, is nothing more than Webster's Dictionary definition of "feminism." I always chuckle when I hear someone say, "I'm for equal rights, but I'm not a feminist"—as if being a feminist was a misdemeanor.

JEANE KIRKPATRICK, ADDRESS TO THE WOMEN'S FORUM (1984)

Kirkpatrick, President Reagan's ambassador to the United Nations, describes from personal experience the difficulties faced by women today in political life.

. . . When I have replied to criticisms of the United States (which is an important part of my job), I have frequently been described as "confrontational": This is an interesting experience for me, since I had never been described as "confrontational" in my life before I went to the United Nations. I reflected a good deal on this "confrontational" label, and on what behavior is described as "confrontational," and whether it is more likely that a woman will be described as "confrontational" than a man. In the beginning I thought that I was described as "confrontational" because we adopted a policy inside the United Nations that, when the United States was publicly attacked, we would defend ourselves. We would address the charge and examine the record. That was a policy of the U.S. government. Interestingly enough, it was attributed to me, as a personal characteristic, as demonstrating that I was a confrontational person. It was a while before I noticed that none of my male colleagues, who often delivered more "confrontational" speeches than I, were labelled as "confrontational."

In thinking about this "confrontational" label, I have concluded that it is extremely unlikely that any woman who arrives at a very high level in any public activity is confrontational. If they were, they would have long since been eliminated. To achieve a significant level of recognition in our society, it is necessary to pass through numerous doors in which males are the gatekeepers. It is highly unlikely that any woman with a confrontational style would make it through more than one of those doors.

In fact, most successful women have become expert at avoiding confrontations. At Georgetown, for example, I managed to stay out of the most incredible faculty-administration "Star Wars," because I had learned to side-step conflicts.

I now think that being tagged as "confrontational" and being a woman in a high position are very closely related. There is a certain level of office the very occupancy of which constitutes a confrontation with conventional expectations. Similarly, I think being described as "tough" and being a woman in public life are very closely related. Again, this is an adjective that was never applied to me before I entered into high politics. Yet, it was not long before the French were calling me the "Femme de Fer," and our own papers were describing me repeatedly as "Reagan's Iron Woman," and most frequently as "tough." I've thought about that, too, and I've come to see here a double-bind: if a woman seems strong, she is called "tough"; if she doesn't seem strong, she's found not strong enough to occupy a high level job in a crunch.

Terms like "tough" and "confrontational" express a certain very general surprise and disapproval at the presence of a woman in arenas in which it is necessary to be—what for males would be considered—normally assertive. Stereotyping has endless variations.

I have recently had a whole new set of adjectives applied to me. They also come as a surprise; they also are clearly sex-related. The key new term is "temperamental." Now, being called "temperamental" is a classically Victorian sexist charge against women. Noting that some six stories had appeared in which White House aides described me as "temperamental," too temperamental to occupy responsible office, one male colleague queried, "What do they mean? Too temperamental once a month?" Who is not familiar with the notion that women are a bit erratic, a bit unstable, hormonally dis-

abled? . . . I found this one downright amusing. Not only is it anachronistic, it utterly ignores the fact that I have led the most extraor-
dinarily stable life; I have lived in the same house for twenty-eight
years, with the same husband, and had the same jobs. Even Dr.
Edgar Berman has approved my performance.

Well, it's all very interesting. I also noticed, as I've watched the
media treatment of Geraldine Ferraro or Ann Gorsuch-Burford, that
there are some identifiable regularities in media response, although
they were very different people in very different roles, different from
each other and from me.

What do I want to say about it all, finally? I want to say that I
think that sexism is alive in the United Nations, in the Secretariat;
it's alive in the U.S. government; it's alive in American politics—
I've seen enough, by the way, of Democratic politics at high levels
to know that it's bipartisan. And I also want to say that sexism is
not unconquerable, if one can avoid getting and staying angry and
wasting one's energies on rage. I don't know how many of you have
recently read *A Room of One's Own*, which remains my own favorite feminist classic. In that beautiful essay, Virginia Woolf talks about
the pitfalls of anger for women, of wasting one's energy, one's self,
on rage. I think that's very important, because if one is angry much
of the time, that anger unbalances one's judgment, consumes one's
energy. If you can avoid the pitfalls of rage and paranoia and can
hang in long enough to prove seriousness and competence, then I
find, in the diplomatic world and in American high politics, too,
then you can develop good relations based on mutual respect with
almost all your colleagues. In the UN, that applies to representatives of countries that don't even grant legal equality to women.

But that is not the end of the inquiry. I still think, even more
clearly than when I wrote *Political Woman* or *The New Presidential Elites*, that the lifestyle in high politics and government may
be peculiarly unattractive to women. I find myself thinking of the
number of women, the relatively high percentage of women, who
withdraw from high politics and government by personal decision—
not because they can't hack it, but because they don't choose to.
High politics involves a weirdly unbalanced kind of lifestyle, which
requires continuous involvement with power. It is not only neces-

sary to work eighty or ninety-hour weeks; that is true of many vocations. It is that the whole enterprise resembles that described by Thomas Hobbes: you know, the "restless striving after power which [one suspects] ceaseth only in death."

I don't know what styles of interaction would be like in politics and government if there were enough women there to affect the way in which business is conducted. Today, any one woman present, whether it's in the UN Security Council, or in our National Security Council, or in the decision arenas of any major power process in our society today, adapts to a male pattern of interaction. To do that for long, you have to like it a lot. You have to need it a lot.

We are back here with the ultimate questions of whether there are identifiable male and female sensibilities and social styles. I tend to think there are; and I tend to think that the patterns of interaction in high politics are peculiarly unattractive to women, that is, to most women I have known (and to me, I might add), as I think these social processes as unattractive to most women as they are inhospitable to them. Neither of these tendencies—if they exist—portend a rapid influx of women into top positions in government, least of all foreign policy.

3

Federalism

The selections in this chapter concern federalism, the American principle of dividing the power of government between the nation and the states.

FEDERALIST 39

Here Publius argues that the newly proposed government, based on what he calls "neither a national nor a federal constitution, but a composition of both," does not violate republican principles.

The last paper having concluded the observations which were meant to introduce a candid survey of the plan of government reported by the convention, we now proceed to the execution of the part of our undertaking. The first question that offers itself is, whether the general form and aspect of the government be strictly republican? It is evident that no other form would be reconcilable with the genius of the people of America; with the fundamental principles of the Revolution; or with that honorable determination, which animates every votary of freedom, to rest all our political experiments on the capacity of mankind for self-government. If the plan of the convention therefore be found to depart from the republican character, its advocates must abandon it as no longer defensible. . . .

If we resort for a criterion, to the different principles on which different forms of government are established, we may define a republic to be, or at least may bestow that name on, a government which derives all its powers directly or indirectly from the great body of the people, and is administered by persons holding their offices during pleasure, for a limited period, or during good behavior. It is essential to such a government that it be derived from the great body of the society, not from an inconsiderable proportion, or a favored class of it; otherwise a handful of tyrannical nobles, exercising their oppressions by a delegation of their powers, might aspire to the rank of republicans, and claim for their government the honorable title of republic. It is sufficient for such a government, that the persons administering it be appointed, either directly or indirectly, by the people; and that they hold their appointments by either of the tenures just specified; otherwise every government in the United States, as well as every other popular government that has been or can be well organized or well executed, would be degraded from the republican character. According to most of them, the chief magistrate himself is so appointed. And according to one, this mode of appointment is extended to one of the coordinate branches of the legislature. According to all the constitutions, also, the tenure of the highest offices is extended to a definite period, and in many instances, both within the legislative and executive departments, to a period of years. According to the provisions of most of the constitutions, again, as well as according to the most respectable and received opinions on the subject, the members of the judiciary department are to retain their offices by the firm tenure of good behavior. . . .

But it was not sufficient, say the adversaries of the proposed Constitution, for the convention to adhere to the republican form. They ought, with equal care, to have preserved the federal form, which regards the Union as a Confederacy of sovereign States; instead of which, they have framed a national government, which regards the Union as a consolidation of the States. And it is asked by what authority this bold and radical innovation was undertaken. The handle which has been made of this objection requires, that it should be examined with some precision.

Without inquiring into the accuracy of the distinction on which the objection is founded, it will be necessary to a just estimate of its force, first to ascertain the real character of the government in question; secondly, to inquire how far the convention were authorized to propose such a government; and thirdly, how far the duty they owed to their country, could supply any defect of regular authority.

First.—In order to ascertain the real character of the government, it may be considered in relation to the foundation on which it is to be established; to the sources from which its ordinary powers are to be drawn; to the operation of those powers; to the extent of them; and to the authority by which future changes in the government are to be introduced.

On examining the first relation, it appears on one hand that the Constitution is to be founded on the assent and ratification of the people of America, given by deputies elected for the special purpose; but on the other, that this assent and ratification is to be given by the people, not as individuals composing one entire nation; but as composing the distinct and independent States to which they respectively belong. It is to be the assent and ratification of the several States, derived from the supreme authority in each State, the authority of the people themselves. The act therefore establishing the Constitution, will not be a national but a federal act.

That it will be a federal and not a national act, as these terms are understood by the objectors, the act of the people as forming so many independent States, not as forming one aggregate nation, is obvious from this single consideration that it is to result neither from the decision of a majority of the people of the Union, nor from that of a majority of the States. It must result from the unanimous assent of the several States that are parties to it, differing no otherwise from their ordinary assent than in its being expressed, not by the legislative authority, but by that of the people themselves. Were the people regarded in this transaction as forming one nation, the will of the majority of the whole people of the United States, would bind the minority, in the same manner as the majority in each State must bind the minority; and the will of the majority must be determined either by a comparison of the individual votes; or by considering the will of a majority of the States, as evidence of the will of a majority of the people of the United States. Neither of these rules has been adopted. Each State in ratifying the Constitution, is considered as a sovereign body independent of all others, and only to be bound by its own voluntary act. In this relation then the new Constitution will, if established, be a federal and not a national constitution.

The next relation is to the sources from which the ordinary powers of government are to be derived. The house of representatives will derive its powers from the people of America; and the people will be represented in the same proportion, and on the same principle, as they are in the legislature of a particular State. So far the government is national not federal. The Senate on the other hand will derive its powers from the States, as political and co-equal societies; and these will be represented on the principle of equality in the Senate, as they now are in the existing Congress. So far the government is federal, not national. The executive power will be derived from a very compound source. The immediate election of the President is to be made by the States in their political characters. The votes allotted to them are in a compound ratio, which considers them partly as distinct and co-equal societies, partly as unequal members of the same society. The eventual election, again is to be made by that branch of the legislature which consists of the national representatives; but in this particular act they are to be thrown into the form of individual delegations from so many distinct and co-equal bodies politic. From this aspect of the government, it appears to be of a mixed character presenting at least as many federal as national features.

The difference between a federal and national government as it relates to the operation of the government is supposed to consist in this, that in the former, the powers operate on the political bodies composing the confederacy, in their political capacities: In the latter, on the individual citizens composing the nation, in their individual capacities. On trying the Constitution by this criterion, it falls under the national, not the federal character; though perhaps not so completely, as has been understood. In several cases and particularly in the trial of controversies to which States may be parties, they must be viewed and proceeded against in their collective and political capacities only. So far the national countenance of the government on this side seems to be disfigured by a few federal features. But this blemish is perhaps unavoidable in any plan; and the operation of the government on the people in their individual capacities, in its ordinary and most essential proceedings, may on the whole designate it in this relation a national Government.

But if the Government be national with regard to the operation of its powers, it changes its aspect again when we contemplate it in relation to the extent of its powers. The idea of a national government involves in it, not only an authority over the individual citizens, but an indefinite supremacy over all persons and things, so far as they are objects of lawful government. Among a people consolidated into one nation, this supremacy is completely vested in the national Legislature. Among communities united for particular purposes, it is vested partly in the general, and partly in the municipal legislatures. In the former case, all local authorities are subordinate to the supreme; and may be controlled, directed or abolished by it at pleasure. In the latter the local or municipal authorities form distinct and independent portions of the supremacy, no more subject within their respective spheres to the general authority, than the general authority is subject to them, within its own sphere. In this relation then the proposed government cannot be deemed a national one; since its jurisdiction extends to certain enumerated objects only, and leaves to the several States a residuary and inviolable sovereignty over all other objects. It is true that in controversies relating to the boundary between the two jurisdictions the tribunal which is ultimately to decide, is to be established under the general government. But this does not change the principle of the case. The decision is to be impartially made, according to the rules of the Constitution; and all the usual and most effectual precautions are taken to secure this impartiality. Some such tribunal is clearly essential to prevent an appeal to the sword, and a dissolution of the compact; and that it ought to be established under the general, rather than under the local governments, or to speak more properly, that it could be safely established under the first alone, is a position not likely to be combated.

If we try the Constitution by its last relation, to the authority by which amendments are to be made, we find it neither wholly national, nor wholly federal. Were it wholly national, the supreme and ultimate authority would reside in the majority of the people of the Union; and this authority would be competent at all times, like that of a majority of every national society, to alter or abolish its established government. Were it wholly federal on the other hand, the concurrence of each State in the Union would be essential to every alteration that would be binding on all. The mode provided by the plan of the convention is not founded on either of these principles. In requiring more than a majority, and particularly, in computing the proportion by States, not by citizens, it departs from the national, and advances towards the federal character: in rendering the concurrence of less than the whole number of States sufficient, it loses again the federal, and partakes of the national character.

The proposed Constitution therefore is in strictness neither a national nor a federal constitution, but a composition of both. In its foundation, it is federal, not national; in the sources from which the ordinary powers of the government are drawn, it is partly federal, and partly national: in the operation of these powers, it is national, not federal: in the extent of them again, it is federal, not national; and finally, in the authoritative mode of introducing amendments, it is neither wholly federal, nor wholly national.

THOMAS JEFFERSON, *NOTES ON THE STATE OF VIRGINIA* (1784)

Jefferson praises the agrarian way of life for its promotion of self-sufficiency and virtue. Those qualities, he believes, are necessary for republican citizens. He opposed the establishment of a powerful and necessarily commerce-oriented national government. Hence he also opposed a flexible interpretation of the powers of Congress under the Constitution.

We never had an interior trade of any importance. Our exterior commerce has suffered very much from the beginning of the present contest. During this time we have manufactured within our families the most necessary articles of clothing. Those of cotton will bear some comparison with the same kinds of manufacture in Europe; but those of wool, flax and hemp are very coarse, unsightly, and unpleasant; and such is our attachment to agriculture, and such our preference for foreign manufactures, that be it wise or unwise, our people will certainly return as soon as they can, to the raising raw materials, and exchanging them for finer manufactures than they are able to execute themselves.

The political economists of Europe have established it as a principle, that every State should endeavor to manufacture for itself; and this principle, like many others, we transfer to America, without calculating the difference of circumstance which should often produce a difference of result. In Europe the lands are either cultivated, or locked up against the cultivator. Manufacture must therefore be resorted to of necessity not of choice, to support the surplus of their people. But we have an immensity of land courting the industry of the husbandman. Is it best then that all our citizens should be employed in its improvement, or that one half should be called off from that to exercise manufactures and handicraft arts for the other? Those who labor in the earth are the chosen people of God, if ever He had a chosen people, whose breasts He has made His peculiar deposit for substantial and genuine virtue. It is the focus in which he keeps alive that sacred fire, which otherwise might escape from the face of the earth. Corruption of morals in the mass of cultivators is a phenomenon of which no age nor nation has furnished an example. It is the mark set on those, who, not looking up to heaven, to their own soil and industry, as does the husbandman, for their subsistence, depend for it on casualties and caprice of customers. Dependence begets subservience and venality, suffocates the germ of virtue, and prepares fit tools for the designs of ambition. This, the natural progress and consequence of the arts, has sometimes perhaps been retarded by accidental circumstances; but, generally speaking, the proportion which the aggregate of the other classes of citizens bears in any State to that of its husbandmen, is the proportion of its unsound to its healthy parts, and is a good enough barometer whereby to measure its degree of corruption. While we have land to labor then, let us never wish to see our citizens occupied at a workbench, or twirling a distaff. Carpenters, masons, smiths, are wanting in husbandry; but, for the general operations of manufacture, let our workshops remain in Europe. It is better to carry provisions and materials to workmen there, than bring them to the provisions and materials, and with them their manners and principles. The loss by the transportation of commodities across the Atlantic will be made up in happiness and permanence of government. The mobs of great cities add just so much to the support of pure government, as sores do to the strength of the human body. It is the manners and spirit of a people which preserve a republic in vigor. A degeneracy in these is a canker which soon eats to the heart of its laws and constitution.

McCULLOCH v. MARYLAND (1819)

This is the classic argument for a flexible or broad interpretation of Congress' powers under the Constitution. The case involves the constitutionality of Maryland's law imposing a tax on operations of the Baltimore branch of the Bank of the United States. In order to reach a decision, the Court was compelled to consider the fundamental question of whether Congress has the power to incorporate a bank.

CHIEF JUSTICE MARSHALL delivered the opinion of the Court. . . .

In the case now to be determined, the defendant, a sovereign State, denies the obligation of a law enacted by the legislature of the Union, and the plaintiff, on his part, contests the validity of an act which has been passed by the legislature of that State. The constitution of our country, in its most interesting and vital parts, is to be considered; the conflicting powers of the government of the Union and of its members, as marked in that constitution, are to be discussed; and an opinion given, which may essentially influence the great operations of government. No tribunal can approach such a question without a deep sense of its importance, and of the awful responsibility involved in its decision. But it must be decided peacefully, or remain a source of hostile legislation, perhaps of hostility of a still more serious nature; and if it is to be so decided, by this tribunal alone can the decision be made. On the Supreme Court of the United States has the Constitution of our country devolved this important duty.

The first question made in the case is, has Congress power to incorporate a bank? . . .

In discussing this question, the counsel for the State of Maryland have deemed it of some importance, in the construction of the Constitution, to consider that instrument not as emanating from the people, but as the act of sovereign and independent states. The powers of the general government, it has been said, are delegated by the states, who alone are truly sovereign; and must be exercised in subordination to the states, who alone possess supreme dominion.

It would be difficult to sustain this proposition. The convention which framed the Constitution was, indeed, elected by the state legislatures. But the instrument, when it came from their hands, was a mere proposal, without obligation, or pretensions to it. It was reported to the then existing Congress of the United States, with a request that it might "be submitted to a convention of delegates, chosen in each state, by the people thereof, under the recommendation of its legislature, for their assent and ratification." This mode of proceeding was adopted; and by the convention, by Congress, and by the state legislatures, the instrument was submitted to the people. They acted upon it, in the only manner in which they can act safely, effectively, and wisely, on such a subject, by assembling in convention. It is true, they assembled in their several states; and where else should they have assembled? No political dreamer was ever wild enough to think of breaking down the lines which separate the states, and of compounding the American people into one common mass. Of consequence, when they act, they act in their states. But the measures they adopt do not, on that account, cease to be the measures of the people themselves, or become the measures of the state governments.

From these conventions the Constitution derives its whole authority. The government proceeds directly from the people; is "ordained and established" in the name of the people; and is declared to be ordained, "in order to form a more perfect union, establish justice, insure domestic tranquility, and secure the blessings of liberty to themselves and to their posterity." The assent of the states, in their sovereign capacity, is implied in calling a convention, and thus submitting that instrument to the people. But the people were at perfect liberty to accept or reject it; and their act was final. It required not the affirmation, and could not be negatived, by the state governments. The Constitution, when thus adopted, was of complete obligation, and bound the state sovereignties.

It has been said, that the people had already surrendered all their powers to the state sovereignties, and had nothing more to give. But, surely, the question whether they may resume and modify the powers granted to government, does not remain to be settled in this country. Much more might the legitimacy of the general government be doubted, had it been created by the states. The powers delegated to the state sovereignties were to be exercised by themselves, not by a distinct and independent sovereignty, created by themselves. To the formation of a league, such as was the Confederation, the state sovereignties were certainly competent. But when, "in order to form a more perfect union," it was deemed necessary to change this alliance into an effective government, possessing great and sovereign powers, and acting directly on the people, the necessity of referring it to the people, and of deriving its powers directly from them, was felt and acknowledged by all.

The government of the Union, then (whatever may be the influence of this fact on the case), is emphatically and truly a government of the people. In form and in substance it emanates from them, its powers are granted by them, and are to be exercised directly on them, and for their benefit.

This government is acknowledged by all to be one of enumerated powers. The principle, that it can exercise only the powers granted to it, would seem too apparent to have required to be enforced by all those arguments which its enlightened friends, while it was depending before the people, found it necessary to urge. That principle is now universally admitted. But the question respecting the extent of the powers actually granted, is perpetually arising, and will probably continue to arise, as long as our system shall exist.

In discussing these questions, the conflicting powers of the general and State governments must be brought into view, and the supremacy of their respective laws, when they are in opposition, must be settled.

If any one proposition could command the universal assent of mankind, we might expect it would be this—that the government of the Union, though limited in its powers, is supreme within its sphere of action. This would seem to result necessarily from its nature. It is the government of all; its powers are delegated by all; it represents all, and acts for all. Though any one State may be willing to control its operations, no State is willing to allow others to control them. The nation, on those subjects on which it can act, must necessarily bind its component parts. But this question is not left to mere reason: the people have, in express terms, decided it, by saying, "this Constitution, and the laws of the United States, which shall be made in pursuance thereof, shall be the supreme law of the land," and by requiring that the members of the State legislatures, and the officers of the executive and judicial departments of the States, shall take the oath of fidelity to it.

The government of the United States, then, though limited in its powers, is supreme; and its laws, when made in pursuance of the Constitution, form the supreme law of the land, "anything in the Constitution or laws of any State to the contrary notwithstanding."

Among the enumerated powers, we do not find that of establishing a bank or creating a corporation. But there is no phrase in the instrument which, like the Articles of Confederation, excludes incidental or implied powers; and which requires that everything granted shall be expressly and minutely described. Even the Tenth Amendment, which was framed for the purpose of quieting the excessive jealousies which had been excited, omits the word "expressly," and declares only that the powers "not delegated to the United States, nor prohibited to the States, are reserved to the States or to the people"; thus leaving the question, whether the particular power which may become the subject of contest has been delegated to the one government, or prohibited to the other, to depend on a fair construction of the whole instrument. The men who drew and adopted this amendment, had experienced the embarrassments resulting from the insertion of this word in the Articles of Confederation, and probably omitted it to avoid those embarrassments. A constitution, to contain an accurate detail of all the subdivisions of which its great powers will admit, and of all the means by which they may be carried into execution, would partake of the prolixity of a legal code, and could scarcely be embraced by the human mind. It would probably never be understood by the public. Its nature, therefore, requires that only its great outlines should be marked, its important objects designated, and the minor ingredients which compose those objects be deduced from the nature of the objects themselves. That this idea was entertained by the framers of the American Constitution, is not only to be inferred from the nature of the instrument, but from the language. Why else were some of the limitations, found in the ninth section of the first article, introduced? It is also, in some degree, warranted by their having omitted to use any restrictive term which might prevent its receiving a fair and just interpretation. In considering this question, then, we must never forget, that it is a constitution we are expounding.

Although, among the enumerated powers of government, we do not find the word "bank," or "incorporation," we find the great powers to lay and collect taxes; to borrow money; to regulate commerce; to declare and conduct a war; and to raise and support armies and navies. The sword and the purse, all the external relations, and no inconsiderable portion of the industry of the nation, are entrusted to its government. It can never be pretended that these vast powers draw after them others of inferior importance, merely because they are inferior. Such an idea can never be advanced. But it may with great reason, be contended that a government, entrusted with such ample powers, on the due execution of which the happiness and prosperity of the nation so vitally depends, must also be entrusted with ample means for their execution. The power being given, it is the interest of the nation to facilitate its execution. It can never be their interest, and cannot be presumed to have been their intention, to clog and embarrass its execution by withholding the most appropriate means. Throughout this vast republic, from the St. Croix to the Gulf of Mexico, from the Atlantic to the Pacific, revenue is to be collected and expended, armies are to be marched and supported. The exigencies of the nation may require, that the treasure raised in the north should be transported to the south, that raised in the east conveyed to the west, or that this order should be reversed. Is that construction of the Constitution to be preferred which would render these operations difficult, hazardous, and expensive? Can we adopt that construction (unless the words imperiously require it) which would impute to the framers of that instrument, when granting these powers for the public good, the intention of impeding their exercise by withholding a choice of means? If, indeed, such be the mandate of the Constitution, we have only to obey; but that instrument does not profess to enumerate the means by which the powers it confers may be executed; nor does it prohibit the creation of a corporation, if the existence of such a being be essential to the beneficial exercise of those powers. It is, then, the subject of fair inquiry, how far such means may be employed. It is not denied, that the powers given to the government imply the ordinary means of execution. That, for example, of raising revenue, and applying it to national purposes, is admitted to imply the power of conveying money from place to place, as the exigencies of the nation may require and of employing the usual means of conveyance. But it is denied that the government has its choice of means; or, that it may employ the most convenient means, if, to employ them, it be necessary to erect a corporation. . . .

We admit, as all must admit, that the powers of the government are limited, and that its limits are not to be transcended. But we think the sound construction of the Constitution must allow to the national legislature that discretion, with respect to the means by which the powers it confers are to be carried into execution, which will enable that body to perform the high duties assigned to it, in the manner most beneficial to the people. Let the end be legitimate, let it be within the scope of the Constitution, and all means which are appropriate, which are plainly adapted to that end, which are not prohibited, but consist with the letter and spirit of the Constitution, are constitutional.

HAMMER v. DAGENHART (1918)

This is an extreme version of the constitutional doctrine of "dual federalism," under which the Court departed from the "national supremacy" position of John Marshall. The case involves the constitutionality of a 1916 law passed by Congress forbidding the interstate shipment of goods manufactured in factories employing child labor.

JUSTICE DAY delivered the opinion of the Court. . . .

The attack upon the act rests upon three propositions: *First.* It is not a regulation of interstate and foreign commerce. *Second.* It contravenes the 10th Amendment to the Constitution. *Third.* It conflicts with the 5th Amendment to the Constitution.

The controlling question for decision is: Is it within the authority of Congress in regulating commerce among the states to prohibit the transportation in interstate commerce of manufactured goods, the product of a factory in which, within thirty days prior to their removal therefrom, children under the age of 14 have been employed or permitted to work, or children between the ages of 14 and 16 years have been employed or permitted to work more than eight hours in any day, or more than six days in any week, or after the hour of 7 o'clock p.m. or before the hour of 6 o'clock a.m.?

The power essential to the passage of this act, the government contends, is found in the commerce clause of the Constitution which authorizes Congress to regulate commerce with foreign nations and among the states.

In *Gibbons v. Ogden* (1824), Chief Justice Marshall, speaking for this court, and defining the extent and nature of the commerce power, said: "It is the power to regulate,—that is, to prescribe the rule by which commerce is to be governed." In other words, the power is one to control the means by which commerce is carried on, which is directly the contrary of the assumed right to forbid commerce from moving and thus destroy it as to particular commodities. But it is insisted that adjudged cases in this court establish the doctrine that the power to regulate given to Congress incidentally includes the authority to prohibit the movement of ordinary commodities, and therefore the subject is not open for discussion. The cases demonstrate the contrary. They rest upon the character of the particular subjects dealt with and the fact that the scope of governmental authority, state or national, possessed over them, is such that the authority to prohibit is, as to them, but the exertion of the power to regulate. . . .

In each of these instances the use of interstate transportation was necessary to the accomplishment of harmful results. In other words, although the power over interstate transportation was to regulate, that could only be accomplished by prohibiting the use of the facilities of interstate commerce to effect the evil intended.

This element is wanting in the present case. The thing intended to be accomplished by this statute is the denial of the facilities of interstate commerce to those manufacturers in the states who employ children within the prohibited ages. The act in its effect does not regulate transportation among the states, but aims to standardize the ages at which children may be employed in mining and manufacturing within the states. The goods shipped are of themselves harmless. The act permits them to be freely shipped after thirty days from the time of their removal from the factory. When offered for shipment, and before transportation begins, the labor of their production is over, and the mere fact that they were intended for interstate commerce transportation does not make their production subject to Federal control under the commerce power.

Commerce "consists of intercourse and traffic . . . and includes the transportation of persons and property, as well as the purchase, sale and exchange of commodities" [ellipsis in *Hammer*]. The making of goods and the mining of coal are not commerce, nor does the fact that these things are to be afterwards shipped, or used in interstate commerce, make their production a part thereof. . . .

Over interstate transportation, or its incidents, the regulatory power of Congress is ample, but the production of articles intended for interstate commerce is a matter of local regulation. "When the commerce begins is determined not by the character of the commodity, nor by the intention of the owner to transfer it to another state for sale, nor by his preparation of it for transportation, but by its actual delivery to a common carrier for transportation, or the actual commencement of its transfer to another state." . . . This principle has been recognized often in this court. . . . If it were otherwise, all manufacture intended for interstate shipment would be brought under federal control to the practical exclusion of the authority of the states,—a result certainly not contemplated by the framers of the Constitution when they vested in Congress the authority to regulate commerce among the states. . . .

It is further contended that the authority of Congress may be exerted to control interstate commerce in the shipment of child-made goods because of the effect of the circulation of such goods in other states where the evil of this class of labor has been recognized by local legislation, and the right to thus employ child labor has been more rigorously restrained than in the state of production. In other words, that the unfair competition thus engendered may be controlled by closing the channels of interstate commerce to manufacturers in those states where the local laws do not meet what Congress deems to be the more just standard of other states.

There is no power vested in Congress to require the states to exercise their police power so as to prevent possible unfair competition. Many causes may cooperate to give one state, by reason of local laws or conditions, an economic advantage over others. The commerce clause was not intended to give to Congress a general authority to equalize such conditions. In some of the states laws have been passed fixing minimum wages for women, in others the local law regulates the hours of labor of women in various employments. Business done in such states may be at an economic disadvantage when compared with states which have no such regulation; surely, this fact does not give Congress the power to deny transportation in interstate commerce to those who carry on business where the hours of labor and the rate of compensation for women have not been fixed by a standard in use in other states and approved by Congress.

The grant of power to Congress over the subject of interstate commerce was to enable it to regulate such commerce, and not to give it authority to control the states in their exercise of the police power over local trade and manufacture.

The grant of authority over a purely Federal matter was not intended to destroy the local power always existing and carefully reserved to the states in the 10th Amendment of the Constitution.

Police regulations relating to the internal trade and affairs of the states have been uniformly recognized as within such control. "This," said this court in *United States v. Dewitt* (1870), "has been so frequently declared by this court, results so obviously from the terms of the Constitution, and has been so fully explained and supported on former occasions, that we think it unnecessary to enter again upon the discussion." . . .

That there should be limitations upon the right to employ children in mines and factories in the interest of their own and the public welfare, all will admit. That such employment is generally deemed to require regulation is shown by the fact that the brief of counsel states that every state in the Union has a law upon the subject, limiting the right to thus employ children. In North Carolina, the state wherein is located the factory in which the employment was had in the present case, no child under twelve years of age is permitted to work.

It may be desirable that such laws be uniform, but our Federal government is one of enumerated powers. . . .

In interpreting the Constitution it must never be forgotten that the nation is made up of states, to which are entrusted the powers of local government. And to them and to the people the powers not expressly delegated to the national government are reserved. . . . The power of the states to regulate their purely internal affairs by such laws as seem wise to the local authority is inherent, and has never been surrendered to the general government. . . . To sustain this statute would not be, in our judgment, a recognition of the lawful exertion of congressional authority over interstate commerce, but would sanction an invasion by the federal power of the control of a matter purely local in its character, and over which no authority has been delegated to Congress in conferring the power to regulate commerce among the states.

We have neither authority nor disposition to question the motives of Congress in enacting this legislation. The purposes intended must be attained consistently with constitutional limitations, and not by an invasion of the powers of the states. This court has no more important function than that which devolves upon it the obligation to preserve inviolate the constitutional limitations upon the exercise of authority, federal and state, to the end that each may continue to discharge, harmoniously with the other, the duties entrusted to it by the Constitution.

In our view the necessary effect of this act is, by means of a prohibition against the movement in interstate commerce of ordinary commercial commodities, to regulate the hours of labor of children in factories and mines within the states, a purely state authority. Thus the act in a twofold sense is repugnant to the Constitution. It not only transcends the authority delegated to Congress over commerce, but also exerts a power as to a purely local matter to which the Federal authority does not extend. The far-reaching result of upholding the act cannot be more plainly indicated than by pointing out that if Congress can thus regulate matters entrusted to local authority by prohibition of the movement of commodities in interstate commerce, all freedom of commerce will be at an end, and the power of the states over local matters may be eliminated, and thus our system of government be practically destroyed.

UNITED STATES v. DARBY (1941)

Here Justice Stone gives the argument for not following the precedent established in Hammer v. Dagenhart. *The case involves the constitutionality of the Fair Labor Standards Act of 1938. The act provided for a comprehensive set of labor standards for persons engaged in interstate commerce or producing goods for that commerce, including minimum wage, maximum hours, and child labor provisions.*

JUSTICE STONE delivered the opinion of the Court. . . .

The motive and purpose of the present regulation is plainly to make effective the Congressional conception of public policy that interstate commerce should not be made the instrument of competition in the distribution of goods produced under substandard labor conditions, which competition is injurious to the commerce and to the states from and to which the commerce flows. The motive and purpose of a regulation of interstate commerce are matters for the legislative judgment upon the exercise of which the Constitution places no restriction and over which the courts are given no control. . . .

Whatever their motive and purpose, regulations of commerce which do not infringe some constitutional prohibition are within the plenary power conferred on Congress by the Commerce Clause. Subject only to that limitation, presently to be considered, we conclude that the prohibition of the shipment interstate of goods produced under the forbidden substandard labor conditions is within the constitutional authority of Congress.

In the more than a century which has elapsed since the decision of *Gibbons v. Ogden*, these principles of constitutional interpretation have been so long and repeatedly recognized by this Court as applicable to the Commerce Clause, that there would be little occasion for repeating them now were it not for the decision of this Court twenty-two years ago in *Hammer v. Dagenhart* (1918). In that case it was held by a bare majority of the Court, over the powerful and now classic dissent of Mr. Justice Holmes setting forth the fundamental issues involved, that Congress was without power to exclude the products of child labor from interstate commerce. The reasoning and conclusion of the Court's opinion there cannot be reconciled with the conclusion which we have reached, that the power of Congress under the Commerce Clause is plenary to exclude any article from interstate commerce subject only to the specific prohibitions of the Constitution.

Hammer v. Dagenhart has not been followed. The distinction on which the decision was rested that Congressional power to prohibit interstate commerce is limited to articles which in themselves have some harmful or deleterious property—a distinction which was novel when made and unsupported by any provision of the Constitution—has long since been abandoned. . . . The thesis of the opinion that the motive of the prohibition or its effect to control in some measure the use or production within the states of the article thus excluded from the commerce can operate to deprive the regulation of its constitutional authority has long since ceased to have force. . . . And finally we have declared "The authority of the federal government over interstate commerce does not differ in extent or character from that retained by the states over intrastate commerce." *United States v. Rock Royal Co-operative* (1939).

The conclusion is inescapable that *Hammer v. Dagenhart* was a departure from the principles which have prevailed in the interpretation of the Commerce Clause both before and since the decision and that such vitality, as a precedent, as it then had has long since been exhausted. It should be and now is overruled.

RONALD REAGAN, THE STATE OF THE UNION ADDRESS (1982)

Here President Reagan introduces a plan for the reinvigoration of state and local governments—a program that he called the New Federalism. Most of this program never became public policy.

. . . [O]ur next major undertaking must be a program—just as bold, just as innovative—to make government again accountable to the people, to make our system of federalism work again.

Our citizens feel they have lost control of even the most basic decisions made about the essential services of Government, such as schools, welfare, roads and even garbage collection. They are right.

A maze of interlocking jurisdictions and levels of Government confronts average citizens in trying to solve even the simplest of problems. They do not know where to turn for answers, who to hold accountable, who to praise, who to blame, who to vote for or against.

The main reason for this is the overpowering growth of Federal grants-in-aid programs during the past few decades.

In 1960, the Federal Government had 132 categorical grant programs, costing $7 billion. When I took office, there were approximately 500, costing nearly $100 billion—13 programs for energy conservation, 36 for pollution control, 66 for social services and 90 for education. The list goes on and on. Here in the Congress, it takes at least 166 committees just to try to keep track of them.

You know and I know that neither the President nor the Congress can properly oversee this jungle of grants-in-aid; indeed, the growth of these grants has led to a distortion in the vital functions of Government. As one Democratic Governor put it recently: "The national Government should be worrying about 'arms control not potholes.'"

Problems Through Growth

. . . Let us solve this problem with a single, bold stroke—the return of some $47 billion in Federal programs to state and local government, together with the means to finance them and a transition period of nearly 10 years to avoid unnecessary disruption. . . .

Starting in fiscal 1984, the Federal Government will assume full responsibility for the cost of the rapidly growing Medicaid program to go along with its existing responsibility for Medicare. As part of a financially equal swap, the states will simultaneously take full responsibility for Aid to Families With Dependent Children and food stamps. This will make welfare less costly and more responsive to genuine need because it will be designed and administered closer to the grass roots and the people it serves.

In 1984, the Federal Government will apply the full proceeds from certain excise taxes to a grassroots trust fund that will belong, in fair shares, to the 50 states. The total amount flowing into this fund will be $28 billion a year.

Over the next four years, the states can use this money in either of two ways. If they want to continue receiving Federal grants in such areas as transportation, education and social services, they can use their trust fund money to pay for the grants or, to the extent they choose to forego the Federal grant programs, they can use their trust fund money on their own, for those or other purposes. There will be a mandatory pass-through of part of these funds to local governments.

By 1988, the states will be in complete control of over 40 Federal grant programs. The trust fund will start to phase out, eventually to disappear, and the excise taxes will be turned over to the states. They can then preserve, lower or raise taxes on their own and fund and manage these programs as they see fit. . . .

Some will also say our states and local communities are not up to the challenge of a new and creative partnership. That might have been true 20 years ago before reforms like reapportionment and the Voting Rights Act, the 10-year extension of which I strongly support. It is no longer true today. This Administration has faith in state and local governments and the constitutional balance envisioned by the Founding Fathers. We also believe in the integrity, decency and sound good sense of grassroots Americans. . . .

GARCIA v. SAN ANTONIO METROPOLITAN TRANSIT AUTHORITY (1985)

San Antonio Metropolitan Transit Authority (SAMTA) is the major provider of public transportation in San Antonio, Texas. In 1979, the Wage and Hour Administration of the U.S. Department of Labor issued an opinion that SAMTA's operations were not immune from the minimum-wage and overtime provisions of the Fair Labor Standards Act (FLSA). In National League of Cities v. Usery (1976), *the Court held that the Tenth Amendment's protection of state sovereignty means that the commerce clause does not empower Congress to regulate the "traditional governmental functions" of the states.*

JUSTICE BLACKMUN delivered the opinion of the Court. . . .

We revisit in these cases an issue raised in *National League of Cities v. Usery* (1976). . . . In that litigation, this Court, by a sharply divided vote, ruled that the Commerce Clause does not empower Congress to enforce the minimum-wage and overtime provisions of the Fair Labor Standards Act (FLSA) against the States "in areas of traditional governmental functions." . . . Although *National League of Cities* supplied some examples of "traditional governmental functions" it did not offer a general explanation of how a "traditional" function is to be distinguished from a "nontraditional" one. Since then, federal and state courts have struggled with the task, thus imposed, of identifying a traditional function for purposes of state immunity under the Commerce Clause. In the present cases, a Federal District Court concluded that municipal ownership and operation of a mass-transit system is a traditional governmental function, and thus under *National League of Cities*, is exempt from the obligations imposed by the FLSA. Faced with the identical question, three Federal Court of Appeals and one state appellate court have reached the opposite conclusion.

Our examination of this "function" standard applied in these and other cases over the last eight years now persuades us that the attempt to draw the boundaries of state regulatory immunity in terms of "traditional governmental function" is not only unworkable but is inconsistent with established principles of federalism, and indeed, with those very federalist principles on which *National League of Cities* purported to rest. That case, accordingly, is overruled. . . .

The central theme of *National League of Cities* was that the States occupy a special position in our constitutional system and that the scope of Congress' authority under the Commerce Clause must reflect that position. . . .

What has proved problematic is not the perception that the Constitution's federal structure imposes limitations on the Commerce Clause, but rather the nature and content of those limitations. . . .

We doubt that courts ultimately can identify principled constitutional limitations on the scope of Congress' Commerce Clause powers over the States merely by relying on *a priori* definitions of state sovereignty. In part, this is because of the elusiveness of objective criteria for "fundamental" elements of state sovereignty, a problem we have witnessed in the search for "traditional governmental functions." There is, however, a more fundamental reason: the sovereignty of the States is limited by the Constitution itself. . . .

. . .The fact that the States remain sovereign as to all powers not vested in Congress or denied them by the Constitution offers no guidance about where the frontier between state and federal power lies. In short, we have no license to employ freestanding conceptions of state sovereignty when measuring congressional authority under the Commerce Clause.

When we look for the States' "residuary and inviolable sovereignty," *The Federalist* No. 39 . . . in the shape of the constitutional scheme rather than in predetermined notions of sovereign power, a different measure of state sovereignty emerges. Apart from the limitation on federal authority inherent in the delegated natures of Congress' Article I powers, the principal means chosen by the Framers to ensure the role of the States in the federal system lies in the structure of the Federal Government itself. It is no novelty to observe that the composition of the Federal Government was designed in large part to protect the States from overreaching by Congress. The Framers thus gave the States a role in the selection both of the Executive and the Legislative Branches of the Federal Government. The States were vested with indirect influence over the House of

Representatives and the Presidency by their control of electoral qualifications and their role in presidential elections. U.S. Const., Art. I, Section 2, and Art. II, Section 1. They were given more direct influence in the Senate, where each State received equal representation and each Senator was to be selected by the legislature of his State. Art. I, Section 3. The significance attached to the States' equal representation in the Senate is underscored by the prohibition of any constitutional amendment divesting a State of equal representation without the State's consent. Art. V.

The extent to which the structure of the Federal Government itself was relied on to insulate the interests of the States is evident in the view of the Framers. James Madison explained that the Federal Government "will partake sufficiency of the spirit [of the States], to be disinclined to invade the rights of the individual States, or the prerogatives of their governments." The *Federalist* No. 46. . . . The Framers chose to rely on a federal system in which special restraints on federal power over the States inhered principally in the workings of the National Government itself, rather than in discrete limitations on the objects of federal authority. State sovereign interests, then, are more properly protected by procedural safeguards inherent in the structure of the federal system than by judicially created limitations on federal power. . . .

We realize that changes in the structure of the Federal Government have taken place since 1789, not the least of which has been the substitution of popular elections of Senators by the adoption of the Seventeenth Amendment in 1913, and that these changes may work to alter the influence of the States in the federal political process. Nonetheless, against this background, we are convinced that the fundamental limitation that the constitutional scheme imposed on the Commerce Clause to protect the "States as States" is one of process rather than one of results. . . .

JUSTICE POWELL, with whom CHIEF JUSTICE BURGER, JUSTICE REHNQUIST, and JUSTICE O'CONNOR join, dissenting. . . .

. . . Whatever effect the Court's decision may have in weakening the application of *stare decisis*, it is likely to be less important than what the Court has done to the Constitution itself. A unique feature of the United States is the *federal* system of government guaranteed by the Constitution and implicit in the very name of our country. Despite some genuflecting in the Court's opinion to the concept of federalism, today's decision effectively reduces the Tenth Amendment to meaningless rhetoric when Congress acts pursuant to the Commerce Clause. . . .

Today's opinion does not explain how the States' role in the electoral process guarantees that particular exercises of the Commerce Clause power will not infringe on residual State sovereignty. Members of Congress are elected from the various States, but once in office they are members of the federal government. Although the States participate in the Electoral College, this is hardly a reason to view the President as a representative of the States' interest against federal encroachment. We noted recently "the hydraulic pressure inherent within each of the separate Branches to exceed the outer limits of its power" . . . *Immigration and Naturalization Service v. Chadha* . . . (1983). The Court offers no reason to think that this pressure will not operate when Congress seeks to invoke its powers under the Commerce Clause, notwithstanding the electoral role of the States. . . .

More troubling than the logical infirmities in the Court's reasoning is the result of its holding, i.e., that federal political officials, invoking the Commerce Clause, are the sole judges of the limits of their own power. This result is inconsistent with the fundamental principles of our constitutional system. . . . At least since *Marbury v. Madison* it has been the settled province of the federal judiciary "to say what the law is" with respect to the constitutionality of acts of Congress. . . . In rejecting the role of the judiciary in protecting the States from federal overreaching, the Court's opinion offers no explanation for ignoring the teaching of the most famous case in our history.

In our federal system, the States have a major role that cannot be preempted by the national government. As contemporaneous writings and the debates at the ratifying conventions make clear, the States' ratification of the Constitution was predicated on this understanding of federalism. Indeed, the Tenth Amendment was adopted specifically to ensure that the important role promised the States by the proponents of the Constitution was realized. . . .

JUSTICE O'CONNOR, with whom JUSTICE POWELL and JUSTICE REHNQUIST join, dissenting. . . .

The Court today surveys the battle scene of federalism and sounds a retreat. Like Justice Powell, I would prefer to hold the field and, at the very least, render a little aid to the wounded. I join Justice Powell's opinion. I also write separately to note my fundamental disagreement with the majority's views of federalism and the duty of this Court. . . .

The true "essence" of federalism is that the States *as States* have legitimate interest which the National Government is bound to respect even though its laws are supreme. . . . If federalism so conceived and so carefully cultivated by the Framers of our Constitution is to remain meaningful, this Court cannot abdicate its constitutional responsibility to oversee the Federal Government's compliance with its duty to respect the legitimate interests of the States.

The Framers perceived the interstate commerce power to be important but limited, and expected that it would be used primarily if not exclusively to remove interstate tariffs and to regulate maritime affairs and large-scale mercantile enterprise. . . . This perception of a narrow commerce power is important not because it suggests that the commerce power should be as narrowly construed today. Rather, it explains why the Framers could believe the Constitution assured significant state authority even as it bestowed a range of powers, including the commerce power, on the Congress. In an era when interstate commerce represented a tiny fraction of economic activity and most goods and services were produced and consumed close to home, the interstate commerce power left a broad range of activities beyond the reach of Congress.

In the decades since ratification of the Constitution, interstate economic activity has steadily expanded. Industrialization, coupled with advances in transportation and communications, has created a national economy in which virtually every activity occurring within the borders of a State plays a part.

Incidental to this expansion of the commerce power, Congress has been given an ability it lacked prior to the emergence of an integrated national economy. Because virtually every *state* activity, like virtually every activity of a private individual, arguably "affects" interstate commerce, Congress can now supplant the States from the significant sphere of activities envisioned for them by the

Framers. It is in this context that recent changes in the workings of Congress, such as the direct election of Senators and the expanded influence of national interest groups . . . become relevant. These changes may well have lessened the weight Congress gives to the legitimate interest of States as States. As a result, there is now a real risk that Congress will gradually erase the diffusion of power between the state and nation on which the Framers based their faith in the efficiency and vitality of our Republic.

It is worth recalling the . . . passage in *McCulloch v. Maryland* . . . that lies at the source of the recent expansion of the commerce power. "Let the end be legitimate, let it be within the scope of the constitution," Chief Justice Marshall said, "and all means which are appropriate, which are plainly adapted to that end, which are not prohibited, but consist with the letter *and spirit* of the constitution, are constitutional" (emphasis added). The *spirit* of the Tenth Amendment, of course, is that the States will retain their integrity in a system in which the laws of the United States are nevertheless supreme. . . .

It is not enough that the "end be legitimate"; the means to that end chosen by Congress must not contravene the spirit of the Constitution. Thus many of this Court's decisions acknowledge that the means by which national power is exercised must take into account concerns for state autonomy. . . .

4

Constitutional Controversy and Political Change

The selections in this chapter are all expressions of disputes over constitutional interpretation. They have been the engines of political change in the United States.

ALEXIS DE TOCQUEVILLE, *DEMOCRACY IN AMERICA*, VOLUME 2, WHAT SORT OF DESPOTISM DEMOCRATIC NATIONS HAVE TO FEAR (1840)

Here Tocqueville explains how the democratic propensities toward centralization and apathy threaten human liberty.

. . . When the power of the Roman emperors was at its height, the different peoples of the empire still preserved very various customs and mores. Although they obeyed the same monarch, most provinces had a separate administration. There were powerful and active municipalities in profusion, and though the whole government of the empire was concentrated in the hands of the emperor alone and he could, if necessary, decide everything, yet the details of social life and personal everyday existence normally escaped his control.

It is true that the emperors had immense and unchecked power, so that they could use the whole might of the empire to indulge any strange caprice. They often abused this power to deprive a man arbitrarily of life or property. The burden of their tyranny fell most heavily on some, but it never spread over a great number. It had a few main targets and left the rest alone. It was violent, but its extent was limited.

But if a despotism should be established among the democratic nations of our day, it would probably have a different character. It would be more widespread and milder; it would degrade men rather than torment them.

. . . We have seen how, as men become more alike and more nearly equal, public mores becomes more humane and gentle. When there is no citizen with great power or wealth, tyranny in some degree lacks both target and stage. When all fortunes are middling, passions are naturally restrained, imagination limited and pleasures simple. Such universal moderation tempers the sovereign's own spirit and keeps within certain limits the disorderly urges of desire. . . .

Taking into consideration the trivial nature of men's passions now, the softness of their mores, the extent of their education, the purity of their religion, their steady habits of patient work, and the restraint which they all show in the indulgence of both their vices and their virtues, I do not expect their leaders to be tyrants, but rather schoolmasters.

I am trying to imagine under what novel features despotism may appear in the world. In the first place, I see an innumerable multitude of men, alike and equal, constantly circling around in pursuit of the petty and banal pleasures with which they glut their souls. Each of them, withdrawn into himself, is almost unaware of the fate of the rest. Mankind, for him, consists in his children and personal friends. As for the rest of his fellow citizens, they are near enough, but he does not notice them. He touches them but feels nothing. He exists in and for himself, and though he still may have a family, one can at least say that he has not got a fatherland.

Over this kind of men stands an immense, protective power which is alone responsible for securing their enjoyment and watching over their fate. That power is absolute, thoughtful of detail, orderly, provident, and gentle. It would resemble parental authority if, fatherlike, it tried to prepare its charges for a man's life, but on the contrary, it only tries to keep them in perpetual childhood. It likes to see the citizens enjoy themselves, provided that they think of nothing but enjoyment. It gladly works for their happiness but wants to be sole agent and judge of it. It provides for their security, foresees and supplies their necessities, facilitates their pleasures, manages their principal concerns, directs their industry, makes rules of their testaments, and divides their inheritances. Why should it not entirely relieve them from the trouble of thinking and all the cares of living?

Thus it daily makes the exercise of free choice less useful and rarer, restricts the activity of free will within a narrower compass, and little by little robs each citizen of the proper use of his own faculties. Equality has prepared men for all this, predisposing them to endure it and often even regard it as beneficial.

Having thus taken each citizen in turn in its powerful grasp and shaped him to its will, government then extends its embrace to include the whole of society. It covers the whole of social life with a network of petty, complicated rules that are both minute and uniform, through which even men of the greatest originality and the most vigorous temperament cannot force their heads above the crowd. It does not break men's will, but softens, bends, and guides it; it seldom enjoins, but often inhibits, action; it does not destroy anything, but prevents much being born; it is not at all tyrannical, but it hinders, restrains, enervates, stifles and stultifies so much that in the end each nation is no more than a flock of timid and hardworking animals with the government as its shepherd.

I have always thought that this brand of orderly, gentle, peaceful slavery which I have just described could be combined, more easily than is generally supposed, with some of the external forms of freedom, and that there is a possibility of its getting itself established even under the shadow of sovereignty of the people.

Our contemporaries are ever a prey to two conflicting passions: they feel the need of guidance, and they long to stay free. Unable to wipe out these two contradictory instincts, they try to satisfy them both together. Their imagination conceives a government which is unitary, protective, and all-powerful, but elected by the people. Centralization is combined with the sovereignty of the people. That gives them a chance to relax. They console themselves for being under schoolmasters by thinking that they have chosen them themselves. Each individual lets them put the collar on, for he sees that it is not a person, or a class of persons, but society itself which holds the end of the chain.

Under this system the citizens quit their state of dependence just long enough to choose their masters and then fall back into it. . . .

Subjection in petty affairs is manifest daily and touches all citizens indiscriminately. It never drives men to despair, but continually thwarts them and leads them to give up using their free will. It slowly stifles their spirits and enervates their souls, whereas obedience demanded only occasionally in matters of great moment brings servitude into play only from time to time, and its weight falls only on certain people. It does little good to summon those very citizens who have been made so dependent on the central power to choose the representatives of that power from time to time. However important, this brief and occasional exercise of free will does not prevent them from gradually losing the faculty of thinking, feeling, and acting for themselves, so that they will slowly fall below the level of humanity. . . .

ABRAHAM LINCOLN, FINAL TEXT OF THE ADDRESS DELIVERED AT THE DEDICATION OF THE CEMETERY AT GETTYSBURG (1863)

This speech, given in the midst of the Civil War, subtly but profoundly reinterprets the founding principles by putting a greater emphasis on equality as the nation's political goal.

Four score and seven years ago our fathers brought forth on this continent, a new nation, conceived in Liberty, and dedicated to the proposition that all men are created equal.

Now we are engaged in a great civil war, testing whether that nation, or any nation so conceived and so dedicated, can long endure. We are met on a great battle-field of that war. We have come to dedicate a portion of that field, as a final resting place for those who here gave their lives that that nation might live. It is altogether fitting and proper that we should do this.

But, in a larger sense, we can not dedicate—we can not consecrate—we can not hallow—this ground. The brave men, living and dead, who struggled here, have consecrated it, far above our poor power to add or detract. The world will little note, nor long remember what we say here, but it can never forget what they did here. It is for us the living, rather, to be dedicated here to the unfinished work which they who fought here have thus far so nobly advanced. It is rather for us to be here dedicated to the great task remaining before us—that from these honored dead we take increased devotion to that cause for which they gave the last full measure of devotion—that we here highly resolve that these dead shall not have died in vain—that this nation, under God, shall have a new birth of freedom—and that government of the people, by the people, for the people, shall not perish from the earth.

WOODROW WILSON, *CONSTITUTIONAL GOVERNMENT IN THE UNITED STATES* (1908)

Woodrow Wilson was the most thoughtful of those intellectuals who provided the foundation for the "progressive movement." This movement dominated American political thought from the turn of the century until the beginning of U.S. participation in World War I, and still exercises a considerable influence to-day. In Constitutional Government, *Wilson embraces a type of political change produced by a unified popular and principled leadership. To do so, he is compelled to criticize the political vision that guided the Framers of the Constitution.*

The government of the United States was constructed upon the Whig theory of political dynamics, which was a sort of unconscious copy of the Newtonian theory of the universe. In our own day, whenever we discuss the structure or development of anything, whether in nature or in society, we consciously or unconsciously follow Mr. Darwin; but before Mr. Darwin, they followed Newton. Some single law, like the law of gravitation, swung each system of thought and gave it its principle of unity. Every sun, every plant, every free body in the spaces of the heavens, the world itself, is kept in its place and reined to its course by the attraction of bodies that swing with equal order and precision about it, themselves governed by the nice poise and balance of forces which give the whole system of the universe its symmetry and perfect adjustment. The Whigs had tried to give England a similar constitution. They had no wish to destroy the throne, no conscious desire to reduce the king to a mere figurehead, but had intended only to surround and offset him with a system of constitutional checks and balances which should regulate his otherwise arbitrary course and make it at least always calculable.

They had made no clear analysis of the matter in their own thoughts; it has not been the habit of English politicians, or indeed of English-speaking politicians on either side of the water, to be clear theorists. It was left to a Frenchman to point out to the Whigs what they had done. They had striven to make Parliament so influential in the making of laws and so authoritative in the criticism of the king's policy that the king could in no matter have his own way without their cooperation and assent, though they left him free, the while, if he chose, to interpose an absolute veto upon the acts of Parliament. They had striven to secure for the courts of law as great an independence as possible, so that they might be neither overawed by Parliament nor coerced by the king. In brief, as Montesquieu pointed out to them in his lucid way, they had sought to balance executive, legislative, and judiciary off against one another by a series of checks and counterpoises, which Newton might readily have recognized as suggestive of the mechanism of the heavens.

The makers of our federal Constitution followed the scheme as they found it expounded in Montesquieu, followed it with genuine scientific enthusiasm. The admirable expositions of the Federalist read like thoughtful applications of Montesquieu to the political needs and circumstances of America. They are full of the theory of checks and balances. The President is balanced off against Congress, Congress against the President, and each against the courts. Our statesmen of the earlier generations quoted no one so often as Montesquieu, and they quoted him always as a scientific standard in the field of politics. Politics is turned into mechanics under his touch. The theory of gravitation is supreme.

The trouble with the theory is that government is not a machine, but a living thing. It falls, not under the theory of the universe, but under the theory of organic life. It is accountable to Darwin, not to Newton. It is modified by its environment, necessitated by its tasks, shaped to its functions by the sheer pressure of life. No living thing can have its organs offset against each other as checks, and live. On the contrary, its life is dependent upon their quick cooperation, their ready response to the commands of instinct or intelligence, their amicable community of purpose. Government is not a body of blind forces; it is a body of men, with highly differentiated functions, no doubt, in our modern day of specialization, but with a common task and purpose. Their cooperation is indispensable, their warfare fatal. There can be no successful government without leadership or without the intimate, almost instinctive, coordination of the organs of life and action. This is not theory, but fact, and displays its force as fact, whatever theories may be thrown across its track. Living political constitutions must be Darwinian in structure and in practice.

Fortunately, the definitions and prescriptions of our constitutional law, though conceived in the Newtonian spirit and upon the Newtonian principle, are sufficiently broad and elastic to allow for the play of life and circumstance. Though they were Whig theorists, the men who framed the federal Constitution were also practical statesmen with an experienced eye for affairs and a quick practical sagacity in respect of the actual structure of government, and they have given us a thoroughly workable model. If it had in fact been a machine governed by mechanically automatic balances, it would have had no history; but it was not, and its history has been rich with the influences and personalities of the men who have conducted it and made it a living reality. The government of the United States has had a vital and normal organic growth and has proved itself eminently adapted to express the changing temper and purposes of the American people from age to age.

FRANKLIN D. ROOSEVELT, COMMONWEALTH CLUB CAMPAIGN SPEECH (1932)

This speech is Roosevelt's most profound statement of his view of the history and future of America. He "calls for a reappraisal of values," because "The day of enlightened administration has come." He aimed to secure a place for progressive principles in American political discourse by interpreting them as an expansion of the natural rights tradition.

I want to speak not of politics but of government. I want to speak not of parties, but of universal principles. They are not political, except in that larger sense in which a great American once expressed a definition of politics, that nothing in all of human life is foreign to the sciences of politics. . . .

The issue of government has always been whether individual men and women will have to serve some system of government or economics, or whether a system of government and economics exists to serve individual men and women. This question has persistently dominated the discussion of government for many generations. On questions relating to these things men have differed, and for time immemorial it is probable that honest men will continue to differ.

The final word belongs to no man; yet we can still believe in change and in progress. Democracy, as a dear old friend of mine in Indiana, Meredith Nicholson, has called it, is a quest, a never-ending seeking for better things, and in the seeking for these things and the striving for them, there are many roads to follow. But, if we map the course of these roads, we find that there are only two general directions.

When we look about us, we are likely to forget how hard people have worked to win the privilege of government. The growth of the national governments of Europe was a struggle for the development of a centralized force in the nation, strong enough to impose peace upon ruling barons. In many instances the victory of the central government, the creation of a strong central government, was a haven of refuge to the individual. The people preferred the master far away to the exploitation and cruelty of the smaller master near at hand.

But the creators of national government were perforce ruthless men. They were often cruel in their methods, but they did strive steadily toward something that society needed and very much wanted, a strong central state, able to keep the peace, to stamp out civil war, to put the unruly nobleman in his place, and to permit the bulk of individuals to live safely. The man of ruthless force had his place in developing a pioneer country, just as he did in fixing the power of the central government in the development of nations. Society paid him well for his services and its development. When the development among the nations of Europe, however, had been completed, ambition and ruthlessness, having served its term, tended to overstep its mark.

There came a growing feeling that government was conducted for the benefit of a few who thrived unduly at the expense of all. The people sought a balancing—a limiting force. There came gradually, through town councils, trade guilds, national parliaments, by constitution and by popular participation and control, limitations on arbitrary power.

Another factor that tended to limit the power of those who ruled, was the rise of the ethical conception that a ruler bore a responsibility for the welfare of his subjects.

The American colonies were born in this struggle. The American Revolution was a turning point in it. After the revolution the struggle continued and shaped itself in the public life of the country. There were those who because they had seen the confusion which attended the years of war for American independence surrendered to the belief that popular government was essentially dangerous and essentially unworkable. They were honest people, my friends, and we cannot deny that their experience had warranted some measure of fear. The most brilliant, honest and able exponent of this point of view was Hamilton. He was too impatient of slow-moving methods. Fundamentally he believed that the safety of the republic lay in the autocratic strength of its government, that the destiny of individuals was to serve that government, and that fundamentally a great and strong group of central institutions, guided by a small group of able and public spirited citizens, could best direct all government.

But Mr. Jefferson, in the summer of 1776, after drafting the Declaration of Independence turned his mind to the same problem and took a different view. He did not deceive himself with outward forms. Government to him was a means to an end, not an end in itself; it might be either a refuge and a help or a threat and a danger, depending on the circumstances. We find him carefully analyzing the society for which he was to organize a government. "We have no paupers. The great mass of our population is of laborers, our rich who cannot live without labor, either manual or professional, being few and of moderate wealth. Most of the laboring class possess property, cultivate their own lands, have families and from the demand for their labor, are enabled to exact from the rich and the competent such prices as enable them to feed abundantly, clothe above mere decency, to labor moderately and raise their families."

These people, he considered, had two sets of rights, those of "personal competency" and those involved in acquiring and possessing property. By "personal competency" he meant the right of free thinking, freedom of forming and expressing opinions, and freedom of personal living, each man according to his own lights. To insure the first set of rights, a government must so order its functions as not to interfere with the individual. But even Jefferson realized that the exercise of the property rights might so interfere with the rights of the individual that the government, without whose assistance the property rights could not exist, must intervene, not to destroy individualism but to protect it.

You are familiar with the great political duel which followed; and how Hamilton, and his friends, building towards a dominant centralized power were at length defeated in the great election of 1800, by Mr. Jefferson's party. Out of that duel came the two parties, Republican and Democratic, as we know them today.

So began, in American political life, the new day, the day of the individual against the system, the day in which individualism was made the great watchword of American life. The happiest of economic conditions made that day long and splendid. On the Western frontier, land was substantially free. No one, who did not shirk the task of earning a living, was entirely without opportunity to do so. Depressions could, and did, come and go; but they could not alter the fundamental fact that most of the people lived partly by selling their labor and partly by extracting their livelihood from the soil, so that starvation and dislocation were practically impossible. At the very worst there was always the possibility of climbing into a covered wagon and moving west where the untilled prairies afforded a haven for men to whom the East did not provide a place. So great were our natural resources that we could offer this relief not only to our own people, but to the distressed of all the world; we could invite immigration from Europe, and welcome it with open arms. Traditionally, when a depression came a new section of land was opened in the West; and even our temporary misfortune served our manifest destiny.

It was in the middle of the 19th century that a new force was released and a new dream created. The force was what is called the industrial revolution, the advance of steam and machinery and the rise of the forerunners of the modern industrial plant. The dream was the dream of an economic machine, able to raise the standard of living for everyone; to bring luxury within the reach of the humblest; to annihilate distance by steam power and later by electricity, and to release everyone from the drudgery of the heaviest manual toil. It was to be expected that this would necessarily affect government. Heretofore, government had merely been called upon to produce conditions within which people could live happily, labor peacefully, and rest secure. Now it was called upon to aid in the consummation of this new dream. There was, however, a shadow over the dream. To be made real, it required use of the talents of men of tremendous will, and tremendous ambition, since by no other force could the problems of financing and engineering and new developments be brought to a consummation.

So manifest were the advantages of the machine age, however, that the United States fearlessly, cheerfully, and, I think, rightly, accepted the bitter with the sweet. It was thought that no price was too high to pay for the advantages which we could draw from a finished industrial system. The history of the last half century is accordingly in large measure a history of a group of financial Titans, whose methods were not scrutinized with too much care, and who were honored in proportion as they produced the results, irrespective of the means they used. The financiers who pushed the railroads to the Pacific were always ruthless, often wasteful, and frequently corrupt; but they did build railroads, and we have them today. It has been estimated that the American investor paid for the American railway system more than three times over in the process; but despite this fact the net advantage was to the United States. As long as we had free land; as long as population was growing by leaps and bounds; as long as our industrial plants were insufficient to supply our own needs, society chose to give the ambitious man free play and unlimited reward provided only that he produced the economic plant so much desired.

During this period of expansion, there was equal opportunity for all and the business of Government was not to interfere but to assist in the development of industry. This was done at the request of business men themselves. The tariff was originally imposed for the purpose of "fostering our infant industry," a phrase I think the older among you will remember as a political issue not so long ago. The railroads were subsidized, sometimes by grants of money, oftener by grants of land; some of the most valuable oil lands in the United States were granted to assist the financing of the railroad which pushed through the Southwest. A nascent merchant marine was assisted by grants of money, or by mail subsidies, so that our steam shipping might ply the seven seas. Some of my friends tell me that they do not want the Government in business. With this I agree; but I wonder whether they realize the implications of the past. For while it has been American doctrine that the Government must not go into business in competition with private enterprises, still it has been traditional particularly in Republican administrations for business urgently to ask the government to put at private disposal all kinds of government assistance. The same man who tells you that he does not want to see the government interfere in business—and he means it, and has plenty of good reasons for saying so—is the first to go to Washington and ask the government for a prohibitory tariff on his product. When things get just bad enough—as they did two years ago—he will go with equal speed to the United States government and ask for a loan; and the Reconstruction Finance Corporation is the outcome of it. Each group has sought protection from the government for its own special interests, without realizing that the function of government must be to favor no small group at the expense of its duty to protect the rights of personal freedom and of private property of all its citizens.

In retrospect we can now see that the turn of the tide came with the turn of the century. We were reaching our last frontier; there was no more free land and our industrial combinations had become great uncontrolled and irresponsible units of power within the state. Clear-sighted men saw with fear the danger that opportunity would no longer be equal; that the growing corporation, like the feudal baron of old, might threaten the economic freedom of individuals to earn a living. In that hour, our antitrust laws were born. The cry was raised against the great corporations. Theodore Roosevelt, the first great Republican progressive, fought a Presidential campaign on the issue of "trust busting" and talked freely about malefactors of great wealth. If the government had a policy it was rather to turn the clock back, to destroy the large combinations and to return to the time when every man owned his individual small business.

This was impossible; Theodore Roosevelt, abandoning the idea of "trust busting," was forced to work out a difference between "good" trusts and "bad" trusts. The Supreme Court set forth the famous "rule of reason" by which it seems to have meant that a concentration of industrial power was permissible if the method by which it got its power, and the use it made of that power, was reasonable.

Woodrow Wilson, elected in 1912, saw the situation more clearly. Where Jefferson had feared the encroachment of political power on the lives of individuals, Wilson knew that the new power was financial. He saw, in the highly centralized economic system, the despot of the twentieth century, on whom great masses of individuals relied for their safety and their livelihood, and whose irresponsibility and greed (if it were not controlled) would reduce them to starvation and penury. The concentration of financial power had not proceeded so far in 1912 as it has today; but it had grown far enough for Mr. Wilson to realize fully its implications. It is interesting, now, to read his speeches. What is called "radical" today (and I have reason to know whereof I speak) is mild compared to the campaign of Mr. Wilson. "No man can deny," he said, "that the lines of endeavor have more and more narrowed and stiffened; no man who knows anything about the development of industry in this country can have failed to observe that the larger kinds of credit are more and more difficult to obtain unless you obtain them upon terms of uniting your efforts with those who already control the industry of the country, and nobody can fail to observe that every man who tries to set himself up in competition with any process of manufacture which has taken place under the control of large combinations of capital will presently find himself either squeezed out or obliged to sell and allow himself to be absorbed." Had there been no World War, had Mr. Wilson been able to devote eight years to domestic instead of to international affairs, we might have had a wholly different situation at the present time. However, the then distant roar of European cannon, growing ever louder, forced him to abandon the study of this issue. The problem he saw so clearly is left with us as a legacy; and no one of us on either side of the political controversy can deny that it is a matter of grave concern to the government.

A glance at the situation today only too clearly indicates that equality of opportunity as we have known it no longer exists. Our industrial plant is built; the problem just now is whether under existing conditions it is not overbuilt. Our last frontier has long since been reached, and there is practically no more free land. More than half of our people do not live on the farms or on lands and cannot derive a living by cultivating their own property. There is no safety valve in the form of a Western prairie to which those thrown out of work by the Eastern economic machines can go for a new start. We are not able to invite the immigration from Europe to share our plenty. We are now providing a drab living for our own people. . . .

Just as freedom to farm has ceased, so also the opportunity in business has narrowed. It still is true that men can start small enterprises, trusting to native shrewdness and ability to keep abreast of competitors; but area after area has been pre-empted altogether by the great corporations, and even in the fields which still have no great concerns, the small man starts under a handicap. The unfeeling statistics of the past three decades show that the independent business man is running a losing race. Perhaps he is forced to the wall; perhaps he cannot command credit; perhaps he is "squeezed out," in Mr. Wilson's words, by highly organized corporate competitors, as your corner grocery man can tell you. Recently a careful study was made of the concentration of business in the United States. It showed that our economic life was dominated by some six hundred odd corporations who controlled two-thirds of American industry. Ten million small business men divided the other third. More striking still, it appeared that if the process of concentration goes on at the same rate, at the end of another century we shall have all American industry controlled by a dozen corporations, and run by perhaps a hundred men. Put plainly, we are steering a steady course toward economic oligarchy, if we are not there already.

Clearly, all this calls for a re-appraisal of values. A mere builder of more industrial plants, a creator of more railroad systems, an organizer of more corporations, is as likely to be a danger as a help. The day of the great promoter or the financial Titan, to whom we granted anything if only he would build, or develop, is over. Our task now is not discovery or exploitation of natural resources, or necessarily producing more goods. It is the soberer, less dramatic business of administering resources and plants already in hand, of seeking to re-establish foreign markets for our surplus production, of meeting the problem of underconsumption, of adjusting production to consumption, of distributing wealth and products more equitably, of adapting existing economic organizations to the service of the people. The day of enlightened administration has come.

Just as in older times the central government was first a haven of refuge, and then a threat, so now in a closer economic system the central and ambitious financial unit is no longer a servant of national desire, but a danger. I would draw the parallel one step farther. We did not think because national government had become a threat in the 18th century that therefore we should abandon the principle of national government. Nor today should we abandon the principle of strong economic units called corporations, merely because their power is susceptible of easy abuse. In other times we dealt with the problem of an unduly ambitious central government by modifying it gradually into a constitutional democratic government. So today we are modifying and controlling our economic units.

As I see it, the task of government in its relation to business is to assist the development of an economic declaration of rights, an economic constitutional order. This is the common task of statesman and business man. It is the minimum requirement of a more permanently safe order of things. . . .

Every man has a right to life; and this means that he has also a right to make a comfortable living. He may by sloth or crime decline to exercise that right; but it may not be denied him. We have no actual famine or dearth; our industrial and agricultural mechanism can produce enough and to spare. Our government formal and informal, political and economic, owes to every one an avenue to possess himself of a portion of that plenty sufficient for his needs, through his own work.

Every man has a right to his own property; which means a right to be assured, to the fullest extent attainable, in the safety of his savings. By no other means can men carry the burdens of those parts of life which, in the nature of things, afford no chance of labor; childhood, sickness, old age. In all thought of property, this right is paramount; all other property rights must yield to it. If, in accord with this principle, we must restrict the operations of the speculator, the manipulator, even the financier, I believe we must accept the restriction as needful, not to hamper individualism but to protect it. . . .

The government should assume the function of economic regulation only as a last resort, to be tried only when private initiative, inspired by high responsibility, with such assistance and balance as government can give, has finally failed. As yet there has been no final failure, because there has been no attempt; and I decline to assume that this nation is unable to meet the situation.

The final term of the high contract was for liberty and the pursuit of happiness. We have learnt a great deal of both in the past century. We know that individual liberty and individual happiness mean nothing unless both are ordered in the sense that one man's meat is not another man's poison. We know that the old "rights of personal competency"—the right to read, to think, to speak, to choose and live a mode of life, must be respected at all hazards. We know that liberty to do anything which deprives others of those elemental rights is outside the protection of any compact; and that government in this regard is the maintenance of a balance, within which every individual may have a place if he will take it; in which every individual may find safety if he wishes it; in which every individual may attain such power as his ability permits, consistent with his assuming the accompanying responsibility. . . .

Faith in America, faith in our tradition of personal responsibility, faith in our institutions, faith in ourselves demands that we recognize the new terms of the old social contract. We shall fulfill them, as we fulfilled the obligation of the apparent Utopia which Jefferson imagined for us in 1776, and which Jefferson, Roosevelt, and Wilson sought to bring to realization. We must do so, lest a rising tide of misery engendered by our common failure, engulf us all. But failure is not an American habit; and in the strength of great hope we must all shoulder our common load.

FRANKLIN D. ROOSEVELT, ADDRESS TO THE YOUNG DEMOCRATIC CLUBS OF AMERICA (1935)

In this address Roosevelt presents the psychological foundation of his New Deal. Through it the American regime was transformed. The pursuit of happiness and the protection of equality of opportunity become the promise of at least a degree of happiness guaranteed by the institutions of the welfare state.

A man of my generation comes to the councils of the younger warriors in a very different spirit from that in which the older men addressed the youth of my time. Party or professional leaders who talked to us twenty-five or thirty years ago almost inevitably spoke in a mood of achievement and of exultation. They addressed us with the air of those who had won the secret of success for themselves and of permanence of achievement for their country for all generations to come. They assumed that there was a guarantee of final accomplishment for the people of this country and that the grim specter of insecurity and want among the great masses would never haunt this land of plenty as it had widely visited other portions of the world. And so the elders of that day used to tell us, in effect, that the job of youth was merely to copy them and thereby to preserve the great things they had won for us.

I have no desire to underestimate the achievements of the past. We have no right to speak slightingly of the heritage, spiritual and material, that comes down to us. There are lessons that it teaches that we abandon only at our own peril. "Hold fast to that which is permanently true" is still a counsel of wisdom.

While my elders were talking to me about the perfection of America, I did not know then of the lack of opportunity, the lack of education, the lack of many of the essential needs of civilization which existed among millions of our people who lived not alone in the slums of the great cities and in the forgotten corners of rural America but even under the very noses of those who had the advantages and the power of Government of those days.

I say from my heart that no man of my generation has any business to address youth unless he comes to that task not in a spirit of exultation, but in a spirit of humility. I cannot expect you of a newer generation to believe me, of an older generation, if I do not frankly acknowledge that had the generation that brought you into the world been wiser and more provident and more unselfish, you would have been saved from needless difficult problems and needless pain and suffering. We may not have failed you in good intentions but we have certainly not been adequate in results. Your task, therefore, is not only to maintain the best in your heritage, but to labor to lift from the shoulders of the American people some of the burdens that the mistakes of a past generation have placed there.

There was a time when the formula for success was the simple admonition to have a stout heart and willing hands. A great, new country lay open. When life became hard in one place it was necessary only to move on to another. But circumstances have changed all that. Today we can no longer escape into virgin territory: we must master our environment. The youth of this generation finds that the old frontier is occupied, but that science and invention and economic evolution have opened up a new frontier—one not based on geography but on the resourcefulness of men and women applied to the old frontier.

The cruel suffering of the recent depression has taught us unforgettable lessons. We have been compelled by stark necessity to unlearn the too comfortable superstition that the American soil was mystically blessed with every kind of immunity to grave economic maladjustments, and that the American spirit of individualism—all alone and unhelped by the cooperative efforts of Government—could withstand and repel every form of economic disarrangement or crisis. The severity of the recent depression, toward which we had been heading for a whole generation, has taught us that no economic or social class in the community is so richly endowed and so independent of the general community that it can safeguard its own security, let alone assure security for the general community.

The very objectives of young people have changed. In the older days a great financial fortune was too often the goal. To rule through wealth, or through the power of wealth, fired our imagination. This was the dream of the golden ladder—each individual for himself.

It is my firm belief that the newer generation of America has a different dream. You place emphasis on sufficiency of life, rather than on a plethora of riches. You think of the security for yourself and your family that will give you good health, good food, good education, good working conditions, and the opportunity for normal recreation and occasional travel. Your advancement, you hope, is along a broad highway on which thousands of your fellow men and women are advancing with you.

You and I know that this modern economic world of ours is governed by rules and regulations vastly more complex than those laid down in the days of Adam Smith or John Stuart Mill. They faced simpler mechanical processes and social needs. It is worth remembering, for example, that the business corporation, as we know it, did not exist in the days of Washington and Hamilton and Jefferson. Private businesses then were conducted solely by individuals or by partnerships in which every member was immediately and wholly responsible for success or failure. Facts are relentless. We must adjust our ideas to the facts of today.

Our concepts of the regulation of money and credit and industrial competition, of the relation of employer and employee, created for the old civilization, are being modified to save our economic structure from confusion, destruction and paralysis. The rules that governed the relationship between an employer and employee in the blacksmith's shop in the days of Washington cannot, of necessity, govern the relationship between the fifty thousand employees of a great corporation and the infinitely complex and diffused ownership of that corporation. If fifty thousand employees spoke with fifty thousand voices, there would be a modern Tower of Babel. That is why we insist on their right to choose their representatives to bargain collectively in their behalf with their employer. In the case of the employees, every individual employee will know in his daily work whether he is adequately represented or not. In the case of the hundreds of thousands of stockholders in the present-day ownership of great corporations, however, their knowledge of the success of the management is based too often solely on a financial balance sheet. Things may go wrong in the management without their being aware of it for a year, or for many years to come. Without their day-to-day knowledge they may be exploited and their investments jeopardized. Therefore, we have come to the recognition of the need of simple but adequate public protection for the rights of the investing public.

A rudimentary concept of credit control appropriate for financing the economic life of a Nation of 3,000,000 people can hardly be urged as a means of directing and protecting the welfare of our twentieth-century industrialism. The simple banking rules of Hamilton's day, when all the transactions of a fair-sized bank could be kept in the neat penmanship of a clerk in one large ledger, fail to protect the millions of individual depositors of a great modern banking institution. And so it goes through all the range of economic life. Aggressive enterprise and shrewd invention have been at work on our economic machine. Our rules of conduct for the operation of that machine must be subjected to the same constant development. . . .

FRANKLIN D. ROOSEVELT, FIRESIDE CHAT ON PARTY PRIMARIES (1938)

This radio address was Roosevelt's effort to convince Democratic voters to oust anti-New Deal Democrats from Congress in the party primaries. Though the effort failed, it did serve to reorient U.S. politics around the principled distinction between liberalism and conservatism.

In the coming primaries in all parties, there will be many clashes between two schools of thought, generally classified as liberal and conservative. Roughly speaking, the liberal school of thought recognizes that the new conditions throughout the world call for new remedies.

Those of us in America who hold to this school of thought, insist that these new remedies can be adopted and successfully maintained in this country under our present form of government if we use government as an instrument of cooperation to provide these remedies. We believe that we can solve our problems through continuing effort, through democratic processes instead of Fascism or Communism. We are opposed to the kind of moratorium on reform which, in effect, is reaction itself.

Be it clearly understood, however, that when I use the word "liberal," I mean the believer in progressive principles of democratic, representative government and not the wild man who, in effect, leans in the direction of Communism, for that is just as dangerous as Fascism.

The opposing or conservative school of thought, as a general proposition, does not recognize the need for Government itself to step in and take action to meet these new problems. It believes that individual initiative and private philanthropy will solve them—that we ought to repeal many of the things we have done and go back, for instance, to the old gold standard, or stop all this business of old age pensions and unemployment insurance, or repeal the Securities and Exchange Act, or let monopolies thrive unchecked—return, in effect, to the kind of Government we had in the twenties.

Assuming the mental capacity of all the candidates, the important question which it seems to me the primary voter must ask is this: "To which of these general schools of thought does the candidate belong?"

As President of the United States, I am not asking the voters of the country to vote for Democrats next November as opposed to Republicans or members of any other party. Nor am I, as President, taking part in Democratic primaries.

As the head of the Democratic Party, however, charged with the responsibility of carrying out the definitely liberal declaration of principles set forth in the 1936 Democratic platform, I feel that I have every right to speak in those few instances where there may be a clear issue between candidates for a Democratic nomination involving these principles, or involving a clear misuse of my own name. . . .

THE PORT HURON STATEMENT (1962)

This is the founding document of the Students for a Democratic Society (SDS), the most theoretically inclined of the groups making up the New Left Movement of the 1960s and early 1970s. It claims to go beyond liberalism in the direction of radicalism.

Making values explicit—an initial task in establishing alternatives—is an activity that has been devalued and corrupted. The conventional moral terms of the age, the politician moralities—"free world," "people's democracies"—reflect realities poorly, if at all, and seem to function more as ruling myths than as descriptive principles. But neither has our experience in the universities brought us moral enlightenment. Our professors and administrators sacrifice controversy to public relations; their curriculums change more slowly than the living events of the world; their skills and silence are purchased by investors in the arms race; passion is called unscholastic. The questions we might want raised—What is really important? Can we live in a different and better way? If we wanted to change society, how would we do it?—are not thought to be questions of a "fruitful, empirical nature," and thus are brushed aside.

Unlike youth in other countries we are used to moral leadership being exercised and moral dimensions being clarified by our elders.

But today, for us, not even the liberal and socialist preachments of the past seem adequate to the forms of the present. Consider the old slogans: Capitalism Cannot Reform Itself, United Front Against Fascism, General Strike, All Out on May Day. Or, more recently, No Cooperation with Commies and Fellow Travelers, Ideologies are Exhausted, Bipartisanship, No Utopias. These are incomplete, and there are few new prophets. It has been said that our liberal and socialist predecessors were plagued by vision without program, while our own generation is plagued by program without vision. All around us there is astute grasp of method, technique—the committee, the ad hoc group, the lobbyist, the hard and soft sell, the make, the projected image—but, if pressed critically, such expertise is incompetent to explain its implicit ideals. It is highly fashionable to identify oneself by old categories, or by naming a respected political figure, or by explaining "how we would vote" on various issues.

Theoretic chaos has replaced the idealistic thinking of old—and, unable to reconstitute theoretic order, men have condemned idealism itself. Doubt has replaced hopefulness—and men act out a defeatism that is labeled realistic. The decline of utopia and hope is in fact one of the defining features of social life today. The reasons are various: the dreams of the older left were perverted by Stalinism and never recreated; the congressional stalemate makes men narrow their view of the possible; the specialization of human activity leaves little room for sweeping thought; the horrors of the twentieth century, symbolized in the gas ovens and concentration camps and atom bombs, have blasted hopefulness. To be idealistic is to be considered apocalyptic, deluded. To have no serious aspirations, on the contrary, is to be "tough-minded."

In suggesting social goals and values, therefore, we are aware of entering a sphere of some disrepute. Perhaps matured by the past, we have no sure formulas, no closed theories—but that does not mean values are beyond discussion and tentative determination. A first task of any social movement is to convince people that the search for orienting theories and the creation of human values is complex but worthwhile. We are aware that to avoid platitudes we must analyze the concrete conditions of social order. But to direct such an analysis we must use the guideposts of basic principles. Our own social values involve conceptions of human beings, human relationships, and social systems.

We regard *men* as infinitely precious and possessed of unfulfilled capacities for reason, freedom, and love. In affirming these principles we are aware of countering perhaps the dominant conceptions of man in the twentieth century: that he is a thing to be manipulated, and that he is inherently incapable of directing his own affairs. We oppose the depersonalization that reduces human beings to the status of things—if anything, the brutalities of the twentieth century teach that means and ends are intimately related, that vague appeals to "posterity" cannot justify the mutilations of the present. We oppose, too, the doctrine of human incompetence because it rests essentially on the modern fact that men have been "competently" manipulated into incompetence—we see little reason why men cannot meet with increasing skill the complexities and responsibilities of their situation, if society is organized not for minority, but for majority, participation in decision-making.

Men have unrealized potential for self-cultivation, self-direction, self-understanding, and creativity. It is this potential that we regard as crucial and to which we appeal, not to the human potentiality for violence, unreason, and submission to authority. The goal of man and society should be human independence: a concern not with the image of popularity but with finding a meaning in life that is personally authentic; a quality of mind not compulsively driven by a sense of powerlessness, nor one which unthinkingly adopts status values, nor one which represses all threats to its habits, but one which has full, spontaneous access to present and past experiences, one which easily unites the fragmented parts of personal history, one which openly faces problems which are troubling and unresolved; one with an intuitive awareness of possibilities, an active sense of curiosity, an ability and willingness to learn.

This kind of independence does not mean egotistic individualism—the object is not to have one's way so much as it is to have a way that is one's own. Nor do we deify man—we merely have faith in his potential.

Human relationships should involve fraternity and honesty. Human interdependence is contemporary fact; human brotherhood must be willed, however, as a condition of future survival and as the most appropriate form of social relations. Personal links between man and man are needed, especially to go beyond the partial and fragmentary bonds of function that bind men only as worker to worker, employer to employee, teacher to student, American to Russian.

Loneliness, estrangement, isolation describe the vast distance between man and man today. These dominant tendencies cannot be overcome by better personnel management, nor by improved gadgets, but only when a love of man overcomes the idolatrous worship of things by man. As the individualism we affirm is not egoism, the selflessness we affirm is not self-elimination. On the contrary, we believe in generosity of a kind that imprints one's unique individual qualities in the relation to other men, and to all human activity. Further, to dislike isolation is not to favor the abolition of privacy; the latter differs from isolation in that it occurs or is abolished according to individual will.

We would replace power rotted in possession, privilege, or circumstance by power and uniqueness rooted in love, reflectiveness, reason, and creativity. As a social system we seek the establishment of a democracy of individual participation, governed by two central aims: that the individual share in those social decisions determining the quality and direction of his life; that society be organized to encourage independence in men and provide the media for their common participation.

LYNDON JOHNSON, THE STATE
OF THE UNION ADDRESS (1964)

The War on Poverty, the heart of Johnson's Great Society agenda for reform, aimed to eradicate—rather than merely alleviate—what Franklin Roosevelt called the "cruel suffering" of poverty.

This administration today, here and now, declares unconditional war on poverty in America. I urge this Congress and all Americans to join with me in that effort.

It will not be a short or easy struggle, no single weapon or strategy will suffice, but we shall not rest until that war is won. The richest Nation on earth can afford to win it. We cannot afford to lose it. One thousand dollars invested in salvaging an unemployable youth today can return $40,000 or more in his lifetime. . . .

Very often a lack of jobs and money is not the cause of poverty, but the symptom. The cause may lie deeper—in our failure to give our fellow citizens a fair chance to develop their own capacities, in a lack of education and training, in a lack of medical care and housing, in a lack of decent communities in which to live and bring up their children.

But whatever the cause, our joint Federal-local effort must pursue poverty, pursue it wherever it exists—in city slums and small towns, in sharecropper shacks or in migrant workers camps, on Indian Reservations, among whites as well as Negroes, among the young as well as the aged, in the boom towns and in the depressed areas.

Our aim is not only to relieve the symptom of poverty, but to cure it and, above all, to prevent it. No single piece of legislation, however, is going to suffice.

We will launch a special effort in the chronically distressed areas of Appalachia. We must expand our small but our successful area redevelopment program.

We must enact youth employment legislation to put jobless, aimless, hopeless youngsters to work on useful projects.

We must distribute more food to the needy through a broader food stamp program.

We must create a National Service Corps to help the economically handicapped of our own country as the Peace Corps now helps those abroad.

We must modernize our unemployment insurance and establish a high-level commission on automation. If we have the brain power to invent these machines, we have the brain power to make certain that they are a boon and not a bane to humanity.

We must extend the coverage of our minimum wage laws to more than 2 million workers now lacking this basic protection of purchasing power.

We must, by including special school aid funds as part of our education program, improve the quality of teaching, training, and counseling in our hardest hit areas.

We must build more libraries in every area and more hospitals and nursing homes under the Hill-Burton Act, and train more nurses to staff them.

We must provide hospital insurance for our older citizens financed by every worker and his employer under Social Security, contributing no more than $1 a month during the employee's working career to protect him in his old age in a dignified manner without cost to the Treasury, against the devastating hardship of prolonged or repeated illness.

We must, as a part of a revised housing and urban renewal program, give more help to those displaced by slum clearance, provide more housing for our poor and our elderly, and seek as our ultimate goal in our free enterprise system a decent home for every American family.

We must help obtain more modern mass transit within our communities as well as low-cost transportation between them.

Above all, we must release $11 billion of tax reduction into the private spending stream to create new jobs and new markets in every area of this land.

These programs are obviously not for the poor or the underprivileged alone. Every American will benefit by the extension of social security to cover the hospital costs of their aged parents. Every American community will benefit from the construction or modernization of schools, libraries, hospitals, and nursing homes, from the training of more nurses and from the improvement of urban renewal in public transit. And every individual American taxpayer and every corporate taxpayer will benefit from the earliest possible passage of the pending tax bill from both the new investment it will bring and the new jobs that it will create.

LYNDON JOHNSON, THE COMMENCEMENT ADDRESS AT THE UNIVERSITY OF MICHIGAN (1964)

President Johnson's Great Society program of welfare reform

*and expansion sought to show that Americans, despite their
affluence, were devoted to more than "soulless wealth."*

For a century we labored to settle and to subdue a continent. For
half a century we called upon unbounded invention and untiring
industry to create an order of plenty for all of our people.

The challenge of the next half century is whether we have the
wisdom to use that wealth to enrich and elevate our national life,
and to advance the quality of our American civilization.

Your imagination, your initiative, and your indignation will determine whether we build a society where progress is the servant
of our needs, or a society where old values and new visions are
buried under unbridled growth. For in your time we have the opportunity to move not only toward the rich society and the powerful
society, but upward to the Great Society.

The Great Society rests on abundance and liberty for all. It demands an end to poverty and racial injustice, to which we are totally
committed in our time. But that is just the beginning.

The Great Society is a place where every child can find knowledge to enrich his mind and to enlarge his talents. It is a place where
leisure is a welcome chance to build and reflect, not a feared cause
of boredom and restlessness. It is a place where the city of man
serves not only the needs of the body and the demands of commerce but the desire for beauty and the hunger for community.

It is a place where man can renew contact with nature. It is a
place which honors creation for its own sake and for what it adds
to the understanding of the race. It is a place where men are more
concerned with the quality of their goals than the quantity of their
goods.

But most of all, the Great Society is not a safe harbor, a resting
place, a final objective, a finished work. It is a challenge constantly
renewed, beckoning us toward a destiny where the meaning of our
lives matches the marvelous products of our labor.

So I want to talk to you today about three places where we begin to build the Great Society—in our cities, in our countryside,
and in our classrooms.

Many of you will live to see the day, perhaps 50 years from now,
when there will be 400 million Americans—four-fifths of them in

urban areas. In the remainder of this century urban population will double, city land will double, and we will have to build homes, highways, and facilities equal to all those built since this country was first settled. So in the next 40 years we must rebuild the entire urban United States.

Aristotle said: "Men come together in cities in order to live, but they remain together in order to live the good life." It is harder and harder to live the good life in American cities today.

The catalog of ills is long: there is the decay of the centers and the despoiling of the suburbs. There is not enough housing for our people or transportation for our traffic. Open land is vanishing and old landmarks are violated.

Worst of all, expansion is eroding the precious and time-honored values of community with neighbors and communion with nature. The loss of these values breeds loneliness and boredom and indifference.

Our society will never be great until our cities are great. Today the frontier of imagination and innovation is inside those cities and not beyond their borders.

New experiments are already going on. It will be the task of your generation to make the American city a place where future generations will come, not only to live but to live the good life. . . .

While our Government has many programs directed at those issues, I do not pretend that we have the full answer to those problems.

But I do promise this: We are going to assemble the best thought and the broadest knowledge from all over the world to find those answers for America. I intend to establish working groups to prepare a series of White House conferences and meetings—on the cities, on natural beauty, on the quality of education, and on other emerging challenges. And from these meetings and from this inspiration and from these studies we will begin to set our course toward the Great Society. . . .

Will you join in the battle to build the Great Society, to prove that our material progress is only the foundation on which we build a richer life of mind and spirit?

There are those timid souls who say this battle cannot be won; that we are condemned to a soulless wealth. I do not agree. We have the power to shape the civilization that we want. But we need your will, your labor, your hearts, if we are to build that kind of society.

RONALD REAGAN, THE STATE OF THE UNION ADDRESS (1982)

This is a wide-ranging critique of the uncontrolled develop-ment of the welfare state established by Roosevelt's New Deal and expanded by Johnson's Great Society. Reagan does, how-ever, see the necessity of a "safety net" provided by government to counter the most brutal effects of economic liberty.

Changing Face of Government

It is my duty to report to you tonight on the progress we have made in our relations with other nations, on the foundation we have carefully laid for our economic recovery and, finally, on a bold and spirited initiative that I believe can change the face of American government and make it again the servant of the people.

Seldom have the stakes been higher for America. What we do and say here will make all the difference to auto workers in De-troit, lumberjacks in the Northwest, and steelworkers in Steubenville who are in the unemployment lines, to black teenagers in Newark and Chicago; to hard-pressed farmers and small businessmen and to millions of everyday Americans who harbor the simple wish of a safe and financially secure future for their children.

To understand the State of the Union, we must look not only at where we are and where we are going but at where we've been. The situation at this time last year was truly ominous.

The last decade has seen a series of recessions. There was a recession in 1970, another in 1974, and again in the spring of 1980. Each time, unemployment increased and inflation soon turned up again. We coined the word "stagflation" to describe this.

Government's response to these recessions was to pump up the money supply and increase spending. . . .

Faith in Government

A year ago, Americans' faith in their governmental process was steadily declining. Six out of ten Americans were saying they were pessimistic about their future.

A new kind of defeatism was heard. Some said our domestic problems were uncontrollable—that we had to learn to live with the seemingly endless cycles of high inflation and high unemployment.

There were also pessimistic predictions about the relationship between our Administration and this Congress. It was said we could never work together. Well, those predictions were wrong.

The record is clear, and I believe history will remember this as an era of American renewal, remember this Administration as an Administration of change and remember this Congress as a Congress of destiny.

Together, we not only cut the increase in Government spending nearly in half, we brought about the largest tax reductions and the most sweeping changes in our tax structure since the beginning of this century. And because we indexed future taxes to the rate of inflation, we took away Government's built-in profit on inflation and its hidden incentive to grow larger at the expense of American workers.

Together, after 50 years of taking power away from the hands of the people in their states and local communities we have started returning power and resources to them.

Together, we have cut the growth of new Federal regulations nearly in half. In 1982, there were 23,000 fewer pages in the Federal Register, which lists new regulations, than there were in 1980.

By deregulating oil, we have come closer to achieving energy independence and helped bring down the costs of gasoline and heating fuel.

Together, we have created an effective Federal strike force to combat waste and fraud in Government. In just six months it has saved the taxpayers more than $2 billion, and it's only getting started.

Together, we have begun to mobilize the private sector—not to duplicate wasteful and discredited Government programs but to bring thousands of Americans into a volunteer effort to help solve many of America's social problems.

Together, we have begun to restore that margin of military safety that ensures peace. Our country's uniform is being worn once again with pride.

Together, we have made a new beginning, but we have only begun.

Inaugural Address Warning

No one pretends that the way ahead will be easy. In my inaugural address last year, I warned that the "ills we suffer have come upon us over several decades. They will not go away in days, weeks or months, but they will go away . . . because we as Americans have the capacity now, as we've had in the past, to do whatever needs to be done to preserve this last and greatest bastion of freedom" [ellipsis in Reagan's address].

The economy will face difficult moments in the months ahead. But, the program for economic recovery that is in place will pull the economy out of its slump and put us on the road to prosperity and stable growth by the latter half of this year.

That is why I can report to you tonight that in the near future the State of the Union and the economy will be better—much better—if we summon the strength to continue on the course we have charted.

And so the question: If the fundamentals are in place, what now?

Two things. First, we must understand what is happening at the moment to the economy. Our current problems are not the product of the recovery program that is only just now getting under way, as some would have you believe; they are the inheritance of decades of tax and tax, spend and spend.

Second, because our economic problems are deeply rooted and will not respond to quick political fixes, we must stick to our carefully integrated plan for recovery. That plan is based on four common-sense fundamentals: continued reduction of the growth in Federal spending, preserving the individual and business tax reductions that will stimulate saving and investment, removing unnecessary Federal regulations to spark productivity and maintaining a healthy dollar and a stable monetary policy—the latter a responsibility of the Federal Reserve System. . . .

Contrary to some of the wild charges you may have heard, this Administration has not and will not turn its back on America's elderly or America's poor. Under the new budget, funding for social insurance programs will be more than double the amount spent only six years ago.

But it would be foolish to pretend that these or any programs cannot be made more efficient and economical.

The entitlement programs that make up our safety net for the truly needy have worthy goals and many deserving recipients. We will protect them. But there is only one way to see to it that these programs really help those whom they were designed to help, and that is to bring their spiraling costs under control.

Today we face the absurd situation of a Federal budget with three-quarters of its expenditures routinely referred to as "uncontrollable," and a large part of this goes to entitlement programs.

Committee after committee of this Congress has heard witness after witness describe many of these programs as poorly administered and rife with waste and fraud. Virtually every American who shops in a local supermarket is aware of the daily abuses that take place in the food stamp program—which has grown by 16,000 percent in the last 15 years. Another example is Medicare and Medicaid—programs with worthy goals but whose costs have increased from $11.2 billion to almost $60 billion, more than five times as much, in just 10 years.

Waste and fraud are serious problems. Back in 1980, Federal investigators testified before one of your committees that "corruption has permeated virtually every area of the Medicare and Medicaid health care industry." One official said many of the people who are cheating the system were "very confident that nothing was going to happen to them."

Aiding "Greedy," Not "Needy"

Well, something is going to happen. Not only the taxpayers are defrauded—the people with real dependency on these programs are deprived of what they need because available resources are going not to the needy but to the greedy.

The time has come to control the uncontrollable.

In August we made a start. I signed a bill to reduce the growth of these programs by $44 billion over the next three years, while at the same time preserving essential services for the truly needy. Shortly you will receive from me a message on further reforms we intend to install—some new, but others long recommended by your own Congressional committees. I ask you to help make these savings for the American taxpayer.

The savings we propose in entitlement programs will total some $63 billion over four years and will, without affecting Social Security, go a long way toward bringing Federal spending under control.

But don't be fooled by those who proclaim that spending cuts will deprive the elderly, the needy and the helpless. The Federal Government will still subsidize 95 million meals every day. That's one out of seven of all the meals served in America. Head Start, senior nutrition programs, and child welfare programs will not be cut from the levels we proposed last year. More than one-half billion dollars has been proposed for minority business assistance. And research at the National Institutes of Health will be increased by over $100 million. While meeting all these needs, we intend to plug unwarranted tax loopholes and strengthen the law which requires all large corporations to pay a minimum tax.

I am confident the economic program we have put into operation will protect the needy while it triggers a recovery that will benefit all Americans. It will stimulate the economy, result in increased savings and thus provide capital for expansion, mortgages for home building and jobs for the unemployed.

MARIO M. CUOMO, SPEECH DELIVERED AT HARVARD CLASS DAY (1985)

Cuomo, governor of New York from 1983 to 1995, is easily the most articulate spokesman for the Democratic party's tradition of liberalism today.

It might be hard for you to think about on this special day, but there are people in this country who despise Harvard and everything it stands for. To them, Harvard is everything wrong with America, a perverse and corruptive force. The invention of sociological and intellectual devils.

These people who feel this way even have a name for themselves.

They call themselves . . . "Yalies."

Other people don't so much hate Harvard as misunderstand it.

They think all Harvard graduates look like Arthur Schlesinger and sound like Ted Kennedy.

Those are some of the perceptions—or misperceptions—of Harvard. But at bottom they're all rooted in one fact: Harvard is synonymous with excellence.

Even the hardcore "Harvard-haters" know that although they might not like what Harvard does, it does it better than any place else.

They can't deny the standard Harvard has set for the entire enterprise of American education, or the rigorous academic training that's made its sons and daughters leaders in every phase of our national life.

And it belongs to you, Harvard's newest graduates.

By getting into Harvard—and now by getting out—you've won a special distinction for yourselves, becoming living links in one of the oldest and finest of America's traditions.

Wherever you go, Harvard will go with you.

And even if you don't travel around with a scarlet letter "H" emblazoned on your sweater, or sound like you're from Boston, or order your clothes from L. L. Bean, people are going to discover soon enough where you went to school.

They'll know because of what you'll do, the learning and intellect you'll bring to bear on your work, the depth and breadth of your talents.

They'll know from your ambition. To be recognized. To distinguish yourselves. To be successful. To measure up to Harvard's standards: to be the best.

That instinct to strive for personal success, that ambition, is a large part of the reason for this nation's extraordinary emergence and growth.

America was born in outrageous ambition, so bold as to be improbable.

The deprived, the oppressed, the impoverished, the powerless from all over the globe came here with little more than the desire to realize themselves. They carved a refuge out of the wilderness and then, in two hundred years, built it into the most powerful nation on earth. A place that has multiplied success for generation after generation of its children.

I'm one of those children. I know the story—the desire—because I saw it in my own parents. They came from another part of the world, uneducated, friendless, destitute, but driven . . . with ambition. To succeed materially. Not in any grand or global way but just for themselves and their family.

And they did.

They allowed their children to live at a level of security and assurance and comfort that they neither enjoyed nor even understood themselves.

That instinct is alive in you.

It has been honed and refined by this great university. But it is alive in you.

If you choose, you will become the leaders of industry. The pioneers of science and medicine. The great teachers and deans.

The brilliant lawyers and jurists. You will earn and wield influence. You will be comfortable in material things. In all likelihood you will eventually be wealthy.

And most of the nation will commend that success and respect you for your striving. And they should. It's your birthright as Americans.

But along with the ability to succeed, Harvard has given you something more.

Harvard has taught you that there is more to the full life than M.B.A.'s, Ph.D.'s, IRA's, stocks and bonds. More than brass plaques on mahogany doors, and mortgages and deeds and European vacations and the sweet green of the exchequer.

Harvard has taught you that America's greatness has been more than a saga of rugged individuals and lone rangers, solitary sojourners who rode to the horizon, alone, seeking their own fortunes.

America's greatness has not been just in the strength and success of individuals but in the ability of its leaders to teach compassion, to create a collective generosity that pooled our strengths and used them to help the vulnerable, to try to fill the gaps created by some inscrutable fate.

America has always been more than J. P. Morgan and Henry Ford and Commodore Vanderbilt. It's always been the people—and the leaders they raised up—who've asked with Rabbi Hillel, "If I am not for myself—who is for me? But if I am for myself alone—what am I?"

America's greatness has always been more than Horatio Alger. It's been in America's achieving enormous strength and then opening its heart to the world, and saying with Pope John Paul, "Freedom and riches and strength bring responsibility. We cannot leave to the poor and the disadvantaged only the crumbs from the feast. Rather, we must treat the less fortunate as guests."

Think about it.

For fifty years, from the Great Depression on, America allowed millions of its children to rise from poverty and anonymity to affluence and fame. We used our strength to lift up those who without our help would have never been able to reach the first rung of the ladder of success. And we grew stronger with the strength these people brought us.

For fifty years we prized words like "guts" and "grit" and "victory." But we weren't afraid to use other words like "heart" and "compassion" and even "love."

For fifty years we thought of this nation as a family, those aboard the wagon train reaching out to all the others, striving always to leave no one behind, at the side of the trail.

With our collective strength we built hospitals and homes and schools, believing that the only way we could truly succeed—not just as individuals but as a nation—was together.

We built an America of great expectations. . . .

Of liberty and justice and opportunity for all.

We struggled to provide those things for everyone. For brown, black and white. For every state and every region and every town.

We, the people, created a government that enabled us to do together, as a country, what no one of us could do so well—or at all—by ourselves.

With that government, we reached out constantly to include the excluded: impoverished immigrants, the victims of slavery and prejudice, women, those who couldn't speak the language, people born blind or disabled.

We did it hesitantly at times—sometimes reluctantly. But gradually—inexorably—we moved always toward the light.

With the leadership of Harvard graduates named Roosevelt and Kennedy, we found new ways to help people off their knees so one day they could stand on their own two feet.

New ways to train the unemployed, to rebuild neighborhoods, to send the young to college, to save the environment, to care for the elderly, to bring hope and opportunity to those who'd tasted precious little of either.

We used the wealth of states like Massachusetts and New York to settle the west and irrigate its fields.

We built dams in the south and parks in the northwest, invested in the southwest, dredged the harbors of the east.

We bridged mountains and rivers, preserved forests and farmlands; fed the hungry of this world . . . and reached for the stars.

And we made it.

With our government, we made excellence more than the privilege of a lucky few, the possession of an elite. With the help of our government, the children of Ellis Island joined the descendants of Plymouth Rock in creating a society always struggling to be fair as well as free.

For fifty years, from 1932 on, we showed the world the shape of what could be.

America was always the future.

Then, we changed course.

We still used the language of opportunity. The music was the same. But the reality was different.

We decided that for fifty years we had been wrong. We had reached too high. We had aspired too grandly.

We had too much ambition.

Without admitting that it was a retreat, we withdrew from our position as world leader and said, "We've decided there's only enough room for some of us . . . the strongest and fittest of us . . . in the wagon train."

Despite all the better mousetraps we've designed, despite all the wonderful stories of rags-to-riches, despite the examples of success and comfort—even exotic luxury—despite the bunting and the martial music, despite our Olympic medals, the truth is we've grown more timid. More afraid. Less confident. Not more selfish as individuals . . . but less confident as a nation.

And all the cheering and all the flags and all the elegant speeches with proud references to "Our America" cannot change the truth.

The glare from the shining city of condominiums and corporate towers cannot blind us to the reality that we are now in fact a tale of two cities, one prospering, the other suffering.

We may want to deny it, we may choose to ignore it, we may resent those who remind us of it, but it's still the truth.

Look around.

Look past the country clubs, and the islands of wealth to the nine million people who've sunk into poverty in the past five years.

One out of every four American children is now being raised in poverty; for blacks, it's one out of every two.

There are more homeless than at any time since the Great Depression.

Hunger—real hunger—has reappeared in our midst.

While the grandchildren of immigrants rise to new success, drive Mercedes Benzes, and build walls of shrubbery around their communities, more and more people sleep on heating grates in the streets of our cities.

And consider the philosophy that we as a people are being asked to accept.

The only way we can prosper, it's said, is to rape the land, to level the forests, to allow the pollution of the water and the air.

The way to help people pull themselves out of poverty, we're told, is to leave them to their own devices.

Let their suffering be their inspiration. Eventually it will drive them to greater self-help . . . and then success.

We should surrender, we're told, the aspirations and expectations that for half-a-century motivated and infused America—the hope that we could create a society where millions didn't have to go hungry or cold, go without an education or the chance to work, or even a roof over their heads; that we could do it without bankrupting ourselves, without destroying the ambition of the already-strong or confiscating the wealth of the already-rich.

Now we're told this was all idealistic and weak. We can't afford compassion anymore. We have to be hard and macho.

We have to electrocute more convicts. We have to support governments that torture their own people. We have to buy bigger weapons. And deny impoverished nations the help they need.

We have to settle for less than we once believed we were capable of.

Seven percent unemployment—the symbol of failure five years ago—is now the signal of recovery.

Consider as well the idea embodied in the current proposal for tax reform. It epitomizes this new world of shrunken aspiration and diminished confidence, especially insofar as it would double tax the most troubled of our states.

It suggests to the American people that the only way we can make our tax law better—fairer and more efficient—is to sacrifice some in the interests of the rest. To punish some regions so that others may thrive. It's a great game of winners and losers—in which a blind evenhandedness is confused with equity. It says that in order to reduce the rates for some people at the bottom of the economic ladder it's also necessary to give special advantage to the oil companies, to cut in half the tax rate for the richest people in the country and punish all the states and communities that have borne the burdens of the immigrants and the poor.

We have to be content if ten or twenty or fifty percent of the people are able to make it because that's all the opportunity we're capable of.

We are being asked to consent to a retreat from the sense of the common good, from caring about each other, from the central thread of western culture and American history—from intelligent compassion.

In this new dispensation, convenience replaces compassion, self-interest takes precedence before family or community, the satisfaction of individual ambition precludes consideration of mercy or justice or our neighbor.

And . . . I'm afraid, it's a philosophy that's succeeding.

More money for missiles, for bombs, for megatonnage. Less to feed babies, less for people in wheelchairs, less for those trapped on the margins of our society—women without work, children without dreams.

More help for the wealthiest, more poor than ever and a tax reform that punishes the middle class, the great mass of Americans either striving toward wealth or trying to avoid poverty.

And the temptation for those of us who are already comfortable to accept—even to profess—this philosophy is great.

The temptation is always there for the rich to see the poor as the victims of their own lack of ambition. For the strong to hoard their strength. For the golden circle of success to close in upon itself.

It's easier for those of us who've made it . . . to wave the flag and invoke all the symbols and poetry of patriotism than it is to insist our patriotism be translated into the prose of government, into programs that buy some opportunity for a child in Roxbury.

DAN QUAYLE, RESTORING BASIC VALUES, STRENGTHENING THE FAMILY (1992)

This speech was the most controversial of the 1992 presidential campaign. It aroused the indignation of the media, but it probably also did the Bush-Quayle campaign some good. Television fans may wonder whether Murphy Brown was a good example for Vice President Quayle to use to support his argument. President Clinton's secretary of health and human services, Donna Shalala, later expressed her agreement with Quayle's choice.

. . . When I have been asked during these last weeks who caused the riots and killings in L.A., my answer has been direct and simple: Who is to blame for the riots? The rioters are to blame. Who is to blame for the killings? The killers are to blame. Yes, I can understand how people were shocked and outraged by the verdict in the Rodney King trial. But there is simply no excuse for the mayhem that followed. To apologize or in any way to excuse what happened is wrong. It is a betrayal of all those people equally outraged and equally disadvantaged who did not loot and did not riot—and who were in many cases victims of the rioters. No matter how much you may disagree with the verdict, the riots were wrong. And if we as a society don't condemn what is wrong, how can we teach our children what is right?

But after condemning the riots, we do need to try to understand the underlying situation.

In a nutshell: I believe the lawless social anarchy which we saw is directly related to the breakdown of family structure, personal responsibility and social order in too many areas of our society. For the poor the situation is compounded by a welfare ethos that impedes individual efforts to move ahead in society, and hampers their ability to take advantage of the opportunities America offers.

If we don't succeed in addressing these fundamental problems, and in restoring basic values, any attempt to fix what's broken will fail. But one reason I believe we won't fail is that we have come so far in the last 25 years.

There is no question that this country has had a terrible problem with race and racism. The evil of slavery has left a long legacy. But we have faced racism squarely, and we have made progress in the past quarter century. The landmark civil rights bills of the 1960's removed legal barriers to allow full participation by blacks in the economic, social and political life of the nation. By any measure the America of 1992 is more equalitarian, more integrated, and offers more opportunities to black Americans—and all other minority group members—than the America of 1964. There is more to be done. But I think that all of us can be proud of our progress.

And let's be specific about one aspect of this progress: This country now has a black middle class that barely existed a quarter century ago. Since 1967 the median income of black two parent families has risen by 60 percent in real terms. The number of black college graduates has skyrocketed. Black men and women have achieved real political power—black mayors head 48 of our largest cities, including Los Angeles. These are achievements.

But as we all know, there is another side to that bright landscape. During this period of progress, we have also developed a culture of poverty—some call it an underclass—that is far more violent and harder to escape than it was a generation ago.

The poor you always have with you, Scripture tells us. And in America we have always had poor people. But in this dynamic, prosperous nation, poverty has traditionally been a stage through which people pass on their way to joining the great middle class. And if one generation didn't get very far up the ladder—their ambitious, better-educated children would.

But the underclass seems to be a new phenomenon. It is a group whose members are dependent on welfare for very long stretches, and whose men are often drawn into lives of crime. There is far too little upward mobility, because the underclass is disconnected from the rules of American society. And these problems have, unfortunately, been particularly acute for Black Americans. . . .

I think we can all agree that government's first obligation is to maintain order. We are a nation of laws, not looting. It has become clear that the riots were fueled by the vicious gangs that terrorize the inner cities. We are committed to breaking those gangs and restoring law and order. . . .

. . . If a single mother raising her children in the ghetto has to worry about drive-by shootings, drug deals, or whether her children will join gangs and die violently, her difficult task becomes impossible. We're for law and order because we can't expect children to learn in dangerous schools. We're for law and order because if property isn't protected, who will build businesses? . . .

Safety is absolutely necessary. But it's not sufficient. Our urban strategy is to empower the poor by giving them control over their lives. To do that, our urban agenda includes:

—Fully funding the Home-ownership and Opportunity for People Everywhere program. HOPE—as we call it—will help public housing residents become homeowners. Subsidized housing all too often merely made rich investors richer. Home ownership will give the poor a stake in their neighborhoods, and a chance to build equity.

—Creating enterprise zones by slashing taxes in targeting areas, including a zero capital gains tax, to spur entrepreneurship, economic development, and job creation in inner cities.

—Instituting our education strategy, AMERICA 2000, to raise academic standards and to give the poor the same choices about how and where to educate their children as rich people.

—Promoting welfare reform to remove the penalties for marriage, create incentives for saving, and give communities greater control over how the programs are administered.

These programs are empowerment programs. . . . Empowering the poor will strengthen families. And right now, the failure of our families is hurting America deeply. When families fail, society fails. The anarchy and lack of structure in our inner cities are testament to how quickly civilization falls apart when the family foundation cracks. Children need love and discipline. They need mothers and fathers. A welfare check is not a husband. The state is not a father. It is from parents that children learn how to behave in society; it is from parents above all that children come to understand values and themselves as men and women, mothers and fathers.

And for those concerned about children growing up in poverty, we should know this: marriage is probably the best anti-poverty program of all. Among families headed by married couples today, there is a poverty rate of 5.7 percent. But 33.4 percent of families headed by a single mother are in poverty today.

Nature abhors a vacuum. Where there are no mature, responsible men around to teach boys how to be good men, gangs serve in their place. In fact, gangs have become a surrogate family for much of a generation of inner-city boys. I recently visited with some former gang members in Albuquerque, New Mexico. In a private meeting, they told me why they had joined gangs. These teenage boys said that gangs gave them a sense of security. They made them feel wanted, and useful. They got support from their friends. And, they said, "It was like having a family." "Like family"—unfortunately, that says it all. . . .

Answers to our problems won't be easy.

We can start by dismantling a welfare system that encourages dependency and subsidizes broken families. We can attach conditions—such as school attendance, or work—to welfare. We can limit the time a recipient gets benefits. We can stop penalizing marriage for welfare mothers. We can enforce child support payments.

Ultimately, however, marriage is a moral issue that requires cultural consensus, and the use of social sanctions. Bearing babies irresponsibly is, simply, wrong. Failing to support children one has fathered is wrong. We must be unequivocal about this.

It doesn't help matters when prime time TV has Murphy Brown—a character who supposedly epitomizes today's intelligent, highly paid, professional woman—mocking the importance of fathers, by bearing a child alone, and calling it just another "lifestyle choice."

I know it is not fashionable to talk about moral values, but we need to do it. Even though our cultural leaders in Hollywood, network TV, the national newspapers routinely jeer at them, I think that most of us in this room know that some things are good, and other things are wrong. Now it's time to make the discussion public.

It's time to talk again about family, hard work, integrity, and personal responsibility. We cannot be embarrassed out of our belief that two parents, married to each other, are better in most cases for children than one. That honest work is better than hand-outs—or crime. That we are our brother's keepers. That it's worth making an effort, even when the rewards aren't immediate. . . .

BILL CLINTON, REMARKS TO THE CONVOCATION OF THE CHURCH OF GOD IN CHRIST, MEMPHIS (1993)

President Clinton, with his emphasis on family, church, and "the spirit," means to distance himself from those Democrats who are too attached to the institutions of government for solutions to our social problems. But he also calls for specific forms of government action to support and supplement personal responsibility.

. . . I guess what I really want to say to you today, my fellow Americans, is that we can . . . still fail unless we meet the great crisis of the spirit that is gripping America today.

When I leave you, Congressman Ford and I are going to a Baptist church near here to a town meeting he's having on health care and violence. I tell you, unless we do something about crime and violence and drugs that [are] ravaging the community, we will not be able to repair this country.

If Martin Luther King . . . were to reappear by my side today and give us a report card on the last 25 years, what would he say? You did a good job, he would say, voting and electing people who formerly were not electable because of the color of their skin. You have more political power, and that is good. You did a good job, he would say, letting people who have the ability to do so live wherever they want to live, go wherever they want to go in this great country. You did a good job, he would say, elevating people of color into the ranks of the United States Armed Forces to the very top or into the very top of our Government. You did a very good job, he would say. He would say, you did a good job creating a black middle class of people who really are doing well, and the middle class is growing more among African-Americans than among non-African-Americans. You did a good job. You did a good job in opening opportunity.

But he would say, I did not live and die to see the American family destroyed. I did not live and die to see 13-year-old boys get automatic weapons and gun down 9-year-olds just for the kick of it. I did not live and die to see young people destroy their own lives with drugs and then build fortunes destroying the lives of others. That is not what I came here to do. I fought for freedom, he would say, but not for the freedom of people to kill each other with reckless abandon, not for the freedom of children to have children and the fathers of the children walk away from them and abandon them as if they don't amount to anything. I fought for people to have the right to work but not to have whole communities and people abandoned. This is not what I lived and died for. . . .

Now when we read that foreign visitors come to our shores and are killed at random in our fine State of Florida, when we see our children planning their funeral, when the American people are finally coming to grips with the accumulated wave of crime and violence and the breakdown of family and community and the increase in drugs and the decrease in jobs, I think finally we may be ready to do something about it. And there is something for each of us to do. There are changes we can make from the outside in, that's the job of the President and the Congress and the Governors and the Mayors and the social service agencies. Then there's some changes we're going to have to make from inside out, or the others won't matter. That's what that magnificent song was about, wasn't it? Sometimes there are no answers from the outside in; sometimes all the answers have to come from the values and the stirrings and the voices that speak to us from within.

So we are beginning. We are trying to pass a bill to make our people safer, to put another 100,000 police officers on the street, to provide boot camps instead of prisons for young people who can still be rescued, to provide more safety in our schools, to restrict the availability of these awful assault weapons, to pass the Brady bill and at least require people to have their criminal background checked before they get a gun, and to say, if you're not old enough to vote and you're not old enough to go to war, you ought not to own a handgun, and you ought not to use one unless you're on a target range.

We want to pass a health care bill that will make drug treatment available for everyone. We have to have drug treatment and education available to everyone and especially those who are in prison who are coming out. We have a drug czar now in Lee Brown, who was the police chief of Atlanta, of Houston, of New York, who understands these things. And when the Congress comes back next year we will be moving forward on that.

We need this crime bill now. We ought to give it to the American people for Christmas. And we need to move forward on all these other fronts. But I say to you, my fellow Americans, we need some other things as well. I do not believe we can repair the basic fabric of society until people who are willing to work have work. Work organizes life. It gives structure and discipline to life. It gives meaning and self-esteem to people who are parents. It gives a role model to children.

The famous African-American sociologist William Julius Wilson has written a stunning book called "The Truly Disadvantaged," in which he chronicles in breathtaking terms how the inner cities of our country have crumbled as work has disappeared. And we must find a way, through public and private sources, to enhance the attractiveness of the American people who live there to get investment there. We cannot, I submit to you, repair the American community and restore the American family until we provide the structure, the value, the discipline and the reward that work gives.

I read a wonderful speech the other day given at Howard University in a lecture series funded by Bill and Camille Cosby, in which the speaker said, "I grew up in Anacostia years ago. Even then it was all black, and it was a very poor neighborhood. But you know, when I was a child in Anacostia, 100 percent African-American neighborhood, a very poor neighborhood, we had a crime rate that was lower than the average of the crime rate of our city. Why? Because we had coherent families. We had coherent communities. The people who filled the church on Sunday lived in the same place they went to church. The guy that owned the drugstore lived down the street. The person that owned the grocery store lived in our community. We were whole." And I say to you, we have to make our people whole again. This church has stood for that. Why do you think you have 5 million members in this country? Because people know you are filled with the spirit of God to do the right thing in this life by them.

So I say to you, we have to make a partnership, all the Government Agencies, all the business folks, but where there are not families, where there is no hope, where there is no order, where we are reducing the size of our armed services because we have won the cold war, who will be there to give structure, discipline and love to these children? You must do that. And we must help you.

Scripture says, you are the salt of the Earth, and the light of the world. That if your light shines before men they will give glory to the Father in heaven. That is what we must do. How would we explain it to Martin Luther King if he showed up today and said, yes, we won the cold war. Yes, the biggest threat that all of us grew up under, communism and nuclear war, communism gone, nuclear war receding. Yes, we developed all these miraculous technologies. Yes, we all have got a VCR in our home. It's interesting. Yes, we get 50 channels on the cable. Yes, without regard to race, if you work hard and play by the rules, you can get in to a service academy or a good college, you'll do just great. How would we explain to him all these kids getting killed and killing each other? How would we justify the things that we permit that no other country in the world would permit? How could we explain that we gave people the freedom to succeed, and we created conditions in which millions abuse that freedom to destroy things that make life worth living and life itself? We cannot.

And so I say to you today, my fellow Americans, you gave me this job, and we're making progress on the things you hired me to do. But unless we deal with the ravages of crime and drugs and violence and unless we recognize that it's due to the breakdown of the family, the community, and the disappearance of jobs, and unless we say some of this cannot be done by Government, because we have to reach deep inside to the values, the spirit, the soul and the truth of human nature, none of the other things we seek to do will ever take us where we need to go. . . .

VÁCLAV HAVEL, ADDRESS TO A JOINT SESSION OF CONGRESS (1990)

Havel, president of the Czech Republic, is an internationally known playwright and philosopher. But he achieved his greatest fame as a dissident, a vigorous and often jailed opponent of the communist rule his country suffered under until 1989. His friendly criticism of America here is from a dissident perspective.

. . . I've only been president for two months, and I've never attended any schools for presidents. My only school was life itself. Therefore I don't want to burden you any longer with my political thoughts, but instead will move on to an area that is more familiar to me. This is what I earlier called the philosophical aspect of those changes taking place in our corner of the world, changes that affect people everywhere.

As long as people are people, democracy in the full sense of the word will never be more than an ideal. One can approach it as one would a horizon, in ways that may be better or worse, but it can never be fully attained. In this sense you too are merely working towards democracy. You have thousands of problems of all kinds, as all countries do. But you have one great advantage: you have been moving towards democracy uninterruptedly for more than two hundred years, and your journey towards that horizon has never been cut short by totalitarianism. Czechs and Slovaks, despite their humanist traditions going back to the first millennium, have worked towards democracy for a mere twenty years, between the two world wars, and now for the three and a half months since November 17th of last year.

The advantage that you have over us is obvious.

The Communist version of totalitarianism has left both our nations, Czechs and Slovaks—as it has all the nations of the Soviet Union and other countries that the Soviet Union has subjugated in its time—a legacy of countless dead, an infinite spectrum of human suffering, profound economic decline, and above all enormous human humiliation. It has brought us horrors that fortunately you have not known.

At the same time, however—unintentionally, of course, it has given us something positive: a special capacity that sometimes allows us to see a little further than someone who has not undergone this bitter experience. A person who cannot move and live an even partially normal life, because he is pinned under a boulder, has more time to think about his hopes than someone who is not trapped in this way.

What I am trying to say is this: we all have things to learn from you, from how to educate our offspring or elect our representatives to how to organize our economic life so that it will lead to prosperity, not poverty. But it needn't only be a question of the well-educated, the powerful and the wealthy offering assistance to someone who has nothing and who therefore has nothing to offer in return.

We too can offer you something: our experience and the knowledge that springs from it. This is a subject for books, many of which have been written, and many of which have yet to appear. I shall therefore limit myself to a single idea.

This specific experience I speak of has given me one great certainty: that consciousness precedes Being, and not the other way around, as the Marxists claim.

For this reason, the salvation of our world can be found only in the human heart, in the power of humans to reflect, in human meekness and responsibility.

Without a global revolution in the sphere of human consciousness, nothing will change for the better in the sphere of our Being as humans, and the catastrophe towards which this world is headed— be it ecological, social, demographic, or a general breakdown of civilization—will be unavoidable. If we are no longer threatened by world war, or by the danger that the absurd mountains of nuclear weapons might blow up the world, this does not mean that we have definitely won. This is actually far from being a final victory.

We are still a long way from that "family of man"; in fact, we seem to be receding from the ideal rather than drawing closer to it. Interests of all kinds—personal, selfish, state, national, group and, if you like, corporate—still considerably outweigh genuinely common and global concerns. We are still under the sway of the destructive and enormously arrogant belief that man is the pinnacle of creation, and not just a part of it, and that he is therefore permitted everything.

There are many who say that they are concerned not for themselves but for the cause, while it is obvious that they are out for themselves and not for the cause at all. We are still destroying the planet that was entrusted to us along with its environment. We still close our eyes to the world's growing social, cultural and ethnic conflicts. Every once in a while we say that the anonymous megamachinery that we have created for ourselves no longer serves us but rather has enslaved us yet still we fail to do anything about it.

In other words, we still don't know how to put morality above politics, science and economics. We are still incapable of understanding that the only genuine grounding for all our actions—if they are to be moral—is responsibility. Responsibility to something higher than family, country, company, success. Responsibility to the order of Being, where all our actions are indelibly recorded and where, and only where, they will be properly judged.

The interpreter or mediator between us and this higher authority is what is traditionally referred to as human conscience.

If I subordinate my political behavior to the imperative given me by my conscience, then I can't go far wrong. If, on the contrary, I weren't guided by this voice, then not even ten presidential schools with 2,000 of the best political scientists in the world could help me.

That is why I ultimately decided, after much resistance, to accept the burden of political responsibility.

I'm not the first, nor will I be the last intellectual to do this. On the contrary, I feel that there will be more and more of them all the time. If the hope of the world lies in human consciousness, then it's clear that intellectuals cannot forever avoid their share of responsibility for the world, hiding their distaste for politics under a supposed need for independence.

It's easy to have independence on your program, leaving it to others to put that program into action. If everyone thought that way, pretty soon no one would be independent at all.

I feel that you Americans should have no difficulty understanding all this. Did not the best minds of your country, people we might call intellectuals, write your famous Declaration of Independence, your Bill of Rights, your Constitution; and didn't they—most important of all—take upon themselves the responsibility of putting these ideas into practice? The worker from Branik in Prague to whom your president referred in his State of the Union message this year is far from being the only person in Czechoslovakia, let alone the world, who is inspired by these great documents. They inspire us all. They inspire us despite the fact that they are over two hundred years old. They inspire us to be citizens.

When Thomas Jefferson wrote that "Governments are instituted among Men deriving their just Powers from the Consent of the Governed," it was a simple and important act of the human spirit.

What gave meaning to that act, however, was the fact that the author backed it up with his life. It was not just his words, but his deed as well.

I shall close by repeating what I said at the beginning: history has accelerated. I believe that once again it will be the human mind that perceives this acceleration, comprehends its shape, and transforms its own words into deeds.

Thank you.

5

President and Congress

The selections in this chapter concern the two "political" branches of the national government, the presidency and Congress. They consider both the purpose of each branch and the conflicts between them.

FEDERALIST 57

Here Madison defends the relatively small number of seats apportioned by the Constitution to the House of Representatives from the Anti-Federalist accusation that the result will be the creation of an ambitious and selfish aristocracy.

The *third* charge against the House of Representatives is, that it will be taken from that class of citizens which will have least sympathy with the mass of the people, and be most likely to aim at an ambitious sacrifice of the many to the aggrandizement of the few.

Of all the objections which have been framed against the Federal Constitution, this is perhaps the most extraordinary. Whilst the objection itself is levelled against a pretended oligarchy, the principle of it strikes at the very root of republican government.

The aim of every political Constitution is or ought to be first to obtain for rulers, men who possess most wisdom to discern, and most virtue to pursue the common good of the society; and in the next place, to take the most effectual precautions for keeping them virtuous, whilst they continue to hold their public trust. The elective mode of obtaining rulers is the characteristic policy of republican government. The means relied on in this form of government for preventing their degeneracy are numerous and various. The most effectual one is such a limitation of the term of appointments, as will maintain a proper responsibility to the people.

Let me now ask what circumstance there is in the Constitution of the House of Representatives, that violates the principles of republican government; or favors the elevation of the few on the ruins of the many? Let me ask whether every circumstance is not, on the contrary, strictly conformable to these principles; and scrupulously impartial to the rights and pretensions of every class and description of citizens?

Who are to be the electors of the Federal Representatives? Not the rich more than the poor; not the learned more than the ignorant; not the haughty heirs of distinguished names, more than the humble sons of obscure and unpropitious fortune. The electors are to be the great body of the people of the United States. They are to be the same who exercise the right in every State of electing the correspondent branch of the Legislature of the State.

Who are to be the objects of popular choice? Every citizen whose merit may recommend him to the esteem and confidence of his country. No qualification of wealth, of birth, of religious faith, or of civil profession, is permitted to fetter the judgment or disappoint the inclination of the people.

If we consider the situation of the men on whom the free suffrages of their fellow citizens may confer the representative trust, we shall find it involving every security which can be devised or desired for their fidelity to their constituents.

In the first place, as they will have been distinguished by the preference of their fellow citizens, we are to presume, that in general, they will be somewhat distinguished also, by those qualities which entitle them to it, and which promise a sincere and scrupulous regard to the nature of their engagements.

In the second place, they will enter into the public service under circumstances which cannot fail to produce a temporary affection at least to their constituents. There is in every breast a responsibility to marks of honor, of favor, of esteem, and of confidence, which, apart from all considerations of interest, is some pledge for grateful and benevolent returns. Ingratitude is a common topic of declamation against human nature; and it must be confessed, that instances of it are but too frequent and flagrant both in public and in private life. But the universal and extreme indignation which it inspires, is itself a proof of the energy and prevalence of the contrary sentiment.

In the third place, these ties which bind the representative to his constituents are strengthened by motives of a more selfish nature. His pride and vanity attach him to a form of government which favors his pretensions, and gives him a share in its honors and distinctions. Whatever hopes or projects might be entertained by a few aspiring characters, it must generally happen that a great proportion of the men deriving their advancement from their influence with the people, would have more to hope from a preservation of the favor, than from innovations in the government subversive of the authority of the people.

All these securities however would be found very insufficient without the restraint of frequent elections. Hence, in the fourth place, the House of Representatives is so constituted as to support in the members an habitual recollection of their dependence on the people. Before the sentiments impressed on their minds by the mode of their elevation, can be effaced by the exercise of power, they will be compelled to anticipate the moment when their power is to cease, when their exercise of it is to be reviewed, and when they must descend to the level from which they were raised; there for ever to remain, unless a faithful discharge of their trust shall have established their title to a renewal of it.

I will add as a fifth circumstance in the situation of the House of Representatives, restraining them from oppressive measures, that they can make no law which will not have its full operation on themselves and their friends, as well as on the great mass of the society. This has always been deemed one of the strongest bonds by which human policy can connect the rulers and the people together. It creates between them that communion of interests and sympathy of sentiments of which few governments have furnished examples; but without which every government degenerates into tyranny. If it be asked what is to restrain the House of Representatives from making legal discriminations in favor of themselves and a particular class of the society? I answer, the genius of the whole system, the nature of just and constitutional laws, and above all the vigilant and manly spirit which actuates the people of America, a spirit which nourishes freedom, and in return is nourished by it.

If this spirit shall ever be so far debased as to tolerate a law not obligatory on the Legislature as well as on the people, the people will be prepared to tolerate anything but liberty.

Such will be the relation between the House of Representatives and their constituents. Duty, gratitude, interest, ambition itself, are the chords by which they will be bound to fidelity and sympathy with the great mass of the people. It is possible that these may all the insufficient to controul the caprice and wickedness of man. But are they not all the government will admit, and that human prudence can devise? Are they not the genuine and the characteristic means by which Republican Government provides for the liberty and happiness of the people? Are they not the identical means on which every State Government in the Union, relies for the attainment of these important ends? What then are we to understand by the objection which this paper has combated? What are we to say to the men who profess the most flaming zeal for Republican Government, yet boldly impeach the fundamental principle of it; who pretend to be champions for the right and the capacity of the people to chuse their own rulers, yet maintain that they will prefer those only who will immediately and infallibly betray the trust committed to them?

Were the objection to be read by one who had not seen the mode prescribed by the Constitution for the choice of representatives, he could suppose nothing less than that some unreasonable qualification of property was annexed to the right of suffrage; or that the right of eligibility was limited to persons of particular families or fortunes; or at least that the mode prescribed by the State Constitutions was in some respect or other very grossly departed from. We have seen how far such a supposition would err as to the two first points. Nor would it in fact be less erroneous as to the last. The only difference discoverable between the two cases, is, that each representative of the United States will be elected by five or six thousand citizens; whilst in the individual States the election of a representative is left to about as many hundred. Will it be pretended that this difference is sufficient to justify an attachment to the State Governments and an abhorrence to the Federal Government? If this be the point on which the objection turns, it deserves to be examined.

Is it supported by *reason*? This cannot be said, without maintaining that five or six thousand citizens are less capable of choosing a fit representative, or more liable to be corrupted by an unfit one, than five or six hundred. Reason, on the contrary assures us, that as in so great a number, a fit representative would be most likely to be found, so the choice would be less likely to be diverted from him, by the intrigues of the ambitious, or the bribes of the rich.

Is the *consequence* from this doctrine admissible? If we say that five or six hundred citizens are as many as can jointly exercise their right of suffrage, must we not deprive the people of the immediate choice of their public servants in every instance where the administration of the government does not require as many of them as will amount to one for that number of citizens?

Is the doctrine warranted by *facts*? It was shown in the last paper, that the real representation in the British House of Commons very little exceeds the proportion of one for every thirty thousand inhabitants. Besides a variety of powerful causes, not existing here, and which favor in that country, the pretensions of rank and wealth, no person is eligible as a representative of a country, unless he possess real estate of the clear value of six hundred pounds sterling per year; nor of a city or borough, unless he possess a like estate of half that annual value. To this qualification on the part of the county representatives, is added another on the part of the county electors, which restrains the right of suffrage to persons having a freehold estate of the annual value of more than twenty pounds sterling according to the present rate of money. Notwithstanding these unfavorable circumstances, and notwithstanding some very unequal laws in the British code, it cannot be said that the representatives of the nation have elevated the few on the ruins of the many.

But we need not resort to foreign experience on this subject. Our own is explicit and decisive. The districts in New Hampshire in which the Senators are chosen immediately by the people are nearly as large as will be necessary for her representatives in the Congress. Those of Massachusetts are larger, than will be necessary for that purpose. And those of New York still more so. In the last State the members of the Assembly, for the cities and counties of New York and Albany, are elected by very nearly as many voters, as will be entitled to a representative in the Congress, calculating on the number of sixty-five representatives only. It makes no difference that in these senatorial districts and counties, a number of representatives are voted for by each elector at the same time. If the same electors, at the same time are capable of choosing four or five representatives, they cannot be incapable of choosing one. Pennsylvania is an additional example. Some of her counties which elect her State representatives, are almost as large as her districts will be by which her Federal Representatives will be elected. The city of Philadelphia is supposed to contain between fifty and sixty thousand souls. It will therefore form nearly two districts for the choice of Federal Representatives. It forms however but one county, in which every elector votes for each of its representatives in the State Legislature. And what may appear to be still more directly to our purpose, the whole city actually elects a *single member* for the executive council. This is the case in all the other counties of the State.

Are not these facts the most satisfactory proofs of the fallacy which has been employed against the branch of the Federal Government under consideration? Has it appeared on trial that the Senators of New Hampshire, Massachusetts, and New York; or the Executive Council of Pennsylvania; or the members of the Assembly in the two last States, have betrayed any peculiar disposition to sacrifice the many to the few; or are in any respect less worthy of their places than the representatives and magistrates appointed in other States, by very small divisions of the people?

But there are cases of a stronger complexion than any which I have yet quoted. One branch of the Legislature of Connecticut is so constituted that each member of it is elected by the whole State. So is the Governor of that State, of Massachusetts, and of this State, and the President of New Hampshire. I leave every man to decide whether the result of any one of these experiments can be said to countenance a suspicion that a diffusive mode of choosing representatives of the people tends to elevate traitors, and to undermine the public liberty.

FEDERALIST 63

Here Publius discusses some of the advantages of the Senate in securing enlightened, stable, and responsible policy.

A fifth desideratum, illustrating the utility of a Senate, is the want of a due sense of national character. Without a select and stable member of the government, the esteem of foreign powers will not only be forfeited by an unenlightened and variable policy, proceeding from the causes already mentioned, but the national councils will not possess that sensibility to the opinion of the world, which is perhaps not less necessary in order to merit, than it is to obtain its respect and confidence.

An attention to the judgment of other nations is important to every government for two reasons: the one is, that independently of the merits of any particular plan or measure, it is desirable, on various accounts, that it should appear to other nations as the offspring of a wise and honorable policy; the second is that in doubtful cases, particularly where the national councils may be warped by some strong passion or momentary interest, the presumed or known opinion of the impartial world may be the best guide that can be followed. What has not America lost by her want of character with foreign nations; and how many errors and follies would she not have avoided, if the justice and propriety of her measures had, in every instance, been previously tried by the light in which they would probably appear to the unbiased part of mankind?

Yet however requisite a sense of national character may be, it is evident that it can never be sufficiently possessed by a numerous and changeable body. It can only be found in a number so small that a sensible degree of the praise and blame of public measures may be the portion of each individual; or in an assembly so durably invested with public trust, that the pride and consequence of its members may be sensibly incorporated with the reputation and prosperity of the community. The half-yearly representatives of Rhode Island would probably have been little affected in their deliberations on the iniquitous measures of that State by arguments drawn from the light in which such measures would be viewed by foreign nations, or even by the sister States; whilst it can scarcely be doubted that if the concurrence of a select and stable body had been necessary, a regard to national character alone would have prevented the calamities under which that misguided people is now laboring.

I add, as a *sixth* defect, the want, in some important cases, of a due responsibility in the government to the people, arising from that frequency of elections which in other cases produces this responsibility. This remark will, perhaps, appear not only new, but paradoxical. It must nevertheless be acknowledged, when explained, to be as undeniable as it is important.

Responsibility, in order to be reasonable, must be limited to objects to be effectual, must relate to operations of that power, of which a ready and proper judgment can be formed by the constituents. The objects of government may be divided into two general classes: the one depending on measures which have singly an immediate and sensible operation; the other depending on a succession of well-chosen and well-connected measures, which have a gradual and perhaps unobserved operation. The importance of the latter description to the collective and permanent welfare of every country needs no explanation. And yet it is evident that an assembly elected for so short a term as to be unable to provide more than one or two links in a chain of measures, on which the general welfare may essentially depend, ought not to be answerable for the final result any more than a steward or tenant, engaged for one year, could be justly made to answer for places or improvements which could not be accomplished in less than half a dozen years. Nor is it possible for the people to estimate the *share* of influence which their annual assemblies may respectively have on events resulting from the mixed transactions of several years. It is sufficiently difficult, at any rate, to preserve a personal responsibility in the members of a *numerous* body, for such acts of the body as have an immediate, detached, and palpable operation on its constituents.

The proper remedy for this defect must be an additional body in the legislative department, which, having sufficient permanency to provide for such objects as require a continued attention, and a train of measures, may be justly and effectually answerable for the attainment of those objects.

Thus far I have considered the circumstances which point out the necessity of a well-constructed Senate only as they relate to the representatives of the people. To a people as little blinded by prejudice or corrupted by flattery as those whom I address, I shall not scruple to add that such an institution may be sometimes necessary as a defence to the people against their own temporary errors and delusions. As the cool and deliberate sense of the community ought, in all governments, and actually will, in all free governments, ultimately prevail over the views of the rulers; so there are particular moments in public affairs when the people, stimulated by some irregular passion, or some illicit advantage, or misled by the artful misrepresentations of interested men, may call for measures which they themselves will afterwards be the most ready to lament and condemn. In these critical moments, how salutary will be the interference of some temperate and respectable body of citizens, in order to check the misguided career and to suspend the blow meditated by the people against themselves, until reason, justice, and truth can regain their authority over the public mind? What bitter anguish would not the people of Athens have often escaped if their government had contained so provident a safeguard against the tyranny of their own passions? Popular liberty might then have escaped the indelible reproach of decreeing to the same citizens the hemlock on one day and statues on the next.

It may be suggested that a people spread over an extensive region cannot, like the crowded inhabitants of a small district, be subject to the infection of violent passions or to the danger of combining in pursuit of unjust measures. I am far from denying that this is a distinction of peculiar importance. I have, on the contrary, endeavored in a former paper to show that it is one of the principal recommendations of a confederated republic. At the same time, this advantage ought not to be considered as superseding the use of auxiliary precautions. . . .

FEDERALIST 70

Federalist 70 and 71 are part of Publius's defense of the Constitution's "energetic" executive.

There is an idea, which is not without its advocates, that a vigorous executive is inconsistent with the genius of republican government. The enlightened well-wishers to this species of government must at least hope that the supposition is destitute of foundation; since they can never admit its truth without at the same time admitting the condemnation of their own principles. Energy in the executive is a leading character in the definition of good government. It is essential to the protection of the community against foreign attacks; it is not less essential to the steady administration of the laws; to the protection of property against those irregular and high-handed combinations which sometimes interrupt the ordinary course of justice; to the security of liberty against the enterprises and assaults of ambition, of faction, and of anarchy. Every man the least conversant in Roman history, knows how often that republic was obliged to take refuge in the absolute power of a single man under the formidable title of dictator, as well as against the intrigues of ambitious individuals who aspired to the tyranny, and the seditions of whole classes of the community whose conduct threatened the existence of all government, as against the invasions of external enemies who menaced the conquest and destruction of Rome.

There can be no need, however, to multiply arguments or examples on this head. A feeble executive implies a feeble execution of the government. A feeble execution is but another phrase for a bad execution; and a government ill executed, whatever it may be in theory, must be in practice a bad government.

Taking it for granted, therefore, that all men of sense will agree in the necessity of an energetic executive, it will only remain to inquire, what are the ingredients which constitute this energy? How far can they be combined with those other ingredients which constitute safety in the republican sense? And how far does this combination characterize the plan which has been reported by the convention?

The ingredients which constitute energy in the executive are unity; duration; an adequate provision for its support; and competent powers.

The ingredients which constitute safety in the republican sense are a due dependence on the people, and a due responsibility.

Those politicians and statesmen who have been the most celebrated for the soundness of their principles and for the justice of their views have declared in favor of a single executive and a numerous legislature. They have with great propriety, considered energy as the most necessary qualification of the former, and have regarded this as most applicable to power in a single hand; while they have with equal propriety considered the latter as best adapted to deliberation and wisdom, and best calculated to conciliate the confidence of the people and to secure their privileges and interests.

FEDERALIST 71

Duration in office has been mentioned as the second requisite to the energy of the executive authority. This has relation to two objects: to the personal firmness of the executive magistrate in the employment of his constitutional powers, and to the stability of the system of administration which may have been adopted under his auspices. With regard to the first, it must be evident that the longer the duration in office, the greater will be the probability of obtaining so important an advantage. It is a general principle of human nature that a man will be interested in whatever he possesses, in proportion to the firmness or precariousness of the tenure by which he holds it; will be less attached to what he holds by a momentary or uncertain title, than to what he enjoys by a durable or certain title; and, of course, will be willing to risk more for the sake of the one than for the sake of the other. This remark is not less applicable to a political privilege, or honor, or trust, than to any article of ordinary property. The inference from it is that a man acting in the capacity of chief magistrate, under a consciousness that in a very short time he must lay down his office, will be apt to feel himself too little interested in it to hazard any material censure or perplexity from the independent exertion of his powers, or from encountering the ill-humors, however transient, which may happen to prevail, either in a considerable part of the society itself, or even in a predominant faction in the legislative body. If the case should only be that he might lay it down, unless continued by a new choice, and if he should be desirous of being continued, his wishes, conspiring with his fears, would tend still more powerfully to corrupt his integrity, or debase his fortitude. In either case, feebleness and irresolution must be the characteristics of the station.

There are some who would be inclined to regard the servile pliancy of the executive to a prevailing current, either in the community or in the legislature, as its best recommendation. But such men entertain very crude notions, as well of the purposes for which government was instituted, as of the true means by which the public happiness may be promoted. The republican principle demands that the deliberate sense of the community should govern the conduct of those to whom they entrust the management of their affairs; but it does not require an unqualified complaisance to every sudden breeze of passion, or to every transient impulse which the people may receive from the arts of men, who flatter their prejudices to betray their interests. It is a just observation that the people commonly intend the PUBLIC GOOD. This often applies to their very errors. But their good sense would despise the adulator who should pretend that they always reason right about the means of promoting it. They know from experience that they sometimes err; and the wonder is that they so seldom err as they do, beset as they continually are by the wiles of parasites and sycophants, by the snares of the ambitious, the avaricious, the desperate, by the artifices of men who possess their confidence more than they deserve it, and of those who seek to possess rather than to deserve it. When occasions present themselves in which the interests of the people are at variance with their inclinations, it is the duty of the persons whom they have appointed to be the guardians of those interests, to withstand the temporary delusion in order to give them time and opportunity for more cool and sedate reflection. Instances might be cited in which a conduct of this kind has saved the people from very fatal consequences of their own mistakes, and has procured lasting monuments of their gratitude to the men who had courage and magnanimity enough to serve them at the peril of their displeasure.

But however inclined we might be to insist upon an unbounded complaisance in the executive to the inclinations of the people, we can with no propriety contend for a like complaisance to the humors of the legislature. The latter may sometimes stand in opposition to the former, and at other times the people may be entirely neutral. In either supposition, it is certainly desirable that the executive should be in a situation to dare to act his own opinion with vigor and decision.

FEDERALIST 73

Publius argues that the president's veto power is both a means of self-defense and a way of influencing policy.

The last of the requisites to energy, which have been enumerated, are competent powers. Let us proceed to consider those which are proposed to be vested in the President of the United States.

The first thing that offers itself to our observation is the qualified negative of the President upon the acts or resolutions of the two houses of the legislature; or, in other words, his power of returning all bills with objections, to have the effect of preventing their becoming laws, unless they should afterwards be ratified by two thirds of each of the component members of the legislative body.

The propensity of the legislative department to intrude upon the rights, and to absorb the powers, of the other departments, has been already suggested and repeated; the insufficiency of a mere parchment delineation of the boundaries of each, has also been remarked upon; and the necessity of furnishing each with constitutional arms for its own defence, has been inferred and proved. From these clear and indubitable principles results the propriety of a negative, either absolute or qualified, in the Executive, upon the acts of the legislative branches. Without the one or the other the former would be absolutely unable to defend himself against the depredations of the latter. He might gradually be stripped of his authorities by successive resolutions or annihilated by a single vote. And in the one mode or the other the legislative and executive powers might speedily come to be blended in the same hands. If even no propensity had ever discovered itself in the legislative body to invade the rights of the Executive, the rules of just reasoning and theoretic propriety would of themselves teach us that the one ought not to be left to the mercy of the other, but ought to possess a constitutional and effectual power of self-defence.

But the power in question has a further use. It not only serves as a shield to the Executive, but it furnishes an additional security against the enaction of improper laws. It establishes a salutary check upon the legislative body, calculated to guard the community against the effects of faction, precipitancy, or of any impulse unfriendly to the public good, which may happen to influence a majority of that body.

The propriety of a negative has, upon some occasions, been combated by an observation that it was not to be presumed a single man would possess more virtue and wisdom than a number of men; and that unless this presumption should be entertained, it would be improper to give the executive magistrate any species of control over the legislative body.

But this observation, when examined, will appear rather specious than solid. The propriety of the thing does not turn upon the supposition of superior wisdom or virtue in the Executive, but upon, the supposition that the legislature will not be infallible; that the love of power may sometimes betray it into a disposition to encroach upon the rights of other members of the government; that a spirit of faction may sometimes pervert its deliberations; that impressions of the moment may sometimes hurry it into measures which itself, on maturer reflection, would condemn. The primary inducement to conferring the power in question upon the Executive is to enable him to defend himself; the secondary one is to increase the chances in favor of the community against the passing of bad laws, through haste, inadvertence, or design. The oftener the measure is brought under examination, the greater the diversity in the situations of those who are to examine it, the less must be the danger of those errors which flow from want of due deliberation, or of those missteps which proceed from the contagion of some common passion or interest. It is far less probable that culpable views of any kind should infect all the parts of the government at the same moment and in relation to the same object, than that they should by turns govern and mislead every one of them.

It may perhaps be said that the power of preventing bad laws includes that of preventing good ones, and may be used to the one purpose as well as to the other. But this objection will have little weight with those who can properly estimate the mischiefs of that inconstancy and mutability in the laws, which form the greatest blemish in the character and genius of our governments. They will consider every institution calculated to restrain the excess of law-making, and to keep things in the same state in which they happen to be at any given period, as much more likely to do good than harm; because it is favorable to greater stability in the system of legislation. The injury which may possibly be done by defeating a few good laws, will be amply compensated by the advantage of preventing a number of bad ones.

Nor is this all. The superior weight and influence of the legislative body in a free government, and the hazard to the Executive in a trial of strength with that body, afford a satisfactory security that the negative would generally be employed with great caution; and there would oftener be room for a charge of timidity than of rashness in the exercise of it. A king of Great Britain, with all his train of sovereign attributes and with all the influence he draws from a thousand sources, would, at this day, hesitate to put a negative upon the joint resolutions of the two houses of Parliament. . . .

If a magistrate so powerful and so well fortified as a British monarch would have scruples about the exercise of the power under consideration, how much greater caution may be reasonably expected in a President of the United States, clothed for the short period of four years with the executive authority of a government wholly and purely republican?

It is evident that there would be greater danger of his not using his power when necessary than of his using it too often, or too much. An argument, indeed, against its expediency has been drawn from this very source. It has been represented . . . as a power odious in appearance, useless in practice. But it will not follow, that because it might be rarely exercised, it would never be exercised. In the case for which it is chiefly designed, that of an immediate attack upon the constitutional rights of the Executive or in a case in which the public good was evidently and palpably sacrificed, a man of tolerable firmness would avail himself of his constitutional means of defence, and would listen to the admonitions of duty and responsibility. In the former supposition, his fortitude would be stimulated by his immediate interest in the power of his office; in the latter, by the probability of the sanction of his constituents, who, though they would naturally incline to the legislative body in a doubtful case, would hardly suffer their partiality to delude them in a very plain case. I speak now with an eye to a magistrate possessing only a common share of firmness. There are men who, under any circumstances, will have the courage to do their duty at every hazard.

But the conventions have pursued a mean in this business, which will both facilitate the exercise of the power vested in this respect in the executive magistrate, and make its efficacy to depend on the sense of a considerable part of the legislature body. Instead of an absolute negative, it is proposed to give the Executive the qualified negative already described. This is a power which would be much more readily exercised than the other. A man who might be afraid to defeat a law by his single VETO, might not scruple to return it for reconsideration; subject to being finally rejected only in the event of more than one third of each house concurring in the sufficiency of his objections. He would be encouraged by the reflection, that if his opposition should prevail, it would embark in it a very respectable proportion of the legislative body, whose influence would be united with his in supporting the propriety of his conduct in the public opinion. A direct and categorical negative has something in the appearance of it more harsh, and more apt to irritate, than the mere suggestion of argumentative objections to be approved or disapproved by those to whom they are addressed. In proportion as it would be less apt to offend, it would be more apt to be exercised; and for this very reason, it may in practice be found more effectual. It is to be hoped that it will not often happen that improper views will govern so large a proportion as two thirds of both branches of the legislature at the same time; and this, too, in spite of the counterposing weight of the Executive. It is at any rate far less probable that this should be the case, than that such views should taint the resolutions and conduct of a bare majority. A power of this nature in the Executive will often have a silent and unperceived, though forcible, operation. When men engaged in unjustifiable pursuits are aware that obstructions may come from a quarter which they cannot control, they will often be restrained by the bare apprehension of opposition, from doing what they would with eagerness rush into, if no such external impediments were to be feared. . . .

ABRAHAM LINCOLN, A MESSAGE TO
CONGRESS IN SPECIAL SESSION (1861)

Lincoln justifies his use of the whole "war power of the government" for several months while Congress was out of session at the beginning of the Civil War.

. . . [T]his issue embraces more than the fate of these United States. It presents to the whole family of man, the question, whether a constitutional republic, or a democracy—a government of the people, by the same people—can, or cannot, maintain its territorial integrity, against its own domestic foes. It presents the question, whether discontented individuals, too few in numbers to control administration, according to organic law, in any case, can always, upon the pretences made in this case, or on any other pretences, or arbitrarily, without any pretence, break up their Government, and thus practically put an end to free government upon the earth. It forces us to ask: "Is there, in all republics, this inherent, and fatal weakness? Must a government, of necessity, be too strong for the liberties of its own people, or too weak to maintain its own existence?"

So viewing the issue, no choice was left but to call out the war power of the government; and so to resist force, employed for its destruction, by force, for its preservation.

Soon after the first call for militia, it was considered a duty to authorize the commanding general, in proper cases, according to his discretion, to suspend the privilege of the writ of habeas corpus; or, in other words, to arrest, and detain, without resort to the ordinary processes and forms of law, such individuals as he might deem dangerous to the public safety. This authority has purposely been exercised but very sparingly. Nevertheless, the legality and propriety of what has been done under it, are questioned; and the attention of the country has been called to the proposition that one who is sworn to "take care that the laws be faithfully executed," should not himself violate them. Of course some consideration was given to the questions of power, and propriety, before this matter was acted upon. The whole of the laws which were required to be faithfully executed, were being resisted, and failing of execution, in nearly one-third of the States. Must they be allowed to finally fail of execution, even had it been perfectly clear, that by the use of the means necessary to their execution, some single law, made in such extreme tenderness of the citizen's liberty, that practically, it relieves more of the guilty, than of the innocent, should, to a very limited extent, be violated? To state the question more directly, are all the laws, but one, to go unexecuted, and the government itself go to pieces, lest that one be violated? Even in such a case, would not the official oath be broken, if the government should be overthrown, when it was believed that disregarding the single law, would tend to preserve it? But it was not believed that this question was presented. It was not believed that any law was violated. The provision of the Constitution that "The privilege of the writ of habeas corpus, shall not be suspended unless when, in cases of rebellion or invasion, the public safety may require it," is equivalent to a provision—is a provision—that such privilege may be suspended when, in cases of rebellion, or invasion, the public safety does require it. It was decided that we have a case of rebellion, and that the public safety does require the qualified suspension of the privilege of the writ which was authorized to be made. Now it is insisted that Congress, and not the Executive, is vested with this power. But the Constitution itself, is silent as to which, or who, is to exercise the power; and as the provision was plainly made for a dangerous emergency, it cannot be believed the Framers of the instrument intended that in every case, the danger should run its course, until Congress could be called together; the very assembling of which might be prevented, as was intended in this case by the rebellion. . . .

This is essentially a People's contest. On the side of the Union, it is a struggle for maintaining in the world, that form and substance of government, whose leading object is, to elevate the condition of men—to lift artificial weights from all shoulders—to clear the paths of laudable pursuit for all—to afford all an unfettered start, and a fair chance, in the race of life. Yielding to partial and temporary departures, from necessity, this is the leading object of the government for whose existence we contend.

I am most happy to believe that the plain people understand, and appreciate this. It is worthy of note, that while in this, the government's hour of trial, large numbers of those in the Army and Navy, who have been favored with the offices, have resigned, and proved false to the hand which had pampered them, not one common soldier or common sailor is known to have deserted his flag.

Great honor is due to those officers who remain true, despite the example of their treacherous associates; but the greatest honor, and most important fact of all, is the unanimous firmness of the common soldiers, and common sailors. To the last man, so far as known, they have successfully resisted the traitorous efforts of those whose commands, but an hour before, they obeyed as absolute law. This is the patriotic instinct of the plain people. They understand, without an argument, that destroying the government, which was made by Washington, means no good to them.

Our popular government has often been called an experiment. Two points in it, our people have already settled—the successful establishing, and the successful administering of it. One still remains—its successful maintenance against a formidable attempt to overthrow it. It is now for them to demonstrate to the world, that those who can fairly carry an election, can also suppress a rebellion—that ballots are the rightful, and peaceful, successors of bullets;

and that when ballots have fairly, and constitutionally, decided, there can be no successful appeal, back to bullets; that there can be no successful appeal, except to ballots themselves, at succeeding elections. Such will be a great lesson of peace; teaching men that what they cannot take by an election, neither can they take it by a war—teaching all, the folly of being the beginners of a war.

And having thus chosen our course, without guile, and with pure purpose, let us renew our trust in God, and go forward without fear, and with manly hearts.

FRANKLIN D. ROOSEVELT, MESSAGE TO CONGRESS (SEPTEMBER 7, 1942)

Perhaps the most aggressive assertion of the president's emergency power came during the early days of World War II. President Roosevelt demanded that Congress immediately repeal a provision of the Emergency Price Control Act which he believed was impeding the war effort. Otherwise, he said, he must accept the responsibility given him by "total war" and act alone.

What is needed . . . is an overall stabilization of prices, salaries, wages, and profits. That is necessary to the continued production of planes and tanks and ships and guns at the present constantly increasing rate.

We cannot hold the actual cost of food and clothing down to approximately the present level beyond October 1. No one can give any assurances that the cost of living can be held down after that date.

Therefore, I ask the Congress to pass legislation under which the President would be specifically authorized to stabilize the cost of living, including the price of all farm commodities. The purpose should be to hold farm prices at parity, or at levels of a recent date, whichever is higher.

I ask the Congress to take this action by the first of October. Inaction on your part by that date will leave me with an inescapable responsibility to the people of this country to see to it that the war effort is no longer imperiled by threat of economic chaos.

In the event that the Congress should fail to act, and act adequately, I shall accept the responsibility, and I will act.

At the same time that farm prices are stabilized, wages can and will be stabilized also. This I will do.

The President has the powers, under the Constitution and under congressional acts, to take measures necessary to avert a disaster which would interfere with the winning of the war.

I have given the most thoughtful consideration to meeting this issue without further reference to the Congress. I have determined, however, on this vital matter to consult with the Congress.

There may be those who will say that, if the situation is as grave as I have stated it to be, I should use my powers and act now. I can only say that I have approached this problem from every angle, and that I have decided that the course of conduct which I am following in this case is consistent with my sense of responsibility as President in time of war, and with my deep and unalterable devotion to the processes of democracy.

The responsibilities of the President in wartime to protect the Nation are very grave. This total war, with our fighting fronts all over the world, makes the use of Executive power far more essential than in any previous war.

If we were invaded, the people of this country would expect the President to use any and all means to repel the invader.

The Revolution and the War between the States were fought on our own soil, but today this war will be won or lost on other continents and remote seas.

I cannot tell what powers may have to be exercised in order to win this war.

The American people can be sure that I will use my powers with a full sense of my responsibility to the Constitution and to my country. The American people can also be sure that I shall not hesitate to use every power vested in me to accomplish the defeat of our enemies in any part of the world where our own safety demands such defeat.

When the war is won, the powers under which I act automatically revert to the people—to whom they belong.

THE WAR POWERS RESOLUTION (1973)

This resolution is most significant as an interpretation by Congress of its war powers under the circumstances of U.S. global military leadership and Cold War. Although it seemed that the possibility of formally declaring war prior to or even "constitutionalizing" after the fact of U.S. involvement in military conflict had become obsolete, Congress asserted that it still had the constitutional responsibility to limit and control such involvement. This resolution was vetoed by President Nixon on constitutional grounds, but his veto was overridden. No president since Nixon has accepted the constitutional interpretation it sets forth.

Section 1541 (a) It is the purpose of this joint resolution to fulfill the intent of the framers of the Constitution of the United States and insure that the collective judgment of both the Congress and the President will apply to the introduction of United States Armed Forces into hostilities, or into situations where imminent involvement in hostilities is clearly indicated by the circumstances, and to the continued use of such forces in hostilities or in such situations. . . .

(b) Under article I, section 8, of the Constitution, it is specifically provided that the Congress shall have the power to make all laws necessary and proper for carrying into execution, not only its own powers but also all other powers vested by the Constitution in the Government of the United States, or in any department or officer hereof.

(c) The constitutional powers of the President as Commander-in-Chief to introduce United States Armed Forces into hostilities, or into situations where imminent involvement in hostilities is clearly indicated by the circumstances, are exercised only pursuant to (1) a declaration of war, (2) specific statutory authorization, or (3) a national emergency created by attack upon the United States, its territories or possessions, or its armed forces. . . .

Section 1542. . . . The President in every possible instance shall consult with Congress before introducing United States Armed Forces into hostilities or into situations where imminent involvement in hostilities is clearly indicated by the circumstances, and after every such introduction shall consult regularly with the Congress until United States Armed Forces are no longer engaged in hostilities or have been removed from such situations. . . .

Section 1543. . . . (a) In the absence of a declaration of war, in any case in which United States Armed Forces are introduced—(1) into hostilities or into situations where imminent involvement in hostilities is clearly indicated by the circumstances; (2) into the territory, airspace or waters of a foreign nation, while equipped for combat, except for deployments which relate solely to supply, replacement, repair, or training of such forces; or (3) in numbers which substantially enlarge United States Armed Forces equipped for combat already located in a foreign nation, the President shall submit within 48 hours to the Speaker of the House of Representatives and to the President pro tempore of the Senate a report, in writing, setting forth—(A) the circumstances necessitating the introduction of the United States Armed Forces; (B) the constitutional and legislative authority under which such introduction took place; and (C) the estimated scope and duration of the hostilities or involvement.

(b) . . . The President shall provide such other information as the Congress may request in the fulfillment of its constitutional responsibilities with respect to committing the Nation to war and to the use of United States Armed Forces abroad. . . .

Section 1544. . . . (b) . . . Within sixty calendar days after a report is submitted or is required to be submitted pursuant to section 1543(a) (1) of this title, whichever is earlier, the President shall terminate any use of United States Armed Forces with respect to which such report was submitted (or required to be submitted), unless the Congress (1) has declared war or has enacted a specific authorization for such use of United States Armed Forces, (2) has extended by law such sixty-day period, or (3) is physically unable to meet as a result of an armed attack upon the United States. Such sixty-day period shall be extended for not more than an additional thirty days if the President determines and certifies to the Congress in writing that unavoidable military necessity respecting the safety of United States Armed Forces requires the continued use of such armed forces in the course of bringing about a prompt removal of such forces.

(c) . . . Notwithstanding subsection (b) of this section, at any time that United States Armed Forces are engaged in hostilities outside the territory of the United States, its possessions and territories without a declaration of war or specific statutory authorization, such forces shall be removed by the President if the Congress so directs by concurrent resolution. . . .

Section 1547. . . . Authority to introduce United States Armed Forces into hostilities or into situations wherein involvement in hostilities is clearly indicated by the circumstances shall not be inferred—(1) from any provision of law (whether or not in effect before November 7, 1973), including any provision contained in any appropriation Act, unless such provision specifically authorizes the introduction within the meaning of this joint resolution; or (2) from any treaty heretofore or hereafter ratified unless such treaty is implemented by legislation specifically authorizing the introduction of United States Armed Forces into hostilities or into such situations and stating that it is intended to constitute specific statutory authorization within the meaning of this joint resolution.

UNITED STATES v. NIXON (1974)

Seven members of President Nixon's administration had been charged by a federal grand jury with conspiracy to defraud the government, and with obstruction of justice. The president himself was named an unindicted co-conspirator. Special prosecutor Leon Jaworski obtained a subpoena directing the president to turn over as evidence certain tape recordings and memoranda of conversations held in the White House. Nixon refused to produce some of this material, claiming executive privilege. The federal district judge rejected this claim, and the president appealed. Executive privilege—the president's power to refuse to produce information requested by other branches of government—is not explicitly granted by the Constitution. It is defended as implied by the nature of the executive's constitutional responsibilities.

CHIEF JUSTICE BURGER delivered the opinion of the Court. . . .

Justiciability

In the District Court, the President's counsel argued that the court lacked jurisdiction to issue the subpoena because the matter was an intrabranch dispute between a subordinate and superior officer of the Executive Branch and hence not subject to judicial resolution. . . . Since the Executive Branch has exclusive authority and absolute discretion to decide whether to prosecute a case, it is contended that a President's decision is final in determining what evidence is to be used in a given criminal case. . . . The Special Prosecutor's demand for the items therefore presents, in the view of the President's counsel, a political question . . . since it involves a "textually demonstrable" grant of power under Art. II. The mere assertion of a claim of an "intrabranch dispute," without more, has never operated to defeat federal jurisdiction. . . .

Our starting point is the nature of the proceeding for which the evidence is sought—here a pending criminal prosecution.

. . . Under the authority of Art. II, Section 2, Congress has vested in the Attorney General the power to conduct the criminal litigation of the United States Government. . . . It has also vested in him the power to appoint subordinate officers to assist him in the discharge of his duties. . . . Acting pursuant to those statutes, the Attorney General has delegated the authority to represent the United States in these particular matters to a Special Prosecutor with unique authority and tenure. The regulation gives the Special Prosecutor explicit power to contest the invocation of executive privilege in the process of seeking evidence deemed relevant to the performance of these specially delegated duties. . . . So long as this regulation is extant it has the force of law. Here at issue is the production or nonproduction of specified evidence deemed by the Special Prosecutor to be relevant and admissible in a pending criminal case. It is sought by one official of the Executive Branch within the scope of his express authority; it is resisted by the Chief Executive on the ground of his duty to preserve the confidentiality of the communications of the President. Whatever the correct answer on the merits, these issues are "of a type which are traditionally justiciable."

The Claim of Privilege

. . . [W]e turn to the claim that the subpoena should be quashed because it demands "confidential conversations between a President and his close advisors that it would be inconsistent with the public interest to produce." . . . The first contention is a broad claim that the separation of powers doctrine precludes judicial review of a President's claim of privilege. The second contention is that if he does not prevail on the claim of absolute privilege, the Court should hold as a matter of constitutional law that the privilege prevails over the subpoena duces tecum.

In the performance of assigned constitutional duties each branch of the Government must initially interpret the Constitution, and the interpretation of its powers by any branch is due great respect from the others. The President's counsel, as we have noted, reads the Constitution as providing an absolute privilege of confidentiality for all Presidential communications. Many decisions of this Court, however, have unequivocally reaffirmed the holding of *Marbury v. Madison* [1803] . . . that "it is emphatically the province and duty of the judicial department to say what the law is.". . .

In support of his claim of absolute privilege, the President's counsel urges two grounds, one of which is common to all governments and one of which is peculiar to our system of separation of powers. The first ground is the valid need for protection of communications between high Government officials and those who advise and assist them in the performance of their manifold duties; the importance of this confidentiality is too plain to require further discussion. Human experience teaches that those who expect public dissemination of their remarks may well temper candor with a concern for appearances and for their own interests to the detriment of the decisionmaking process. Whatever the nature of the privilege of confidentiality of Presidential communications in the exercise of Art. II powers, the privilege can be said to derive from the supremacy of each branch within its own assigned area of constitutional duties. Certain powers and privileges flow from the nature of enumerated powers; the protection of the confidentiality of Presidential communications has similar constitutional underpinnings.

The second ground asserted by the President's counsel in support of the claim of absolute privilege rests on the doctrine of separation of powers. Here it is argued that the independence of the Executive Branch within its own sphere . . . insulates a President from a judicial subpoena in an ongoing criminal prosecution, and thereby protects confidential Presidential communications.

However, neither the doctrine of separation of powers, nor the need for confidentiality of high level communications, without more, can sustain an absolute, unqualified Presidential privilege of immunity from judicial process under all circumstances. The President's need for complete candor and objectivity from advisers calls for great deference from the courts. However, when the privilege depends solely on the broad, undifferentiated claim of public interest in the confidentiality of such conversations, a confrontation with other values arises.

Absent a claim of need to protect military, diplomatic, or sensitive national security secrets, we find it difficult to accept the argument that even the very important interest in confidentiality of Presidential communications is significantly diminished by production of such material for *in camera* inspection with all the protection that a district court will be obliged to provide.

The impediment that an absolute, unqualified privilege would place in the way of the primary constitutional duty of the Judicial Branch to do justice in criminal prosecutions would plainly conflict with the function of the courts under Art. III. . . .

Since we conclude that the legitimate needs of the judicial process may outweigh Presidential privilege, it is necessary to resolve those competing interests in a manner that preserves the essential functions of each branch.

The expectation of a President to the confidentiality of his conversations and correspondence, like the claim of confidentiality of judicial deliberations, for example, has all the values to which we accord deference for the privacy of all citizens and, added to those values, is the necessity for protection of the public interest in candid, objective, and even blunt or harsh opinions in Presidential decisionmaking. . . .

But this presumptive privilege must be considered in light of our historic commitment to the rule of law. . . . The ends of criminal justice would be defeated if judgments were to be founded on a partial or speculative presentation of the facts. The very integrity of the judicial system and public confidence in the system depend on full disclosure of all the facts, within the framework of the rules of evidence. To ensure that justice is done, it is imperative to the function of courts that compulsory process be available for the production of evidence needed either by the prosecution or by the defense. . . . In this case the President challenges a subpoena served on him as a third party requiring the production of materials for use in a criminal prosecution; he does so on the claim that he has a privilege against disclosure of confidential communications. He does not place his claim of privilege on the ground that they are military or diplomatic secrets. As to these areas of Art. II duties the courts have traditionally shown the utmost deference to Presidential responsibilities. . . . No case of the Court, however, has extended this high degree of deference to a President's generalized interest in confidentiality. . . .

On the other hand, the allowance of the privilege to withhold evidence that is demonstrably relevant in a criminal trial would cut deeply into the guarantee of due process of law and gravely impair the basic function of the courts. . . . Without access to specific facts a criminal prosecution may be totally frustrated. . . .

We conclude that when the ground for asserting privilege as to subpoenaed materials sought for use in a criminal trial is based only on the generalized interest in confidentiality, it cannot prevail over the fundamental demands of due process of law in the fair administration of criminal justice. The generalized assertion of privilege must yield to the demonstrated, specific need for evidence in a pending criminal trial.

GERALD FORD, THE NIXON PARDON (1974)

President Nixon's resignation on August 9, 1974, left him subject to indictment, trial, and possible conviction for obstructing justice in the Watergate investigation and related allegations. President Ford used the power given him by the Constitution to grant Nixon a "full, free and absolute pardon . . . for all offenses against the United States which he . . . has committed or may have committed." Ford paid a severe political price for this pardon. He was roundly criticized and his approval rating dropped 20 percentage points in the polls. This pardon probably was decisive in Ford's narrow defeat for reelection.

. . . The Constitution is the supreme law of our land and it governs our actions as citizens. Only the laws of God, which govern our consciences, are superior to it. As we are a nation under God, so I am sworn to uphold our laws with the help of God. And I have sought such guidance and searched my own conscience with special diligence to determine the right thing for me to do with respect to my predecessor in this place, Richard Nixon, and his loyal wife and family.

Theirs is an American tragedy in which we all have played a part. It could go on and on and on, or someone must write "The End" to it.

I have concluded that only I can do that. And if I can, I must. . . . The facts as I see them are that a former President of the United States, instead of enjoying equal treatment with any other citizen accused of violating the law, would be cruelly and excessively penalized either in preserving the presumption of his innocence or in obtaining a speedy determination of his guilt in order to repay a legal debt to society.

During this long period of delay and potential litigation, ugly passions would again be aroused, and our people would again be polarized in their opinions, and the credibility of our free institutions of government would again be challenged at home and abroad. In the end, the courts might well hold that Richard Nixon had been denied due process and the verdict of history would even more be inconclusive with respect to those charges arising out of the period of his presidency of which I am presently aware.

But it is not the ultimate fate of Richard Nixon that most concerns me—though surely it deeply troubles every decent and every compassionate person. My concern is the immediate future of this great country. In this I dare not depend upon my personal sympathy as a longtime friend of the former President nor my professional judgment as a lawyer. And I do not.

As President, my greatest concern must always be the greatest good of all the people of the United States, whose servant I am.

As a man, my first consideration is to be true to my own convictions and my own conscience.

My conscience tells me clearly and certainly that I cannot prolong the bad dreams that continue to reopen a chapter that is closed. My conscience tells me that only I, as President, have the constitutional power to firmly shut and seal this book. My conscience says it is my duty, not merely to proclaim domestic tranquility, but to use every means that I have to ensure it.

I do believe that the buck stops here, that I cannot rely upon public opinion polls to tell me what is right. I do believe that right makes might, and that if I am wrong 10 angels swearing I was right would make no difference. I do believe with all my heart and mind and spirit that I, not as President, but as a humble servant of God, will receive justice without mercy if I fail to show mercy.

Finally, I feel that Richard Nixon and his loved ones have suffered enough and will continue to suffer no matter what I do, no matter what we as a great and good nation can do together to make his goal of peace come true.

Now, therefore, I, Gerald R. Ford, President of the United States, pursuant to the pardon power conferred upon me by Article II, Section 2, of the Constitution, have granted and by these present do grant a full, free, and absolute pardon unto Richard Nixon for all offenses against the United States which he, Richard Nixon, has committed or may have committed or taken part in during the period from January 20, 1969, through August 9, 1974. . . .

THOMAS P. O'NEILL JR., CONGRESS: THE FIRST 200 YEARS (1984)

"Tip" O'Neill was elected to Congress in 1952 and served as Speaker of the House from 1977 to 1985. The years from 1981 to 1993 were a period of "divided government," with the presidency controlled by the Republicans and the House by the Democrats. O'Neill spiritedly defended congressional power and his party's policies against the popular President Reagan.

As we approach the Bicentennial of the Constitution and the Congress it created, it is appropriate to consider how the legislative branch of our federal government has developed during its nearly 200 years of existence. It might be both interesting and useful to see how much Congress has turned out the way the Drafters of the Constitution conceived it, as well as how much of the evolution of Congress was not anticipated by them. . . .

Delegates to the Convention seem to have anticipated that a candidate for president would have to forge an alliance with the House of Representatives in order to attain the presidency. Presidents would not assume office with what has been too often the case in recent years—a highly personal interpretation that they have been given a specific mandate by the American people to whip the Congress into shape and force it to respond to their own interpretation of what is best for the country. On the contrary, the Constitution does not give to the president alone the power to interpret and execute the popular will.

Even during my thirty-some years in Congress, the party system has changed a lot, and some of these changes have hurt the ability of Congress to act effectively. When I first entered the House in 1953, it seemed that most of the members had worked their way up through the ranks to get to the House of Representatives. They had worked for their party on the local or state level and had served in some kind of local office, like mayor or alderman or city commissioner. Perhaps they had served in the state legislature, as I did, and they knew what it meant to follow the leadership and learn the art of legislation. There were not many members in those days who set out on their own with complete disregard for the party to which they belonged. They had some understanding of government and how it works.

The party system is much different today, and I believe it works to our detriment as a Congress. Men and women are elected to the House without having previously held elective office. They can get elected because they raise the money and hire a media consultant and get on television. Some of them do not care about what party they belong to, and they feel as if they owe the party nothing when they take office. The House has always been a difficult body to lead; I do not believe, though, that even Henry Clay, despite the many problems he had with John Randolph of Roanoke who brought his hunting dogs on the floor of the House, ever had to deal with as many independent members as are found in the modern House of Representatives. The result has been a breakdown of party discipline and a refusal to follow party leadership, which leads in turn to congressional paralysis and an inability to act coherently as a legislative body.

Other fundamental changes have occurred in Congress over the past 200 years. Congressional tenures, for instance, have become much longer. Most of the men—there were only men in the Congress in those days—who served in the first years of the Republic stayed for only a term or two. The custom was that a representative would leave his farm or business or profession and go to Washington for a few years. He would stay in a boarding house, eat his meals with other members of the House and Senate, and curse the insects, Washington's heat and humidity, and the open sewer that ran near the Capitol building.

For the first fifty or so Congresses, very few men made a career of service in the House or the Senate. Until about 1880, more than half the men elected to each Congress were first-termers. Service of long duration, like that of Nathaniel Macon (1791–1828), Samuel Smith (1793–1833), and William R. King (1811–16, 1819–44, 1848–52), was most unusual. As we passed into the twentieth century, elective office became more of a career than a temporary public service.

Concurrent with the longer tenure in office, seniority began to acquire greater significance in leadership assignments in the Congress. Throughout the first century or so in the House of Representatives, the Speaker switched committee chairmen as he wished, often naming large numbers of new ones at the beginning of each Congress. His power to do this was enhanced by the relatively short careers of most congressmen of the time. By 1900, when the trend toward longer service in Congress was well-established, it had become accepted practice in both the House and the Senate that a member would move up in seniority as he outlasted other members of his party on a particular committee. When he reached the top of the ladder, he would become the committee chairman, provided that his party had a majority in his branch of the Congress. It still works this way in the Senate.

The House, however, has recently introduced an element of flexibility into the process of committee chair selection. The Democratic Caucus, whose rules control the House as long as the Democrats have a majority, adopted a series of reforms in 1974. These changes require a secret ballot election for committee chairmen at the beginning of each Congress and limit a member to one subcommittee chairmanship. As a practical matter, seniority is still quite important in deciding who will chair a House committee, but it is no longer the only consideration.

There are other developments in the Congress that would surprise the men who drafted the Constitution in 1787. The Constitutional Convention, for example, was able to get by with only one staff person to help with its work. The growth of federal responsibilities and activities over the past 200 years, however, has meant that every branch of the government has increased in size since the first years of the Republic. This is as true for the Congress, which began in 1789 with only ninety-one members and a minuscule staff, as for any other branch.

For their first fifty years, the House and the Senate were able to function without having staff for particular congressional committees. By 1891, the first year for which we have good data, a total of 103 persons worked full-time for congressional committees. This assistance helped ease the committee members' workload, and as committee responsibilities have increased over the past ninety years, the number of committee staff persons has grown to just over 3000. Until almost the end of the nineteenth century, however, there was no such thing as personal staff support for a member of Congress. By 1930, the total of these congressional staffs was some 1569 persons. Fifty years later, some 14,000 individuals served the Congress as personal or committee staff members, an eightfold increase. By comparison, the national budget, for which Congress is responsible, increased by more than 172 times during this same period.

It is not unreasonable to believe that Congress has required an increase in staff assistance to enable it to cope with the growth of the national budget and the increased complexity of the federal government as a whole. The president is able to obtain information and advice from the Office of Management and Budget, the White House staff, and the thousands of analysts, statisticians, and managers elsewhere in the executive branch of the government. If the Congress is to consider legislation, appropriate hundreds of billions of dollars, perform its oversight of executive branch operations, answer millions of letters, and act as ombudsman for harassed constituents, it needs a staff much greater than the one man who served the delegates to the Constitutional Convention in 1787.

Although the role of members of Congress has expanded greatly over the past 200 years, they still have a responsibility to their constituencies. The difference, however, is the scope of these duties. Just over 100 years ago (1882) a congressman from Michigan, Roswell G. Horr, placed in the record an account of the typical constituent-service duties and activities:

> . . . I think it is safe to say that each member of this House receives fifty letters each week; many receive more. . . . Growing out of these letters will be found during each week a large number of errands, a vast amount of what is called department work. One-quarter of them, perhaps, will be from soldiers asking aid in their pension cases, and each soldier is clear in his own mind that the member can help his case out if he will only make it a special case and give it special attention.
>
> Another man writes you to look up some matter in reference to a land patent. Another says his homestead claim should be looked after and he wants you to learn and let him know why he does not receive his full title. Another has invented some machine and the department have [*sic*] declared his discovery to be already supplemented by some former inventor, and have [*sic*] refused his patent. He would like you to go through the Patent Office and look over the patent laws and see if great injustice has not been done in his case. Another has a son or brother in the Regular Army whom he would like to have discharged.
>
> Another has a recreant son whom he would like to get into the Regular Army or Navy. In conformity with these requests you are liable to be called upon, perhaps several times in one week, by these applicants in personam, and they will require you to go at once and exert your enormous powers.

Recall that the members who preceded Representative Horr, as well as those who came along many years after, performed all of these functions personally. The fifty letters a week received by Representative Horr, however, have become more than 5000 a week for the typical member of the House. All of this mail needs to be answered, even if it is only a simple acknowledgement.

Much of this incoming mail is issue-oriented, and the marriage of the computer to the high-speed printer enables a well-organized, well-financed interest group to generate literally millions of letters to Congress on a given topic. If members did not in turn rely upon their own computers and computer operators to respond to this mass-generated correspondence, they would slowly disappear beneath a sea of paper. The computer age is upon us, and for better or worse the Congress has had to adjust its way of doing business to reflect this reality.

Certain realities have not changed. Constituents need help with some agency or department of the executive branch. By the time someone writes his or her member of Congress, you can be fairly certain that a long and frustrating history has already taken place. Many citizens today feel with some justification that too much of government has become large and impersonal. When there is a problem with their Social Security benefits or their Veterans Administration benefits, the ordinary citizen often feels reduced to nothing more than a multi-digit number, dealt with in an impersonal fashion. The member can step in, cut through the Gordian knot of bureaucracy, and see to it that the citizen receives his or her due. Members of Congress have been helping their constituents in this manner since the beginning of the Republic, and I cannot imagine that anyone today would suggest that this is not an appropriate role for the Congress.

Finally, I would like to consider the relationship of the Congress and the president, in its idealized state, as it actually exists, and as I believe it should exist. When most of us were going through what used to be called civics class, we were taught that there were three branches of government at the national level. The legislative branch, we were taught, makes the laws; the executive branch enforces the laws; and the judicial branch interprets the laws. In a general sense, this scheme is correct.

But the distinction between making and enforcing laws has become blurred over the years with the advent of executive branch regulation making and the congressional veto. Even the courts have gone far beyond merely "interpreting" the law and have been performing such executive functions as administering state prison systems and redrawing school district boundaries. I believe that this blurring of duties will continue for the foreseeable future, and no amount of railing for a return to the good old days will do one bit of good.

If I could accomplish one thing as Speaker of the House of Representatives, it would be to teach the American public that the Congress is a coequal branch of the federal government, with its own set of powers and responsibilities. It is not the duty of the House or the Senate to accede to the wishes of the president, just because the president occupies the Oval Office. Indeed, the Congress and the president were intentionally set at cross-purposes by the men who drafted the Constitution. Sometimes a powerful president has been able to dominate the Congress; sometimes the Congress has run over a president. The locus of power in the government swings back and forth between these two branches.

In my own lifetime, the man who was most responsible for concentrating power in the presidency was Franklin D. Roosevelt. A dynamic individual, he knew how to make the Congress bow to his will. After him other presidents, regardless of party, were able to build on Roosevelt's legacy and increase the power of the presidency.

The growth of personal and committee staffs has certainly given the Congress a better chance to meet the president on an equal basis. There are also certain congressionally initiated statutes that have recently increased the power and influence of the House and Senate, specifically the War Powers Act and the anti-impoundment provisions of the Budget Act of 1974.

The War Powers Act was passed over President Richard M. Nixon's veto in 1973 by a Congress that was reasserting its constitutional primacy in the war area. Twice since 1950—in Korea and Vietnam—the United States has found itself in a hot war without a specific congressional declaration of war. Some people might argue that the War Powers Act is too much of a restriction on the president, but I see it as a return to the intent of the Constitution. I see the same principle in the anti-impoundment law incorporated in the Budget Act of 1974, which was largely a reaction to President Nixon's refusal to spend certain funds that had been appropriated by Congress.

In 1972 alone, President Nixon refused to spend $2.5 billion for highway construction, $1.9 billion in defense funds, and $1.5 billion for such programs as food stamps, rural water and waste disposal, and rural electrification. The proper and constitutional way for him to object to these appropriations would have been to veto the appropriations bill. Such action would have given the Congress an opportunity to override him; impoundment—refusing to spend the money that had been appropriated—leaves the Congress high and dry with little means to protest effectively. I believe this law was greatly needed and helps restore a balance to the government. Parenthetically, I would point out that the much-discussed presidential line-item veto would undermine congressional power in the budget process and could result in the elimination of many programs, such as federal aid to libraries or museums, that are favored by a majority of the Congress but opposed by an administration. The anti-impoundment law is the sole protector of these programs today.

The biggest advantage a modern president has is the six o'clock news. Presidents can be on the news every night if they want to—and usually they want to. They can easily make themselves the focus of every major news report, because the president of the United States is unarguably the most powerful individual in the world. And it is precisely for this reason that the Congress has a duty and a responsibility to act to counterbalance this power. The Congress is composed of the collective wisdom of the 435 members of the House and 100 members of the Senate, men and women who bring to the Nation's capital every conceivable combination of education and experience, 535 individuals who together represent the richness and diversity of our country. Who is to say that this group, this Congress, should bow to the wishes of any one individual, no matter who that individual may be? No, the Congress has its own role to play, and it has always been a difficult one. . . .

GEORGE BUSH, MESSAGE TO THE HOUSE OF REPRESENTATIVES RETURNING WITHOUT APPROVAL THE FOREIGN RELATIONS AUTHORIZATION ACT, FISCAL YEARS 1990 AND 1991 (1989)

President Bush, a Republican, faced a hostile Democratic Congress during his four years in office. He was a master at using the veto both to protect the president's constitutional powers and to pursue policy objectives. This message explains why he must veto a congressional attempt to usurp his foreign policy powers.

I am returning herewith without my approval H.R. 1487, the foreign relations authorization bill for fiscal years 1990 and 1991. I am convinced that Section 109 of the bill would impermissibly constrict the conduct of our Nation's foreign policy, for many of the same reasons I set forth in my veto of H.R. 2939 on November 19, 1989. Although this bill contains many desirable provisions, including a number sought by this Administration, it is fatally flawed by the inclusion of Section 109. Under some circumstances, this provision purports to prohibit, under peril of criminal sanctions, the use of U.S. assistance or third-party funds by executive branch officials, and requires Presidential reporting of certain discussions concerning provision of assistance even within the executive branch. Because of its vague and sweeping language, it threatens to subject to criminal investigation a wide range of entirely legitimate diplomatic activity, the authority and responsibility for which is vested in the executive branch by the Constitution. The result would be a dangerous timidity and disarray in the conduct of U.S. foreign policy. Such a result is wholly contrary to the allocation of powers under the Constitution.

The Administration made a good-faith effort to resolve with the Congress the constitutional and other problems contained in the bill. Those efforts have failed, and I must in these circumstances veto this bill.

Among other things, Section 109 of the bill would prohibit officers or employees of the executive branch from using "any United States funds or facilities" to "assist" certain diplomatic enterprises "if the purpose of any such act is the furthering" of certain prohibited activities. This prohibition on use of funds could extend to activities or conversations of any U.S. diplomats who receive a federal salary. The prohibition on use of facilities could also extend to meetings at U.S. embassies, or the use of U.S. word processors or telephones. Those who violate this prohibition would be subject to substantial criminal penalties.

I believe that the limiting provisions set forth therein may allow for a constitutional construction of certain provisions in Section 109; nonetheless, serious constitutional problems remain, and the section as a whole is sufficiently ambiguous to present an unacceptable risk that it will chill the conduct of our Nation's foreign affairs.

Section 109 could be construed to prohibit consultation between U.S. officials and other sovereign nations regarding certain actions that nation may wish to undertake. As I observed in my veto of H.R. 2939, however, it has long been recognized— by the Framers, by the Supreme Court, and by past Congresses— that the President, both personally and through his subordinates in the executive branch, possesses the constitutional authority to communicate freely with representatives of foreign governments, and to recommend to their representatives such courses of action as the President believes are in our Nation's best interest. The prohibition, therefore, would impermissibly circumscribe a fundamental responsibility that the Constitution has entrusted to the President—the protection of our Nation's security through a vigorous representation of our interests abroad. I am not convinced that the limiting provisions are sufficient to resolve this constitutional problem inherent in the section. It would be cold comfort indeed for our diplomats to be assured that these provisions would be available as a defense in a criminal investigation.

Moreover, Section 109 poses profound constitutional problems insofar as it purports to restrict the use of U.S. funds, or facilities in the realm of foreign affairs, because the "purpose" test it establishes is so vague and subjective as to interfere with the President's constitutional role. For courts to attempt to discern the President's state of mind or the state of mind of subordinate executive branch officials in such matter would entangle the judiciary in political disputes and foreign policy questions ill-suited to judicial resolution.

Were Section 109 and its criminal sanctions to be extended to prohibitions existing in current law, it would have a sweeping effect and cause incalculable damage to American foreign policy interests. There are many statutory prohibitions on the provision of U.S. assistance in situations where we would have no objection to others providing assistance or taking other action—such as prohibitions on U.S. assistance to Communist countries even when they are undergoing reform. Were Section 109 applied to this prohibition, it could inhibit vital discussions concerning the provision of assistance of democratizing regimes in Eastern Europe.

The Presidential notification procedures contained in Section 109 also appear designed further to disable the President in the conduct of foreign relations. The provisions would require the President to inform the Congress whenever various types of foreign initiatives are urged by executive branch officials, even if the initiatives are discussed solely within the executive branch—or are discussed with the legislative branch. This provision would interfere with the Nation's need to keep confidential our foreign policy discussions with other countries, as well as our internal planning of such discussions.

In addition to these constitutional problems, Section 109 would hamper the Nation's foreign policy by criminalizing foreign policy disputes, rather than leaving resolution of such disputes to the political process. By making those who formulate and execute foreign policy serve the public under a vague and sweeping prohibition, Section 109 would clearly circumscribe the effective, forceful and entirely lawful representation of the Nation's foreign policy interest. It is neither wise nor fair to expect the men and women of our Foreign Service to represent the Nation with a sword of Damocles over their heads.

It is significant that the Congress has seen fit to extend the prohibitions contained in Section 109 only to the executive branch, and not to Congress itself. The Congress would thus remain free to engage in the very activities proscribed for the executive branch. There is no logical or constitutional basis for such a distinction. . . .

LAMAR ALEXANDER, CUT THEIR PAY AND SEND THEM HOME (1994)

Alexander has been governor of Tennessee, president of the University of Tennessee, and President Bush's secretary of education. Here he offers both a Republican vision of the promise of America's future and a specific proposal for reform.

. . . Our country has become too focused on Washington. So has our Republican Party. At Southern Republican leadership meetings, it seemed all we would do was bring in well-respected people from Washington to talk about Washington issues. I became so exasperated that, in 1986, I helped form something called the Republican Exchange, so we could talk about how to create safe, clean communities where children could grow up healthy, go to a good school, and get a good job, which is what we were supposed to be working on.

In 1985, a group of Republican Congressmen led by Newt Gingrich and several of us activist Republican Governors spent a weekend in the Tennessee mountains to see whether we were really in the same party and on the same song sheet. Of course, we quickly agreed that we were—that good Republican philosophy is to put a harness on the government in Washington, and do what needs to be done in communities and in the private sector.

So this is not a new subject for me. What is new is the number of Americans who want Washington out of their everyday lives and the strength of their feeling about it.

Why This Is the Issue

Why has this happened? I think it's important to go back almost to the beginning of the century to a book that has kept popping up ever since it was written. It's called *The Promise of American Life*, by Herbert Croly. The title is magnificent, the first chapter is also magnificent, but for our time, the rest of the book is wrong. Nevertheless, it's worth paying attention to, because in 1909 Croly wrote that what's unique about this country is the unlimited belief in America's future. That's what is different about America, together with the idea that any of us—from wherever we came—has the opportunity to have a piece of that future.

Croly argued that all of us just doing our own things in our communities didn't add up to enough, that we needed more of a national purpose and national identity. He liked what Lincoln had done and what Teddy Roosevelt was doing. So he argued for a stronger, more activist central government. He believed the federal government's role should be more than just national defense, monetary and commercial regulation, and the enforcement of our constitutional rights. He believed the government in Washington should get into the business of raising children, eradicating poverty, and creating opportunities and prosperity for all Americans.

This belief, which he articulated in a very compelling way, has been at the core of the near ceaseless expansion of the federal government, starting with the progressive era, through the New Deal and the Great Society, to today's supposedly "new" Democrats.

Just think of it: for over 80 years the federal government has been growing and growing, spending and spending, meddling and meddling. Particularly in the last 30 years, those numbers have grown into almost abstract figures. The number of federal employees has grown from just under 1 million in 1939 to almost 3 million today. Federal spending has gone from $715 million in 1913 to nearly $1.5 trillion today. We are now paying more in interest on the national debt than we are on national defense. The number of pages in the Federal Register has gone from 2,619 in 1936 to 61,000 in 1993. (The number of pages went down by over one-third during the Reagan Administration, but it is expected to be back up to 76,000 this year.)

We don't really need these numbers to be convinced. You don't even need to drive across America. We can read the newspapers and look around in our lives to see the continuing growth, spending, and meddling of the government. We can even watch on two channels what is going on in Congress: taxes in the name of creating jobs: "reinventing" welfare one more time from Washington, D.C.; a new national school board; turning the health care system over to the government to run.

One of the best examples of government interference is the GOALS 2000 federal education legislation that passed this year, which some were touting as the greatest bill ever. They're wrong: it takes us in exactly the wrong direction. It creates a national school board; pushes Governors out, and puts Washington experts in; puts the emphasis on "inputs" instead of results; bans tests with consequences; and fails to expand choices of schools for low- and middle-income families. Worst of all, it takes a national movement that the Governors had worked on for nearly ten years and turns it into a federal program. Nothing could be worse for our schools than taking a national education reform movement and turning it into a federal program. . . .

This continuous expansion is one reason for the surge of this exasperation with the government, but there is another fundamental one we ought to recognize. We have gone through a great divide and are entering a very different age. Back when Croly was advocating a large centralized government, it was the industrial age, when more centralization was the way to accomplish great things. It was a time, too, when we started to fall in love with the idea of single solutions to our problems. Expertise and resources from Washington, it was imagined, could solve almost anything.

Now we have entered the age of information, and as the big, centralized industries have discovered, centralized bureaucracy and decision-making don't work very well anymore. This is a time for being fast on your feet, having instant access to information, ideas, and expertise from around the country and the world, dealing with the unexpected, and tailoring activities to fit particular circumstances. A large, central bureaucracy can't do that. That's true in almost every part of American life, and it is certainly true about government. As a result, such a bulky, meddlesome government in Washington has become a relic—it is obsolete. Precisely because life is larger and so much more complicated, we need much less—not much more—government in Washington.

The information age has given Americans in all walks of life the tools and the flexibility to start making more of their own decisions, to share ideas, to develop their own ways of solving problems. The era of the search for a single best way, whether to educate children, to help the down and out, or to preserve natural resources, has given way to our natural inclinations as Americans toward pluralism, creativity, and innovation. The lingering attitude here of "Washington knows best" and the efforts of the government in Washington to tell people in states and communities what to do run in exactly the wrong direction. This, too, adds to the exasperation with the federal government.

What We Need to Do

What can we do about this sense of exasperation?

Well, I think it is clear we need to take Herbert Croly's idea and roll it back in the other direction. We need to create a new promise of American life by getting the government in Washington out of the way. And we need to be very shrewd and hard-nosed about this. The time is right. The country is ready for big changes in Washington. This is going to be a decade of enormous reform—very nearly an uprising—to bring about change in the institutions of our central government.

Because the Democratic Party is so committed to the central government, so insistent on reinventing America from here, this creates an opening a mile wide for the Republican Party. But we have been timid about plowing through that opening. I believe that after 1996 the nation is likely to have a Republican government, that is, a Republican President and a Republican Congress—if for no other reason than because that is the only option that the voters have not yet tried. Republicans could advance that prospect by persuading the American people that, if they choose us, we will respond boldly by sending a good part of the federal government home. But between now and 1996 we must think strategically about this. We must decide upon, agree upon and advance big ideas that will actually work if we are given the opportunity to govern.

What I propose as a first step seems far-fetched, I'm sure, to many here. But I believe it is very mild compared to what may be coming down the pike during the rest of the 1990s.

Cut Their Pay and Send Them Home

We should cut the pay of Members of Congress and send them home. Here's how it would work. Congress could:

1. Convene on January 3rd, just as it now does, pass the authorization bills to help the government run, and go home early in the baseball season.

2. Come back Labor Day, pass the appropriations bills and any other urgent legislation, and be home by Thanksgiving.

3. Cut the pay of Members in half and repeal the rules that keep them from holding real jobs and leading normal lives in their home towns. Pay Members adequate per diem for travel and expenses when they are in Washington.

If Members of Congress would eat more of their meals in diners in Jennings, Louisiana, or in Nashville, or in Billings or in Hartford or anywhere in America, if they lived back in those places and had their roots there, then when these hare-brained ideas come up—turning health care over to the government to run, or reinventing welfare for the seventh time in Washington, or even drafting a rule about whether you can wear a cross or Star of David to work—these ideas would never see the light of day.

I am talking about an old idea, this idea of the citizen legislator, the idea that our political leadership is supposed to be us. The notion is that a part time Congress of community leaders makes a better government than a full-time Congress of career politicians. The country began with such a citizen legislature and operated that way for most of its existence. . . .

This idea—maybe more than any other—would begin to exchange the culture of the company town, and help to shift the focus away from Washington and back to communities.

Critics, of course, are apt to object by arguing that the business of the federal government has become too complicated and intricate to be handled by part-time legislators. I believe that one reason for this is because the work of Congress has expanded to fill the available time. Another reason is that Washington—with all its special interests and experts—also has a tendency to overcomplicate almost everything. Nobody I've seen on my drive has been jumping for joy over Congress's famous deficit reduction package and tax increases, or the 1,400 page health care reform bill. Regular Americans sitting around a kitchen table over a short period of time could come up with more fair, straight-forward, and effective answers. It is possible and usually better to deal with large matters in an uncomplicated way. A time limit would encourage just that. . . .

Cut their pay and send them home. I believe it would dignify Congress, shrink the federal government, and be the most important first step we could take toward the new promise of American life. I also believe, by the way, that this would be the surest way for Newt Gingrich to become the Speaker of the House. Newt and his colleagues are going to stand on the Capitol steps on September 27th and say what a Republican agenda will be in hopes that the people of the country will put them in charge by January. I think a one-item agenda would do it. If they would stand up and say, "Elect us. We'll cut our pay in half and send ourselves home for half a year, take a real job and work alongside you," they would be members of a Republican Congress in January.

CONTRACT WITH AMERICA (1994)

In reaction to four decades of Democratic control of the House, over 300 House Republican challengers and incumbents met on the Capitol steps and promised to pursue certain policy objectives if their party were given control of Congress. The following "contract" was signed and offered to the American people. It helped nationalize the congressional campaign and so contributed to a Republican takeover of the House.

As Republican Members of the House of Representatives and citizens seeking to join that body we propose not just to change its policies, but even more important, to restore the bonds of trust between the people and their elected representatives.

That is why, in this era of official evasion and posturing, we offer indeed a detailed agenda for national renewal, a written commitment with no fine print.

This year's election offers the chance, after four decades of one-party control, to bring to the House a new majority that will transform the way Congress works. That historic change would be the end of government that is too big, too intrusive, and too easy with the public's money. It can be the beginning of a Congress that respects the values and shares the faith of the American family.

Like Lincoln, our first Republican president, we intend to act "with firmness in the right, as God gives us to see the right." To restore accountability to Congress. To end its cycle of scandal and disgrace. To make us all proud again of the way free people govern themselves.

On the first day of the 104th Congress, the new Republican majority will immediately pass the following major reforms, aimed at restoring the faith and trust of the American people in their government.

FIRST, require all laws that apply to the rest of the country also apply equally to the Congress;

SECOND, select a major, independent auditing firm to conduct a comprehensive audit of Congress for waste, fraud or abuse;

THIRD, cut the number of House committees, and cut committee staff by one-third;

FOURTH, limit the terms of all committee chairs;

FIFTH, ban the casting of votes in committee;

SIXTH, require committee meetings to be open to the public;

SEVENTH, require a three-fifths majority vote to pass a tax increase;

EIGHTH, guarantee an honest accounting of our Federal Budget by implementing zero base-line budget.

Thereafter, within the first 100 days of the 104th Congress we shall bring to the House Floor the following bills, each to be given full and open debate, each to be given a clear and fair vote and each to be immediately available this day for public inspection and scrutiny.

1. THE FISCAL RESPONSIBILITY ACT

A balanced budget/tax limitation amendment and a legislative line-item veto to restore fiscal responsibility to an out-of-control Congress, requiring them to live under the same budget constraints as families and businesses.

2. THE TAKING BACK OUR STREETS ACT

An anti-crime package including stronger truth-in-sentencing, "good faith" exclusionary rule exemptions, effective death penalty provisions, and cuts in social spending from this summer's "crime" bill to fund prison construction and additional law enforcement to keep people secure in their neighborhoods and kids safe in their schools.

3. THE PERSONAL RESPONSIBILITY ACT

Discourage illegitimacy and teen pregnancy by prohibiting welfare to minor mothers and denying increased AFDC for additional children while on welfare, cut spending for welfare programs and enact a tough two-years-and-out provision with work requirements to promote individual responsibility.

4. THE FAMILY REINFORCEMENT ACT

Child support enforcement, tax incentives for adoption, strengthening rights of parents in their children's education, stronger child pornography laws, and an elderly dependent care tax credit to reinforce the central role of families in American society.

5. THE AMERICAN DREAM RESTORATION ACT

A $500 per child tax credit, begin repeal of the marriage tax penalty, and creation of American Dream Savings Account to provide middle class tax relief.

6. THE NATIONAL SECURITY RESTORATION ACT

No U.S. troops under U.N. command and restoration of the essential parts of our national security funding to strengthen our national defense and maintain our credibility around the world.

7. THE SENIOR CITIZENS FAIRNESS ACT

Raise the Social Security earnings limit which currently forces seniors out of the work force, repeal the 1993 tax hikes on Social Security benefits and provide tax incentives for private long-term care insurance to let Older Americans keep more of what they have earned over the years.

8. THE JOB CREATION AND WAGE ENHANCEMENT ACT

Small business incentives, capital gains cut and indexation, neutral cost recovery, risk assessment/cost-benefit analysis, strengthening the Regulatory Flexibility Act and unfunded mandate reform to create jobs and raise worker wages.

9. THE COMMON SENSE LEGAL REFORM ACT

"Loser pays" laws, reasonable limits on punitive damages and reform of product liability laws to stem the endless tide of litigation.

10. THE CITIZEN LEGISLATURE ACT

A first-ever vote on term limits to replace career politicians with citizen legislators.

Further, we will instruct the House Budget Committee to report to the floor and we will work to enact additional budget savings, beyond the budget cuts specifically included in the legislation described above, to ensure that the Federal budget deficit will be *less* than it would have been without the enactment of these bills.

Respecting the judgment of our fellow citizens as we seek their mandate for reform, we hereby pledge our names to this Contract with America.

6

Judiciary

This section concerns the power of the judiciary under the Constitution. That power has been mainly judicial review, the power to declare unconstitutional acts both of the other two branches of the national government and of state and local government.

BRUTUS, ESSAY XI (1788)

Brutus, the pseudonym of an Anti-Federalist author, argues for a vote against the ratification of the Constitution because it implies judicial review.

. . . Much has been said and written upon the subject of this new system on both sides, but I have not met with any writer, who has discussed the judicial powers with any degree of accuracy. . . . The real effect of this system of government will . . . be brought home to the feelings of the people through the medium of the judicial power. It is, moreover, of great importance to examine with care the nature and extent of the judicial power, because those who are to be vested with it are to be placed in a situation altogether unprecedented in a free country. They are to be rendered totally independent, both of the people and the legislature, both with respect to their offices and salaries. No errors they may commit can be corrected by any power above them, if any such power there be, nor can they be removed from office for making ever so many erroneous adjudications. . . .

They [the members of the court] will give the sense of every article of the constitution, that may from time to time come before them. And in their decisions they will not confine themselves to any fixed or established rules, but will determine, according to what appears to them, the reason and spirit of the constitution. The opinions of the supreme court, whatever they may be, will have the

241

force of law, because there is no power provided in the constitution, that can correct their errors, or controul their adjudications. From this court there is no appeal. And I conceive the legislature themselves, cannot set aside a judgment of this court, because they are authorized by the constitution to decide in the last resort. The legislature must be controuled by the constitution, and not the constitution by them. They have therefore no more right to set aside any judgment pronounced upon the construction of the constitution, than they have to take from the president, the chief command of the army and navy, and commit it to some other person. The reason is plain; the judicial and executive derive their authority from the same source, that the legislature do theirs; and therefore in all cases, where the constitution does not make the one responsible to, or controulable by the other, they are altogether independent of each other.

The judicial power will operate to effect, in the most certain, but yet silent and imperceptible manner, what is evidently the tendency of the constitution:—I mean, an entire subversion of the legislative, executive and judicial powers of the individual states. Every adjudication of the supreme court, on any question that may arise upon the nature and extent of the general government, will affect the limits of the state jurisdiction. In proportion as the former enlarge the exercise of their powers, will that of the latter be restricted. . . .

This power in the judicial, will enable them to mould the government, into almost any shape they please. . . .

FEDERALIST 78

Publius answers the charge made by Brutus and other Anti-Federalists that the judiciary will be too powerful. He defends the power of judicial review.

We proceed now to an examination of the judiciary department of the proposed government.

In unfolding the defects of the existing Confederation, the utility and necessity of a federal judicature have been clearly pointed out. It is the less necessary to recapitulate the considerations there urged as the propriety of the institution in the abstract is not disputed; the only questions which have been raised being relative to the manner of constituting it, and to its extent. To these points, therefore, our observations shall be confined.

The manner of constituting it seems to embrace these several objects: 1st. The mode of appointing the judges. 2nd. The tenure by which they are to hold their places. 3rd. The partition of the judiciary authority between different courts and their relations to each other.

First. As to the mode of appointing the judges; this is the same with that of appointing the officers of the Union in general, and has been so fully discussed in the two last numbers that nothing can be said here which would not be useless repetition.

Second. As to the tenure by which the judges are to hold their places: this chiefly concerns their duration in office, the provisions for their support, the precautions for their responsibility.

According to the plan of the convention, all judges who may be appointed by the United States are to hold their offices *during good behavior;* which is conformable to the most approved of the State constitutions, and among the rest, to that of this State. Its propriety having been drawn into question by the adversaries of that plan, is no light symptom of the rage for objection, which disorders their imaginations and judgments. The standard of good behavior for the continuance in office of the judicial magistracy is certainly one of the most valuable of the modern improvements in the practice of government. In a monarchy it is an excellent barrier to the despotism of the prince; in a republic it is a no less excellent barrier to the encroachments and oppressions of the representative body. And it is the best expedient which can be devised in any government to secure a steady, upright, and impartial administration of the laws.

Whoever attentively considers the different departments of power must perceive that, in a government in which they are separated from each other, the judiciary, from the nature of its functions, will always be the least dangerous to the political rights of the Constitution; because it will be least in a capacity to annoy or injure them. The executive not only dispenses the honors but holds the sword of the community. The legislature not only commands the purse, but prescribes the rules by which the duties and rights of every citizen are to be regulated. The judiciary, on the contrary, has no influence over either the sword or the purse; no direction either of the strength or of the wealth of the society, and can take no active resolution whatever. It may truly be said to have neither FORCE nor WILL, but merely judgment; and must ultimately depend upon the aid of the executive arm even for the efficacy of its judgments.

This simple view of the matter suggests several important consequences. It proves incontestably that the judiciary is beyond comparison the weakest of the three departments of power [*sic*]; that it can never attack with success either of the other two; and that all possible care is requisite to enable it to defend itself against their attacks. It equally proves that though individual oppression may now and then proceed from the courts of justice, the general liberty of the people can never be endangered from that quarter; I mean so long as the judiciary remains truly distinct from both the legislature and the executive. For I agree, that "there is no liberty, if the power of judging be not separated from the legislative and executive powers." And it proves, in the last place, that as liberty can have nothing to fear from the judiciary alone, but would have every thing to fear from its union with either of the other departments; that as all the effects of such a union might ensue from a dependence of the former on the latter, notwithstanding a nominal and apparent separation; that as, from the natural feebleness of the judiciary, it is in continual jeopardy of being overpowered, awed, or influenced by its co-ordinate branches; and that as nothing can contribute so much to its firmness and independence as permanency in office, this quality may therefore be justly regarded as an indispensable ingredient in its constitution, and, in a great measure, as the citadel of the public justice and the public security.

The complete independence of the courts of justice is peculiarly essential in a limited Constitution. By a limited Constitution, I understand one which contains certain specified exceptions to the legislative authority; such, for instance, as that it shall pass no bills of attainder, no *ex-post-facto* laws, and the like. Limitations of this kind can be preserved in practice no other way than through the medium of courts of justice, whose duty it must be to declare all acts contrary to the manifest tenor of the Constitution void. Without this, all the reservations of particular rights or privileges would amount to nothing.

Some perplexity respecting the rights of the courts to pronounce legislative acts void, because contrary to the Constitution, has arisen from an imagination that the doctrine would imply a superiority of the judiciary to the legislative power. It is urged that the authority which can declare the acts of another void must necessarily be superior to the one whose acts may be declared void. As this doctrine is of great importance in all the American constitutions, a brief discussion of the ground on which it rests cannot be unacceptable.

There is no position which depends on clearer principles than that every act of a delegated authority, contrary to the tenor of the commission under which it is exercised, is void. No legislative act, therefore, contrary to the Constitution, can be valid. To deny this would be to affirm that the deputy is greater than his principal; that the servant is above his master; that the representatives of the people are superior to the people themselves; that men acting by virtue of powers may do not only what their powers do not authorize, but what they forbid.

If it be said that the legislative body are themselves the constitutional judges of their own powers and that the construction they put upon them is conclusive upon the other departments it may be answered that this cannot be the natural presumption where it is not to be collected from any particular provisions in the Constitution. It is not otherwise to be supposed that the Constitution could intend to enable the representatives of the people to substitute their *will* to that of their constituents. It is far more rational to suppose that the courts were designed to be an intermediate body between the people and the legislature in order, among other things, to keep the latter within the limits assigned to their authority. The interpretation of the laws is the proper and peculiar province of the courts. A constitution is, in fact, and must be regarded by the judges, as a fundamental law. It therefore belongs to them to ascertain its meaning as well as the meaning of any particular act proceeding from the legislative body. If there should happen to be an irreconcilable variance between the two, that which has the superior obligation and validity ought, of course, to be preferred; or, in other words, the Constitution ought to be preferred to the statute, the intention of the people to the intention of their agents.

Nor does this conclusion by any means suppose a superiority of the judicial to the legislative power. It only supposes that the power of the people is superior to both, and that where the will of the legislature, declared in its statutes, stands in opposition to that of the people, declared in the Constitution, the judges ought to be governed by the latter rather than the former. They ought to regulate their decisions by the fundamental laws rather than by those which are not fundamental.

This exercise of judicial discretion, in determining between two contradictory laws is exemplified in a familiar instance. It not uncommonly happens that there are two statutes existing at one time, clashing in whole or in part with each other, and neither of them containing any repealing clause or expression. In such a case, it is the province of the courts to liquidate and fix their meaning and operation. So far as they can, by any fair construction, be reconciled to each other, reason and law conspire to dictate that this should be done; where this is impracticable, it becomes a matter of necessity to give effect to one in exclusion of the other. The rule which has obtained in the courts for determining their relative validity is that the last in order of time shall be preferred to the first. But this is a mere rule of construction, not derived from any positive law but from the nature and reason of the thing. It is a rule not enjoined upon the courts by legislative provision but adopted by themselves, as consonant to truth and propriety for the direction of their conduct as interpreters of the law. They thought it reasonable, that between the interfering acts of an *equal* authority, that which was the last indication of its will should have the preference.

But in regard to the interfering acts of a superior and subordinate authority of an original and derivative power, the nature and reason of the thing indicate the converse of that rule as proper to be followed. They teach us that the prior act of a superior ought to be preferred to the subsequent act of an inferior and subordinate authority; and that accordingly, whenever a particular statute contravenes the Constitution, it will be the duty of the judicial tribunals to adhere to the latter and disregard the former.

It can be of no weight to say that the courts, on the pretense of a repugnancy, may substitute their own pleasure to the constitutional intentions of the legislature. This might as well happen in the case of two contradictory statutes; or it might as well happen in every adjudication upon any single statute. The courts must declare the sense of the law; and if they should be disposed to exercise WILL instead of JUDGMENT, the consequence would equally be the substitution of their pleasure to that of the legislative body. The observation, if it proves any thing, would prove that there ought to be no judges distinct from that body.

If, then, the courts of justice are to be considered as the bulwarks of a limited Constitution against legislative encroachments, this consideration will afford a strong argument for the permanent tenure of judicial offices, since nothing will contribute so much as this to that independent spirit in the judges which must be essential to the faithful performance of so arduous a duty.

This independence of the judges is equally requisite to guard the Constitution and the rights of individuals from the effects of those ill humors, which the arts of designing men, or the influence of particular conjunctures, sometimes disseminate among the people themselves, and which, though they speedily give place to better information and more deliberate reflection, have a tendency, in the meantime, to occasion dangerous innovations in the government, and serious oppressions of the minor party in the community. Though I trust the friends of the proposed Constitution will never concur with its enemies in questioning that fundamental principle of republican government which admits the right of the people to alter or abolish the established Constitution whenever they find it inconsistent with their happiness; yet it is not to be inferred from this principle that the representatives of the people, whenever a momentary inclination happens to lay hold of a majority of their constituents, incompatible with the provisions in the existing Constitution, would, on that account, be justifiable in a violation of those provisions; or that the courts would be under a greater obligation to connive at infractions in this shape, than when they had proceeded wholly from the cabals of the representative body. Until the people have by some solemn and authoritative act, annulled or changed the established form, it is binding upon themselves collectively, as well as individually; and no presumption, or even knowledge, of their sentiments, can warrant their representatives in a departure from it, prior to such an act. But it is easy to see that it would require an uncommon portion of fortitude in the judges to do their duty as faithful guardians of the Constitution, where legislative invasions of it had been instigated by the major voice of the community.

But it is not with a view to infractions of the Constitution only that the independence of the judges may be an essential safeguard against the effects of occasional ill humors in the society. These sometimes extend no farther than to the injury of the private rights of particular classes of citizens by unjust and partial laws. Here also the firmness of the judicial magistracy is of vast importance in mitigating the severity and confining the operation of such laws. It not only serves to moderate the immediate mischiefs of those which may have been passed, but it operates as a check upon the legislative body in passing them; who, perceiving that obstacles to the success of iniquitous intention are to be expected from the scruples of the courts, are in a manner compelled by the very motives of the injustice they meditate to qualify their attempts. This is a circumstance calculated to have more influence upon the character of our governments, than but few may be aware of. The benefits of the integrity and moderation of the judiciary have already been felt in more States than one; and though they may have displeased those whose sinister expectations they may have disappointed, they must have commanded the esteem and applause of all the virtuous and disinterested. Considerate men of every description ought to prize whatever will tend to beget or fortify that temper in the courts; as no man can be sure that he may not be tomorrow the victim of a spirit of injustice, by which he may be a gainer today. And every man must now feel that the inevitable tendency of such a spirit is to sap the foundations of public and private confidence, and to introduce in its stead universal distrust and distress.

That inflexible and uniform adherence to the rights of the Constitution, and of individuals, which we perceive to be indispensable in the courts of justice, can certainly not be expected from judges who hold their offices by a temporary commission. Periodical appointments, however regulated, or by whomsoever made, would, in some way or other, be fatal to their necessary independence. If the power of making them was committed either to the executive or legislature, there would be danger of an improper complaisance to the branch which possessed it; if to both, there would be an unwillingness to hazard the displeasure of either; if to the people or to persons chosen by them for the special purpose, there would be too great a disposition to consult popularity to justify a reliance that nothing would be consulted but the Constitution and the laws.

There is yet a further and a weighty reason for the permanency of the judicial offices, which is deducible from the nature of the qualifications they require. It has been frequently remarked, with

great propriety, that voluminous code of laws is one of the inconveniences necessarily connected with the advantages of a free government. To avoid an arbitrary discretion in the courts, it is
indispensable that they should be bound down by strict rules and
precedents, which serve to define and point out their duty in every
particular case that comes before them; and it will readily be conceived from the variety of controversies which grow out of the folly and wickedness of mankind, that the records of those precedents
must unavoidably swell to a very considerable bulk, and must demand long and laborious study to acquire a competent knowledge
of them. Hence it is, that there can be but few men in the society
who will have sufficient skill in the laws to qualify them for the
stations of judges. And making the proper deductions for the ordinary depravity of human nature, the number must be still smaller
of those who unite the requisite integrity with the requisite knowledge. These considerations apprise us that the government can have
no great option between fit characters; and that a temporary duration in office, which would naturally discourage such characters
from quitting a lucrative line of practice to accept a seat on the
bench, would have a tendency to throw the administration of justice into hands less able, and less well qualified, to conduct it with
utility and dignity. In the present circumstances of this country and
in those in which it is likely to be for a long time to come, the
disadvantages on this score would be greater than they may at first
sight appear; but it must be confessed that they are far inferior to
those which present themselves under the other aspects of the
subject.

Upon the whole, there can be no room to doubt that the convention acted wisely in copying from the models of those constitutions
which have established *good behavior* as the tenure of their judicial offices, in point of duration; and that so far from being blamable
on this account, their plan would have been inexcusably defective
if it had wanted this important feature of good government. The
experience of Great Britain affords an illustrious comment on the
excellence of the institution.

MARBURY v. MADISON (1803)

*This case is the judicial defense of the constitutionality of ju-
dicial review. It involves one of a number of last-minute
judicial appointments made by the outgoing Adams adminis-*

tration in early 1801. When Thomas Jefferson assumed the presidency in March 1801, he discovered that the commission appointing William Marbury to be justice of the peace for the District of Columbia had not been delivered. John Marshall, who had been Adams's secretary of state as well as chief justice, had failed to process the commission before leaving office. Jefferson, angered by the large number of last-minute appointments, ordered his own secretary of state, James Madison, not to follow through with delivering the commission. Marbury applied to the Supreme Court for a writ of mandamus, through which the Court could require Madison to deliver the commission. Congress had given to the Court the power to issue writs in cases of this sort under a provision of the Judiciary Act of 1789.

CHIEF JUSTICE MARSHALL delivered the opinion of the Court. . . .

It is then the opinion of the court,

1. That, by signing the commission of Mr. Marbury, the President of the United States appointed him a justice of peace for the county of Washington in the District of Columbia; and that the seal of the United States, affixed thereto by the Secretary of State, is conclusive testimony of the verity of the signature, and of the completion of the appointment; and that the appointment conferred on him a legal right to the office for the space of five years.

2. That, having this legal title to the office, he has a consequent right to the commission; a refusal to deliver, which is a plain violation of that right, for which the laws of his country afford him a remedy.

It remains to be inquired whether, 3. He is entitled to the remedy for which he applies. This depends on, 1. The nature of the writ applied for and 2. The power of this court. 1st. The nature of the writ.

Blackstone, in the 3d volume of his Commentaries, page 110, defines a mandamus to be "a command issuing in the king's name from the court of king's bench, and directed to any person, corporation, or inferior court of judicature within the king's dominions, requiring them to do some particular thing therein specified, which appertains to their office and duty, and which the court of king's bench has previously determined, or at least supposes, to be consonant to right and justice . . ." [ellipsis in *Marbury*].

This, then, is a plain case for a mandamus, either to deliver the commission, or a copy of it from the record; and it only remains to be inquired,

Whether it can issue from this court.

The act to establish the judicial courts of the United States authorizes the Supreme Court "to issue writs of mandamus, in cases warranted by the principles and usages of law, to any courts appointed, or persons holding office, under the authority of the United States."

The Secretary of State, being a person holding an office under the authority of the United States, is precisely within the letter of the description, and if this court is not authorized to issue a writ of mandamus to such an officer, it must be because the law is unconstitutional, and therefore absolutely incapable of conferring the authority, and assigning the duties which its words purport to confer and assign.

The Constitution vests the whole judicial power of the United States in one Supreme Court, and such inferior courts as Congress shall, from time to time, ordain and establish. This power is expressly extended to all cases arising under the laws of the United States; and consequently, in some form may be exercised over the present case, because the right claimed is given by a law of the United States.

In the distribution of this power it is declared that "the Supreme Court shall have original jurisdiction in all cases affecting ambassadors, other public ministers and consuls, and those in which a state shall be a party. In all other cases, the Supreme Court shall have appellate jurisdiction."

It has been insisted at the bar, that as the original grant of jurisdiction, to the Supreme and inferior courts, is general, and the clause assigning original jurisdiction to the Supreme Court contains no negative or restrictive words, the power remains to the legislature to assign original jurisdiction to that court in other cases than those specified in the article which has been recited; provided those cases belong to the judicial power of the United States.

If it had been intended to leave it in the discretion of the legislature to apportion the judicial power between the Supreme and inferior courts according to the will of that body, it would certainly have been useless to have proceeded further than to have defined the judicial power, and the tribunals in which it should be vested. The subsequent part of the section is mere surplusage, is entirely without meaning, if such is to be the construction. If Congress remains at liberty to give this court appellate jurisdiction, where the Constitution has declared their jurisdiction shall be original; and original jurisdiction where the Constitution has declared it shall be appellate; the distribution of jurisdiction, made in the Constitution, is form without substance.

Affirmative words are often, in their operation, negative of other objects than those affirmed; and in this case, a negative or exclusive sense must be given to them, or they have no operation at all.

It cannot be presumed that any clause in the Constitution is intended to be without effect; and, therefore, such a construction is inadmissible, unless the words require it. . . .

To enable this court, then, to issue a mandamus, it must be shown to be an exercise of appellate jurisdiction, or to be necessary to enable them to exercise appellate jurisdiction.

It has been stated at the bar that the appellate jurisdiction may be exercised in a variety of forms, and that, if it be the will of the legislature that a mandamus should be used for that purpose, that will must be obeyed. This is true, yet the jurisdiction must be appellate, not original.

It is the essential criterion of appellate jurisdiction that it revises and corrects the proceedings in a cause already instituted, and does not create that cause. Although, therefore, a mandamus may be directed to courts, yet to issue such a writ to an officer for the delivery of a paper is in effect the same as to sustain an original action for that paper, and, therefore, seems not to belong to appellate, but to original jurisdiction. Neither is it necessary in such a case as this, to enable the court to exercise its appellate jurisdiction.

The authority, therefore, given to the Supreme Court by the act establishing the judicial courts of the United States, to issue writs of mandamus to public officers, appears not to be warranted by the Constitution; and it becomes necessary to inquire whether a jurisdiction so conferred can be exercised.

The question, whether an act repugnant to the Constitution can become the law of the land, is a question deeply interesting to the United States; but, happily, not of an intricacy proportioned to its interest. It seems only necessary to recognize certain principles, supposed to have been long and well established, to decide it.

That the people have an original right to establish, for their future government, such principles as, in their opinion, shall most conduce to their own happiness, is the basis on which the whole American fabric has been erected. The exercise of this original right is a very great exertion; nor can it, nor ought it, to be frequently repeated. The principles, therefore, so established, are deemed fundamental. And as the authority from which they proceed is supreme, and can seldom act, they are designed to be permanent.

This original and supreme will organizes the government, and assigns to different departments their respective powers. It may either stop here, or establish certain limits not to be transcended by those departments.

The government of the United States is of the latter description. The powers of the legislature are defined and limited; and that those limits may not be mistaken, or forgotten, the Constitution is written. To what purpose are powers limited, and to what purpose is that limitation committed to writing, if these limits may, at any time, be passed by those intended to be restrained? The distinction between a government with limited and unlimited powers is abolished, if those limits do not confine the persons on whom they are imposed, and if acts prohibited and acts allowed are of equal obligation. It is a proposition too plain to be contested, that the Constitution controls any legislative act repugnant to it; or, that the legislature may alter the Constitution by an ordinary act.

Between these alternatives there is no middle ground. The Constitution is either a superior paramount law, unchangeable by ordinary means, or it is on a level with ordinary legislative acts, and, like other acts, is alterable when the legislature shall please to alter it.

If the former part of the alternative be true, then a legislative act contrary to the Constitution, is not law; if the latter part be true, then written constitutions are absurd attempts, on the part of the people, to limit a power in its own nature illimitable.

Certainly all those who have framed written constitutions contemplate them as forming the fundamental and paramount law of the nation, and consequently, the theory of every such government must be, that an act of the legislature, repugnant to the constitution, is void.

This theory is essentially attached to a written constitution, and is consequently to be considered, by this court, as one of the fundamental principles of our society. It is not, therefore, to be lost sight of in the further consideration of this subject.

If an act of the legislature, repugnant to the constitution, is void, does it, notwithstanding its invalidity, bind the courts, and oblige them to give it effect? Or, in other words, though it be not law, does it constitute a rule as operative as if it was a law? This would be to overthrow in fact what was established in theory; and would seem, at first view, an absurdity too gross to be insisted on. It shall, however, receive a more attentive consideration.

It is emphatically the province and duty of the judicial department to say what the law is. Those who apply the rule to particular cases, must of necessity expound and interpret that rule. If two laws conflict with each other, the courts must decide on the operation of each.

So if a law be in opposition to the Constitution; if both the law and the Constitution apply to a particular case, so that the court must either decide that case conformably to the law, disregarding the Constitution; or conformably to the Constitution, disregarding the law; the court must determine which of these conflicting rules governs the case. This is of the very essence of judicial duty.

If, then, the courts are to regard the Constitution, and the Constitution is superior to any ordinary act of the legislature, the

Constitution, and not such ordinary act, must govern the case to which they both apply. . . .

The judicial power of the United States is extended to all cases arising under the Constitution.

Could it be the intention of those who gave this power to say that, in using it, the Constitution should not be looked into? That a case arising under the Constitution should be decided without examining the instrument under which it arises?

This is too extravagant to be maintained.

In some cases then, the Constitution must be looked into by the judges. And if they can open it at all, what part of it are they forbidden to read or to obey?

There are many other parts of the Constitution which serve to illustrate this subject.

It is declared that "no tax or duty shall be laid on articles exported from any state." Suppose a duty on the export of cotton, of tobacco, or of flour; and a suit instituted to recover it. Ought judgment to be rendered in such a case? Ought the judges to close their eyes on the Constitution, and only see the law? . . .

Why does a judge swear to discharge his duties agreeably to the Constitution of the United States, if that Constitution forms no rule for his government—if it is closed upon him, and cannot be inspected by him? If such be the real state of things, this is worse than solemn mockery. To prescribe, or to take this oath, becomes equally a crime.

It is also not entirely unworthy of observation, that in declaring what shall be the *supreme* law of the land, the *Constitution* itself is first mentioned; and not the laws of the United States generally, but those only which shall be made in *pursuance* of the Constitution, have that rank.

Thus, the particular phraseology of the Constitution of the United States confirms and strengthens the principle, supposed to be essential to all written constitutions, that a law repugnant to the

Constitution is void; and that *courts,* as well as other departments, are bound by that instrument.

The rule must be discharged.

ABRAHAM LINCOLN, FIRST INAUGURAL ADDRESS (1861)

Lincoln, of course, thought the pro-slavery interpretation of the Constitution by the Supreme Court in Dred Scott *was wrong. Here he shows how the other departments of government and the people ought to view such errors. He denies that "constitutional questions" are simply answered by the Court. Citizens cannot be understood to have consented to the surrender of their own judgments.*

. . . I do not forget the position assumed by some, that constitutional questions are to be decided by the Supreme Court; nor do I deny that such decisions must be binding in any case, upon the parties to a suit, as to the object of that suit, while they are also entitled to a very high respect and consideration, in all parallel cases, by all other departments of government. And while it is obviously possible that such decision may be erroneous in any given case, still the evil effect following it, being limited to that particular case, with the chance that it may be over-ruled, and never become a precedent for other cases, can better be borne, than could the evils of a different practice. At the same time the candid citizen must confess that if the policy of the government is to be irrevocably fixed by decisions of the Supreme Court, the instant they are made, in ordinary litigation between parties, in personal actions, the people will have ceased to be their own rulers, having to that extent, practically resigned their government, into the hands of the eminent tribunal. Nor is there, in this view, any assault upon the court, or the judges. It is a duty, from which they may not shrink, to decide cases properly brought before them; and it is no fault of theirs if others seek to turn their decisions to political purposes. . . .

WILLIAM J. BRENNAN JR., SPEECH TO THE TEXT AND TEACHING SYMPOSIUM, GEORGETOWN UNIVERSITY (1985)

Justice Brennan was the most thoughtful and insistent critic of the doctrine of "original intent" on the contemporary Supreme

*Court. His comments should be compared carefully with those
of Judge Robert Bork, which follow.*

It will perhaps not surprise you that the text I have chosen for
exploration is the amended Constitution of the United States, which,
of course, entrenches the Bill of Rights and the Civil War amendments, and draws sustenance from the bedrock principles of another great text, the Magna Carta. So fashioned, the Constitution
embodies the aspiration to social justice, brotherhood, and human
dignity that brought this nation into being. The Declaration of Independence, the Constitution and the Bill of Rights solemnly committed the United States to be a country where the dignity and rights
of all persons were equal before all authority. In all candor we must
concede that part of this egalitarianism in America has been more
pretension than realized fact. But we are an aspiring people, a people with faith in progress. Our amended Constitution is the lodestar
for our aspirations. Like every text worth reading, it is not crystal-
line. The phrasing is broad and the limitations of its provisions are
not clearly marked. Its majestic generalities and ennobling pronouncements are both luminous and obscure. This ambiguity of
course calls forth interpretation, the interaction of reader and text.
The encounter with the constitutional text has been, in many sens-
es, my life's work. . . .

There are those who find legitimacy in fidelity to what they call
"the intentions of the Framers." In its most doctrinaire incarnation,
this view demands that Justices discern exactly what the Framers
thought about the question under consideration and simply follow
that intention in resolving the case before them. It is a view that
feigns self-effacing deference to the specific judgments of those who
forged our original social compact. But in truth it is little more than
arrogance cloaked as humility. It is arrogant to pretend that from
our vantage we can gauge accurately the intent of the Framers on
application of principle to specific, contemporary questions. All too
often, sources of potential enlightenment such as records of the
ratification debates provide sparse or ambiguous evidence of the
original intention. Typically, all that can be gleaned is that the Framers themselves did not agree about the application or meaning of
particular constitutional provisions, and hid their differences in
cloaks of generality. Indeed, it is far from clear whose intention is
relevant—that of the drafters, the congressional disputants, or the
ratifiers in the states?—or even whether the idea of an original inten-

tion is a coherent way of thinking about a jointly drafted document drawing its authority from a general assent of the states. And apart from the problematic nature of the sources, our distance of two centuries cannot but work as a prism refracting all we perceive. One cannot help but speculate that the chorus of lamentations calling for interpretation faithful to "original intention"—and proposing nullification of interpretations that fail this quick litmus test—must inevitably come from persons who have no familiarity with the historical record.

Perhaps most importantly, while proponents of this facile historicism justify it as a depoliticization of the judiciary, the political underpinnings of such a choice should not escape notice. A position that upholds constitutional claims only if they were within the specific contemplation of the Framers in effect establishes a presumption of resolving textual ambiguities against the claim of constitutional right. It is far from clear what justifies such a presumption against claims of right. Nothing intrinsic in the nature of interpretation—if there is such a thing as the "nature" of interpretation— commands such a passive approach to ambiguity. This is a choice not less political than any other; it expresses antipathy to claims of the minority rights against the majority. Those who would restrict claims of right to the values of 1789 specifically articulated in the Constitution turn a blind eye to social progress and eschew adaptation of overarching principles to changes of social circumstance.

Another perhaps more sophisticated response to the potential power of judicial interpretation stresses democratic theory: because ours is a government of the people's elected representatives, substantive value choices should by and large be left to them. This view emphasizes not the transcendent historical authority of the Framers but the predominant contemporary authority of the elected branches of government. Yet it has similar consequences for the nature of proper judicial interpretation. Faith in the majoritarian process counsels restraint. Even under more expansive formulations of this approach, judicial review is appropriate only to the extent of ensuring that the people are heard by their representatives, rather than as a separate, substantive value. When, by contrast, society tosses up to the Supreme Court a dispute that would require invalidation of a legislature's substantive policy choice, the Court generally would stay its hand because the Constitution was meant as a plan of government and not as an embodiment of fundamental substantive values.

The view that all matters of substantive policy should be resolved through the majoritarian process has appeal under some circumstances, but I think it ultimately will not do. Unabashed enshrinement of majority will would permit the imposition of a social caste system or wholesale confiscation of property so long as a majority of the authorized legislative body, fairly elected, approved. Our Constitution could not abide such a situation. It is the very purpose of a Constitution—and particularly of the Bill of Rights—to declare certain values transcendent, beyond the reach of temporary political majorities. The majoritarian process cannot be expected to rectify claims of minority right that arise as a response to the outcomes of that very majoritarian process. . . .

Faith in democracy is one thing, blind faith quite another. Those who drafted our Constitution understood the difference. One cannot read the text without admitting that it embodies substantive value choices; it places certain values beyond the power of any legislature. Obvious are the separation of powers; the privilege of the Writ of Habeas Corpus; prohibition of Bills of Attainder and *ex post facto* laws; prohibition of cruel and unusual punishments; the requirement of just compensation for official taking of property; the prohibition of laws tending to establish religion or enjoining the free exercise of religion; and, since the Civil War, the banishment of slavery and official race discrimination. With respect to at least such principles, we simply have not constituted ourselves as strict utilitarians. While the Constitution may be amended, such amendments require an immense effort by the People as a whole.

To remain faithful to the content of the Constitution, therefore, an approach to interpreting the text must account for the existence of these substantive value choices, and must accept the ambiguity inherent in the effort to apply them to modern circumstances. The Framers were discerning fundamental principles through struggles against particular malefactions of the Crown; the struggle shapes the particular contours of the articulated principles. But our acceptance of the fundamental principles has not and should not bind us to those precise, at times anachronistic, contours. Successive generations of Americans have continued to respect these fundamental choices and adopt them as their own guide to evaluating quite different historical practices. Each generation has the choice to overrule or add to the fundamental principles enunciated by the Framers; the Constitution can be amended or it can be ignored. Yet with respect to its fundamental principles, the text has suffered neither fate. . . .

We current Justices read the Constitution in the only way that we can: as Twentieth Century Americans. We look to the history of the time of framing and to the intervening history of interpretation. But the ultimate question must be, what do the words of the text mean in our time? For the genius of the Constitution rests not in any static meaning it might have had in a world that is dead and gone, but in the adaptability of its great principles to cope with current problems and current needs. What the constitutional fundamentals meant to the wisdom of other times cannot be their measure to the vision of their time. . . .

Interpretation must account for the transformative purpose of the text. Our Constitution was not intended to preserve a preexisting society but to make a new one, to put in place new principles that the prior political community had not sufficiently recognized. Thus, for example, when we interpret the Civil War Amendments to the charter—abolishing slavery, guaranteeing blacks equality under law, and guaranteeing blacks the right to vote—we must remember that those who put them in place had no desire to enshrine the status quo. Their goal was to make over their world, to eliminate all vestige of slave caste. . . .

The Constitution on its face is, in large measure, a structuring text, a blueprint for government. And when the text is not prescribing the form of government[,] it is limiting the powers of that government. The original document, before addition of any of the amendments, does not speak primarily of the rights of man, but of the abilities and disabilities of government. When one reflects upon the text's preoccupation with the scope of government as well as its shape, however, one comes to understand that what this text is about is the relationship of the individual and the state. The text marks the metes and bounds of official authority and individual autonomy. When one studies the boundary that the text marks out, one gets a sense of the vision of the individual embodied in the Constitution.

As augmented by the Bill of Rights and the Civil War Amendments, this text is a sparkling vision of the supremacy of the human dignity of every individual. This vision is reflected in the very choice of democratic self-governance: the supreme value of a democracy is the presumed worth of each individual. And this vision manifests itself most dramatically in the specific prohibitions of the Bill of Rights, a term which I henceforth will apply to describe not only the original first eight amendments, but the Civil War amendments as well. It is a vision that has guided us as a people throughout our history, although the precise rules by which we have protected fundamental human dignity have been transformed over time in response to both transformations of social condition and evolution of our concepts of human dignity.

Until the end of the nineteenth century, freedom and dignity in our country found meaningful protection in the institution of real property. In a society still largely agricultural, a piece of land provided men not just with sustenance but with the means of economic independence, a necessary precondition of political independence and expression. Not surprisingly, property relationships formed the heart of litigation and of legal practice, and lawyers and judges tended to think stable property relationships the highest aim of the law.

But the days when common law property relationships dominated litigation and legal practice are past. To a growing extent economic existence now depends on less certain relationships with government—licenses, employment, contracts, subsidies, unemployment benefits, tax exemptions, welfare and the like. Government participation in the economic existence of individuals is pervasive and deep. Administrative matters and other dealings with government are at the epicenter of the exploding law. We turn to government and to the law for controls which would never have been expected or tolerated before this century, when a man's answer to economic oppression or difficulty was to move two hundred miles west. Now hundreds of thousands of Americans live entire lives without any real prospect of the dignity and autonomy that ownership of real property could confer. Protection of the human dignity of such citizens requires a much modified view of the proper relationship of individual and state. . . .

I do not mean to suggest that we have in the last quarter century achieved a comprehensive definition of the constitutional ideal of human dignity. We are still striving toward that goal, and doubtless it will be an eternal quest. For if the interaction of the Justice and the constitutional text over the years confirms any single proposition, it is that the demands of human dignity will never cease to evolve.

Indeed, I cannot in good conscience refrain from mention of one grave and crucial respect in which we continue, in my judgment, to fall short of the constitutional vision of human dignity. It is in our continued tolerance of State-administered execution as a form of punishment. I make it a practice not to comment on the constitutional issues that come before the Court, but my position on this issue, of course, has been for some time fixed and immutable. I think I can venture some thoughts on this particular subject without transgressing my usual guideline too severely.

As I interpret the Constitution, capital punishment is under all circumstances cruel and unusual punishment prohibited by the Eighth and Fourteenth Amendments. This is a position of which I imagine you are not unaware. Much discussion of the merits of capital punishment has in recent years focused on the potential arbitrariness that attends its administration, and I have no doubt that such arbitrariness is a grave wrong. But for me, the wrong of capital punishment transcends such procedural issues. As I have said in my opinions, I view the Eighth Amendment's prohibition of cruel and unusual punishments as embodying to a unique degree moral principles that substantively restrain the punishments our civilized society may impose on those persons who transgress its laws. Foremost among the moral principles recognized in our cases and inherent in the prohibition is the primary principle that the State, even as it punishes, must treat its citizens in a manner consistent with their intrinsic worth as human beings. A punishment must not be so severe as to be utterly and irreversibly degrading to the very essence of human dignity. Death for whatever crime and under all circumstances is a truly awesome punishment. The most vile murder does not, in my view, release the State from constitutional restraints on the destruction of human dignity. Yet an executed person has lost the very right to have rights, now or ever. For me, then, the fatal constitutional infirmity of capital punishment is that it treats members of the human race as nonhumans, as objects to be toyed with and discarded. It is, indeed, "cruel and unusual." It is thus inconsistent with the fundamental premise of that Clause that even the most base criminal remains a human being possessed of some potential, at least, for common human dignity.

This is an interpretation to which a majority of my fellow Justices—not to mention, it would seem, a majority of my fellow countrymen—do not subscribe. Perhaps you find my adherence to it, and my recurrent publication of it, simply contrary, tiresome, or quixotic. Or perhaps you see in it a refusal to abide by the judicial principle of *stare decisis*, obedience to precedent. In my judgment, however, the unique interpretive role of the Supreme Court with respect to the Constitution demands some flexibility with respect to the call of *stare decisis*. Because we are the last word on the meaning of the Constitution, our views must be subject to revision over time, or the Constitution falls captive, again, to the anachronistic views of long-gone generations. I mentioned earlier the judge's role in seeking out the community's interpretation of the Constitution's text. Yet, again in my judgment, when a Justice perceives an interpretation of the text to have departed so far from its essential meaning, that Justice is bound, by larger constitutional duty to the community, to expose the departure and point toward a different path. On this issue, the death penalty, I hope to embody a community striving for human dignity for all, although perhaps not yet arrived. . . .

ROBERT H. BORK, INTERPRETING
THE CONSTITUTION (1987)

Judge Bork, nominated for the Supreme Court by President Reagan and then rejected by the Senate, argues here for the continuing relevance of the Framers' intentions.

The American ideal of democracy lives in constant tension with the American ideal of judicial review under the Constitution in the service of individual liberties. It is a tension that sometimes erupts in bitter partisanship. That has happened regularly since the days of the Jeffersonian assaults upon the Supreme Court headed by Chief Justice John Marshall down to our time. On its bicentennial we are still arguing about how courts should apply the Constitution.

The problem is the resolution of what has been called the Madisonian dilemma. The name comes from the man who, more than any other, was responsible for the fact that we have a Constitution, and this specific Constitution rather than another. The United States was founded as a Madisonian system, one that allows majorities to govern wide and important areas of life simply because they are majorities, but which also holds that individuals have some freedoms that must be exempt from majority control. The dilemma is that neither the majority nor the minority can be trusted to define the proper spheres of democratic authority and individual liberty.

It has come to be thought that the resolution of this dilemma is primarily the function of the judiciary and, ultimately and especially, of the Supreme Court.

That is an awesome responsibility and we require a strong theory of how we should go about discharging it. In [the words of legal scholar and Yale University Law School Professor] Alexander M. Bickel, judges must achieve "a rigorous general accord between judicial supremacy and democratic theory, so that the boundaries of the one [can] be described with some precision in terms of the other." We do not now have such an accord, or at least not one upon which we all agree.

How should a judge go about the task of deciding constitutional cases? Should he or she try to enforce the intentions of the founders, the intentions underlying each clause of the Constitution, or should the judge attempt to decide constitutional cases according to the morality of today's society? There is no doubt that American morality has undergone significant changes from the late eighteenth century.

My answer—and it is by no means universally accepted—is that the judge is required to seek and apply the intentions of the founders. The reason is that a judge has no legitimate power to set at naught the decisions made by the elected representatives of the American people unless he or she is required to do so by law. What does it mean to say that the Constitution is law? It means that the words of the document, and their historical meaning, constrain judgment. The words must control judges every bit as much as they control legislators, executives and citizens.

The various systems of moral philosophy that legal academics propound as guides to constitutional adjudication are not capable of constraining the judge. They are capable, instead, of producing any result the judge, or the professor, wants. They also lack democratic legitimacy because there is no reason why those of us who have our moral visions should be governed by some judge's personal moral views.

A judge who applies what he believes to be the morality of our time will in fact be applying his or her own morality. If the judge were correct about society's morality today, he would find no reason to declare any law unconstitutional because that morality is reflected in today's statutes. What elected representatives decide is the best evidence we have of our society's morality. That morality cannot be allowed to cut back freedoms guaranteed by the Constitution and it can always add to freedoms by statute. It is a great mistake to suppose that courts are the only guardians of our liberties. Very important freedoms have been secured or created by statute. But my main point is that a judge has no legitimate warrant to make up the Constitution out of morality, and the judge who looks outside the historic Constitution looks inside himself, and nowhere else.

The philosophy of original intent takes the values the founders specified in the various provisions of the Constitution and applies them to the different circumstances of today's world. That is not easy or mechanical, but it is also not impossible. Courts do the same sort of thing every day with respect to statutes, contracts, wills, and, indeed, with respect to the original intention underlying a Supreme Court opinion. These are all forms of law that govern judges as well as citizens. If judges began to construe statutes or contracts according to moral philosophy rather than the intentions underlying them, we would all agree that the judges were not applying law but creating it at wholesale.

So it is with the Constitution. The Constitution can be law only if it is applied as intended. That is why only a philosophy of original intention is legitimate for judges.

ROE v. WADE (1973)

This case concerns an unmarried woman in Texas who wished to terminate her pregnancy by abortion. Texas law prohibited abortions except those performed by a physician for the purpose of saving the life of the woman. The Court's decision here invalidated restrictive abortion laws in almost all of the states.

JUSTICE BLACKMUN delivered the opinion of the Court. . . .

. . . We forthwith acknowledge our awareness of the sensitive and emotional nature of the abortion controversy, of the vigorous opposing views, even among physicians, and of the deep and seemingly absolute convictions that the subject inspires. One's philosophy, one's experiences, one's exposure to the raw edges of human existence, one's religious training, one's attitudes toward life and family and their values, and the moral standards one establishes and seeks to observe, are all likely to influence and to color one's thinking and conclusions about abortion. . . .

Our task, of course, is to resolve the issue by constitutional measurement free of emotion and of predilections. We seek earnestly to do this, and because we do, we have inquired into, and in this opinion place some emphasis upon, medical and medical-legal history and what that history reveals about man's attitudes toward the abortive procedure over the centuries. . . .

It perhaps is not generally appreciated that the restrictive criminal abortion laws in effect in a majority of States today are of relatively recent vintage. Those laws, generally proscribing abortion or its attempt at any time during pregnancy except when necessary to preserve the pregnant woman's life, are not of ancient or even of common law origin. Instead, they derive from statutory changes effected, for the most part, in the latter half of the 19th century. . . .

It is thus apparent that at common law, at the time of the adoption of our Constitutions, and throughout the major portion of the 19th century, abortion was viewed with less disfavor than under most American statutes currently in effect. . . .

Three reasons have been advanced to explain historically the enactment of criminal abortion laws in the 19th century and to justify their continued existence.

It has been argued occasionally that these laws were the product of a Victorian social concern to discourage illicit sexual conduct. Texas, however, does not advance this justification in the present case, and it appears that no court or commentator has taken the argument seriously. . . .

A second reason is concerned with abortion as a medical procedure. When most criminal abortion laws were first enacted, the procedure was a hazardous one for the woman. This was particularly true prior to the development of antisepsis. . . . Abortion mortality was high. . . .

The third reason is the State's interest—some phrase it in terms of duty—in protecting prenatal life. Some of the argument for this justification rests on the theory that a new human life is present from the moment of conception. The State's interest and general obligation to protect life then extends, it is argued, to prenatal life. Only when the life of the pregnant mother herself is at stake, balanced against the life she carries within her, should the interests of the embryo or fetus not prevail. Logically, of course, a legitimate state interest in this area need not stand or fall on acceptance of the belief that life begins at conception or at some other point prior to live birth. In assessing the State's interest, recognition may be given to the less rigid claim that as long as at least *potential* life is involved, the State may assert interests beyond the protection of the pregnant woman alone. . . .

It is with these interests, and the weight to be attached to them, that this case is concerned. . . .

The Constitution does not explicitly mention any right of privacy. . . . The Court has recognized that a right of personal privacy, or a guarantee of certain areas or zones of privacy, does exist under the Constitution. In varying contexts the Court or individual Justices have indeed found at least the roots of that right in the First Amendment . . . in the Fourth and Fifth Amendments . . . in the penumbras of the Bill of Rights . . . in the Ninth Amendment . . . or in the concept of liberty guaranteed by the first section of the Fourteenth Amendment. . . . These decisions make it clear that only personal rights that can be deemed "fundamental" or "implicit in the concept of ordered liberty" . . . are included in this guarantee of personal privacy. They also make it clear that the right has some extension to activities relating to marriage . . . procreation, contraception, family relationships, and child rearing and education.

The right to privacy, whether it is founded in the Fourteenth Amendment's conception of personal liberty and restriction on state action, as we feel it is, or, as the District Court determined, in the Ninth Amendment's reservation of rights to the people, is broad enough to encompass a woman's decision whether or not to terminate her pregnancy. The detriment that the State would impose upon the pregnant woman by denying this choice altogether is apparent. Specific and direct harm medically diagnosable even in early pregnancy may be involved. Maternity, or additional offspring, may force upon the woman a distressful life and future. Psychological harm may be imminent. Mental and physical health may be taxed by child care. There is also the distress, for all concerned, associated with the unwanted child, and there is the problem of bringing a child into a family already unable, psychologically and otherwise, to care for it. In other cases, as in this one, the additional difficulties and continuing stigma of unwed motherhood may be involved. All these are factors the woman and her responsible physician necessarily will consider in consultation. . . .

We therefore conclude that the right of personal privacy includes the abortion decision, but that this right is not unqualified and must be considered against important state interests in regulation. . . .

Where certain "fundamental rights" are involved, the Court has held that regulation limiting these rights may be justified only by a "compelling state interest," and that legislative enactments must be narrowly drawn to express only the legitimate state interests at stake. . . .

The Constitution does not define "person" in so many words. Section 1 of the Fourteenth Amendment contains three references to "person." The first, in defining "citizens," speaks of "persons born or naturalized in the United States." The word also appears both in the Due Process Clause and in the Equal Protection Clause. "Person" is used in other places in the Constitution. . . . But in nearly all these instances, the use of the word is such that it has application only postnatally. None indicates, with any assurance, that it has any possible prenatal application. . . .

Texas urges that, apart from the Fourteenth Amendment, life begins at conception and is present throughout pregnancy, and that, therefore, the State has a compelling interest in protecting that life from and after conception. We need not resolve the difficult question of when life begins. When those trained in the respective disciplines of medicine, philosophy, and theology are unable to arrive at any consensus, the judiciary, at this point in the development of man's knowledge, is not in a position to speculate as to the answer.

. . . Physicians and their scientific colleagues have regarded that event with less interest and have tended to focus either upon conception or upon live birth or upon the interim point at which the fetus becomes "viable," that is, potentially able to live outside the mother's womb, albeit with artificial aid. Viability is usually placed at about seven months (28 weeks) but may occur earlier, even at 24 weeks. . . . Substantial problems for precise definition . . . are posed, however, by new embryological data that purport to indicate that conception is a "process" over time, rather than an event, and by new medical techniques such as menstrual extraction, the "morning-after" pill, implantation of embryos, artificial insemination, and even artificial wombs.

. . . We do not agree that, by adopting one theory of life, Texas may override the rights of the pregnant woman that are at stake. We repeat, however, that the State does have an important and legitimate interest in preserving and protecting the health of the pregnant woman, whether she be a resident of the State or a nonresident who seeks medical consultation and treatment there, and that it has still *another* important and legitimate interest in protecting the potentiality of human life. These interests are separate and distinct. Each grows in substantiality as the woman approaches term, and at a point during pregnancy, each becomes "compelling."

With respect to the State's important and legitimate interest in the health of the mother, the "compelling" point, in the light of present medical knowledge, is at approximately the end of the first trimester. This is so because of the now established medical fact . . . that until the end of the first trimester mortality in abortion is less than mortality in normal childbirth. It follows that, from and after this point, a State may regulate the abortion procedure to the extent that the regulation reasonably relates to the preservation and protection of maternal health. Examples of permissible state regulation in this area are requirements as to the qualifications of the person who is to perform the abortion, as to whether it must be a hospital or may be a clinic or some other place of less-than-hospital status; as to the licensing of the facility; and the like.

This means, on the other hand, that, for the period of pregnancy prior to the "compelling" point, the attending physician, in consultation with his patient, is free to determine, without regulation by the State, that in his medical judgment the patient's pregnancy should be terminated. If that decision is reached, the judgment may be effectuated by an abortion free of interference by the State. . . .

With respect to the State's important and legitimate interest in potential life, the "compelling" point is at viability. This is so because the fetus then presumably has the capability of meaningful life outside the mother's womb. State regulation protective of fetal life after viability thus has both logical and biological justifications. If the State is interested in protecting fetal life after viability, it may go so far as to proscribe abortion during that period except when it is necessary to preserve the life or health of the mother.

Measured against these standards . . . Texas, in restricting legal abortion to those "procured or attempted by medical advice for the purpose of saving the life of the mother," sweeps too broadly. The statute makes no distinction between abortions performed early in pregnancy and those performed later, and it limits to a single reason, "saving" the mother's life, the legal justification for the procedure. The statute, therefore, cannot survive the constitutional attack made upon it here. . . .

JUSTICE REHNQUIST, dissenting. . . .

The decision here to break the term of pregnancy into three distinct terms and to outline the permissible restrictions the State may impose in each one, . . . partakes more of judicial legislation than it does of a determination of the intent of the drafters of the Fourteenth Amendment.

The fact that a majority of the States, reflecting after all the majority sentiment in those States, have had restrictions on abortions for at least a century seems to me as strong an indication there is that the asserted right to an abortion is not "so rooted in the traditions and conscience of our people as to be ranked as fundamental." . . . Even today, when society's views on abortion are changing, the very existence of the debate is evidence that the "right" to an abortion is not so universally accepted as the appellants would have us believe.

To reach its result the Court necessarily has had to find within the scope of the Fourteenth Amendment a right that was apparently completely unknown to the drafters of the Amendment. As early as 1821, the first state law dealing directly with abortion was enacted by the Connecticut legislature. . . . By the time of the adoption of the Fourteenth Amendment in 1868 there were at least 36 laws enacted by state or territorial legislatures limiting abortion. While many States have amended or updated their laws, 21 of the laws on the books in 1868 remain in effect today. Indeed, the Texas statute struck down today was, as the majority notes, first enacted in 1857 and "has remained substantially unchanged to the present time." . . .

PLANNED PARENTHOOD OF SOUTHEASTERN PENNSYLVANIA v. CASEY (1992)

This case concerned five provisions of the Pennsylvania Abortion Control Act of 1982, which set certain requirements for a woman seeking an abortion. The Court upheld most of those requirements but in a way that reaffirmed its "essential holding" in Roe v. Wade. *The decision to reaffirm* Roe *was made by a 5-4 vote.*

JUSTICE O'CONNOR delivered the opinion of the Court. . . .

After considering the fundamental constitutional questions resolved by *Roe*, principles of institutional integrity, and the rule of *stare decisis*, we are led to conclude this: the essential holding of *Roe v. Wade* should be retained and once again reaffirmed. . . .

Our law affords constitutional protection to personal decisions relating to marriage, procreation, contraception, family relationships, child rearing, and education. . . . These matters, involving the most intimate and personal choices a person may make in a lifetime, choices central to personal dignity and autonomy, are central to the liberty protected by the Fourteenth Amendment. At the heart of liberty is the right to define one's own concept of existence, of meaning, of the universe, and of the mystery of human life. Beliefs about these matters could not define the attributes of personhood were they formed under compulsion of the State.

These considerations begin our analysis of the woman's interest in terminating her pregnancy but cannot end it, for this reason: though the abortion decision may originate within the zone of conscience and belief, it is more than a philosophic exercise. Abortion is a unique act. It is an act fraught with consequences for others: for the woman who must live with the implications of her decision; for the persons who perform and assist in the procedure; for the spouse, family, and society which must confront the knowledge that these procedures exist, procedures some deem nothing short of an act of violence against innocent human life; and, depending on one's beliefs, for the life or potential life that is aborted. Though abortion is conduct, it does not follow that the State is entitled to proscribe it in all instances. That is because the liberty of a woman is at stake in a sense unique to the human condition and so unique to the law. The mother who carries a child to full term is subject to anxieties, to physical constraints, to pain that only she must bear. That these sacrifices have from the beginning of the human race been endured by woman with a pride that ennobles her to the eyes of others and gives to the infant a bond of love cannot alone be grounds for the State to insist she make the sacrifice. Her suffering is too intimate and personal for the State to insist, without more, upon its own vision of the woman's role, however dominant that vision has been in the course of our history and our culture. The destiny of the woman must be shaped to a large extent on her own conception of her spiritual imperatives and her place in society.

It should be recognized, moreover, that in some critical respects the abortion decision is of the same character as the decision to use contraception, to which *Griswold v. Connecticut, Eisenstadt v. Baird*, and *Carey v. Population Services International*, afford constitutional protection. We have no doubt as to the correctness of those decisions. They support the reasoning in *Roe* relating to the woman's liberty because they involve personal decisions concerning not only the meaning of procreation but also human responsibility and respect for it. . . .

No evolution of legal principle has left *Roe*'s doctrinal footings weaker than they were in 1973. No development of constitutional law since the case was decided has implicitly or explicitly left *Roe* behind as a mere survivor of obsolete constitutional thinking.

. . . We have seen how time has overtaken some of *Roe*'s factual assumptions: advances in maternal health care allow for abortions safe to the mother later in pregnancy than was true in 1973, and advances in neonatal care have advanced viability to a point somewhat earlier. But these facts go only to the scheme of time limits on the realization of competing interests, and the divergences from the factual premises of 1973 have no bearing on the validity of *Roe*'s central holding, that viability marks the earliest point at which the

State's interest in fetal life is constitutionally adequate to justify a legislative ban on nontherapeutic abortions. The soundness or unsoundness of that constitutional judgment in no sense turns on whether viability occurs at approximately 28 weeks, as was usual at the time of *Roe*, at 23 to 24 weeks, as it sometimes does today.

. . . The sum of the precedential inquiry to this point shows *Roe*'s underpinnings unweakened in any way affecting its central holding. While it has engendered disapproval, it has not been unworkable. An entire generation has come of age free to assume *Roe*'s concept of liberty in defining the capacity of women to act in society, and to make reproductive decisions; no erosion of principle going to liberty or personal autonomy has left *Roe*'s central holding a doctrinal remnant; *Roe* portends no developments at odds with other precedent for the analysis of personal liberty; and no changes of fact have rendered viability more or less appropriate as the point at which the balance of interests tips. Within the bounds of normal *stare decisis* analysis, then, and subject to the considerations of which it customarily turns, the stronger argument is for affirming *Roe*'s central holding, with whatever degree of personal reluctance any of us may have, not for overruling it.

. . . Our analysis would not be complete, however, without explaining why overruling *Roe*'s central holding would not only reach an unjustifiable result under principles of *stare decisis*, but would seriously weaken the Court's capacity to exercise the judicial power and to function as the Supreme Court of a Nation dedicated to the rule of law. To understand why this would be so it is necessary to understand the source of this Court's authority, the conditions necessary for its preservation, and its relationship to the country's understanding of itself as a constitutional Republic.

The root of American governmental power is revealed most clearly in the instance of the power conferred by the Constitution upon the Judiciary of the United States and specifically upon this Court. As Americans of each succeeding generation are rightly told, the Court cannot buy support for its decisions by spending money and, except to a minor degree, it cannot independently coerce obedience to its decrees. The Court's power lies, rather, in its legitimacy, a product of substance and perception that shows itself in the people's acceptance of the Judiciary as fit to determine what the Nation's law means and to declare what it demands.

The underlying substance of this legitimacy is of course the warrant for the Court's decisions in the Constitution and the lesser sources of legal principle on which the Court draws. That substance is expressed in the Court's opinions, and our contemporary understanding is such that a decision without principled justification would be no judicial act at all. But even when justification is furnished by apposite legal principle, something more is required. Because not every conscientious claim of principled justification will be accepted as such, the justification claimed must be beyond dispute. The Court must take care to speak and act in ways that allow people to accept its decisions on the terms the Court claims for them, as grounded truly in principle, not as compromises with social and political pressures having, as such, no bearing on the principled choices that the Court is obliged to make. Thus, the Court's legitimacy depends on making legally principled decisions under circumstances in which their principled character is sufficiently plausible to be accepted by the Nation. . . .

JUSTICE SCALIA concurring in part and dissenting in part, joined by CHIEF JUSTICE REHNQUIST, JUSTICE WHITE, and JUSTICE THOMAS. . . .

The States may, if they wish, permit abortion-on-demand, but the Constitution does not require them to do so. The permissibility of abortion, and the limitations upon it, are to be resolved like most important questions in our democracy: by citizens trying to persuade one another and then voting. As the Court acknowledges, "where reasonable people disagree the government can adopt one position or the other." The Court is correct in adding the qualification that this "assumes a state of affairs in which the choice does not intrude upon a protected liberty,"—but the crucial part of that qualification is the penultimate word. A State's choice between two positions on which reasonable people can disagree is constitutional even when (as is often the case) it intrudes upon a "liberty" in the absolute sense. Laws against bigamy, for example—which entire societies of reasonable people disagree with—intrude upon men and women's liberty to marry and live with one another. But bigamy happens not to be a liberty specially "protected" by the Constitution. . . .

Roe's mandate for abortion-on-demand destroyed the compromises of the past, rendered compromise impossible for the future, and required the entire issue to be resolved uniformly, at the national level. At the same time, *Roe* created a vast new class of abortion consumers and abortion proponents by eliminating the moral opprobrium that had attached to the act. ("If the Constitution guarantees abortion, how can it be bad?"—not an accurate line of thought, but a natural one.) Many favor all of those developments. . . .

I cannot agree with, indeed I am appalled by, the Court's suggestion that the decision whether to stand by an erroneous constitutional decision must be strongly influenced—against overruling, no less—by the substantial and continuing public opposition the decision has generated. The Court's judgment that any other course would "subvert the Court's legitimacy" must be another consequence of reading the error-filled history book that described the deeply divided country brought together by *Roe*. In my history book, the Court was covered with dishonor and deprived of legitimacy by *Dred Scott v. Sanford* (1857), an erroneous (and widely opposed) opinion that it did not abandon, rather than by *West Coast Hotel Co. v. Parrish* (1937), which produced the famous "switch in time" from the Court's erroneous (and widely opposed) constitutional opposition to the social measures of the New Deal. (Both *Dred Scott* and one line of the cases resisting the New Deal rested upon the concept of "substantive due process" that the Court praises and employs today.)

In truth, I am as distressed as the Court is about the "political pressure" directed to the Court: the marches, the mail, the protests aimed at inducing us to change our opinions. How upsetting it is, that so many of our citizens (good people, not lawless ones, on both sides of this abortion issue, and on various sides of other issues as well) think that we Justices should properly take into account their views, as though we were engaged not in ascertaining an objective law but in determining some kind of social consensus. The Court would profit, I think, from giving less attention to the fact of this distressing phenomenon, and more attention to the cause of it. That cause permeates today's opinion: a new mode of constitutional adjudication that relies not upon text and traditional practice to determine the law, but upon what the Court calls "reasoned judgment," which turns out to be nothing but philosophical predilection and moral intuition. All manner of "liberties," the Court tells us, inhere in the Constitution and are enforceable by this Court—not just those mentioned in the text or established in the traditions of our society. Why even the Ninth Amendment—which says only that "[t]he enumeration in the Constitution of certain rights shall not be construed to deny or disparage others retained by the people"—is, despite our contrary understanding for almost 200 years, a literally boundless source of additional, unnamed, unhinted-at "rights," definable and enforceable by us, through "reasoned judgment."

What makes all this relevant to the bothersome application of "political pressure" against the Court are the twin facts that the American people love democracy and the American people are not fools. As long as this Court thought (and the people thought) that we Justices were doing essentially lawyers' work up here—reading text and discerning our society's traditional understanding of that text—the public pretty much left us alone. Texts and traditions are facts to study, not convictions to demonstrate about. But if in reality our process of constitutional adjudication consists primarily of making value judgments; if we can ignore a long and clear tradition clarifying an ambiguous text; . . . if, as I say, our pronouncement of constitutional law rests primarily on value judgments, then a free and intelligent people's attitude towards us can be expected to be (ought to be) quite different. The people know that their value judgments are quite as good as those taught in any law school—maybe better. If, indeed, the "liberties" protected by the Constitution are, as the Court says, undefined and unbounded, then the people should demonstrate, to protest that we do not implement their values instead of ours. Not only that, but confirmation hearings for new Justices should deteriorate into question-and-answer sessions in which Senators go through a list of their constituents' most favored and most disfavored alleged constitutional rights, and seek the nominee's commitment to support or oppose them. Value judgments, after all, should be voted on, not dictated; and if our Constitution has somehow accidently committed them to the Supreme Court, at least we can have a sort of plebiscite each time a new nominee to that body is put forward. Justice Blackmun not only regards this prospect with equanimity, he solicits it.

RUTH BADER GINSBURG, SPEAKING IN A JUDICIAL VOICE (1992)

This criticism of the Court's argument and sweeping decision in Roe v. Wade *by Ginsburg, President Clinton's first appoin-*

tee to the Supreme Court, is written from a pro-choice perspective.

The seven to two judgment in *Roe v. Wade* declared "violative of the Due Process Clause of the Fourteenth Amendment" a Texas criminal abortion statute that intolerably shackled a woman's autonomy; the Texas law "except[ed] from criminality only a life-saving procedure on behalf of the [pregnant woman]." Suppose the Court had stopped there, rightly declaring unconstitutional the most extreme brand of law in the nation, and had not gone on, as the Court did in *Roe*, to fashion a regime blanketing the subject, a set of rules that displaced virtually every state law then in force. Would there have been the twenty-year controversy we have witnessed, reflected mostly in the Supreme Court's splintering decision in *Planned Parenthood v. Casey*? A less encompassing *Roe*, one that merely struck down the extreme Texas law and went no further on that day, I believe and will summarize why, might have served to reduce rather than to fuel controversy.

In the 1992 *Planned Parenthood* decision, the three controlling Justices accepted as constitutional several restrictions on access to abortion that could not have survived strict adherence to *Roe*. While those Justices did not closely consider the plight of women without means to overcome the restrictions, they added an important strand to the Court's opinions on abortion—they acknowledged the intimate connection between a woman's "ability to control [her] reproductive li[fe]" and her "ability . . . to participate equally in the economic and social life of the Nation." The idea of the woman in control of her destiny and her place in society was less prominent in the *Roe* decision itself, which coupled with the rights of the pregnant woman the free exercise of her physician's medical judgment. The *Roe* decision might have been less of a storm center had it both homed in more precisely on the women's equality dimension of the issue and, correspondingly, attempted nothing more bold at that time than the mode of decisionmaking the Court employed in the 1970s gender classification cases.

The Court ruled in 1973, for example, that married women in the military were entitled to the housing allowance and family medical care benefits that Congress had provided solely for married men in the military. Two years later, the Court held it unconstitutional for a state to allow a parent to stop supporting a daughter once she reached the age of 18, while requiring parental support for a son until he turned 21. In 1975, and again in 1979, the Court declared that state jury-selection systems could not exclude or exempt women as a class. In decisions running from 1975 to 1980, the Court deleted the principal explicitly sex-based classifications in social insurance and worker's compensation schemes. In 1981, the Court said nevermore to a state law designating the husband "head and master" of the household. And in 1982, in an opinion by Justice O'Connor, the Court held that a state could not limit admission to a state nursing college to women only.

The backdrop for these rulings was a phenomenal expansion, in the years from 1961 to 1971, of women's employment outside the home, the civil rights movement of the 1960s and the precedents set in that struggle, and a revived feminist movement, fueled abroad and in the United States by Simone de Beauvoir's remarkable 1949 publication, *The Second Sex*. In the main, the Court invalidated laws that had become obsolete, retained into the 1970s by only a few of the states. In a core set of cases, however, those dealing with social insurance benefits for a worker's spouse or family, the decisions did not utterly condemn the legislature's product. Instead, the Court, in effect, opened a dialogue with the political branches of government. In essence, the Court instructed Congress and state legislatures: rethink ancient positions on these questions. Should you determine that special treatment for women is warranted, i.e., compensatory legislation because of the sunken-in social and economic bias for disadvantage women encounter, we have left you a corridor in which to move. But your classifications must be refined, adopted for remedial reasons, and not rooted in prejudice about "the way women (or men) are." In the meantime, the Court's decrees removed no benefits; instead, they extended to a woman worker's husband, widower, or family benefits Congress had authorized only for members of the male worker's family.

The ball, one might say, was tossed by the Justices back into the legislators' court, where the political forces of the day could operate. The Supreme Court wrote modestly, it put forward no grand philosophy; but by requiring legislative reexamination of once customary sex-based classifications, the Court helped to ensure that laws and regulations would "catch up with a changed world."

Roe v. Wade, in contrast, invited no dialogue with legislators. Instead, it seemed entirely to remove the ball from the legislators' court. In 1973 when *Roe* issued, abortion law was in a state of change across the nation. As the Supreme Court itself noted, there was a marked trend in state legislatures "toward liberalization of abortion statutes." That movement for legislative change ran parallel to another law revision effort then underway—the change from fault to no-fault divorce regimes, a reform that swept through the state legislatures and captured all of them by the mid 1980s.

No measured motion, the *Roe* decision left virtually no state with laws fully conforming to the Court's delineation of abortion regulation still permissible. Around that extraordinary decision, a well-organized and vocal right-to-life movement rallied and succeeded, for a considerable time, in turning the legislative tide in the opposite direction.

Constitutional review by courts is an institution that has been for some two centuries our nation's hallmark and pride. Two extreme modes of court intervention in social change processes, however, have placed stress on the institution. At one extreme, the Supreme Court steps boldly in front of the political process, as some believe it did in *Roe*. At the opposite extreme, the Court in the early part of the twentieth century found—or thrust—itself into the rearguard opposing change, striking down, as unconstitutional, laws embodying a new philosophy of economic regulation at odds with the nineteenth century's laissez-faire approach. Decisions at both of these poles yielded outcries against the judiciary in certain quarters. The Supreme Court, particularly, was labeled "activist" or "imperial," and its precarious position as final arbiter of constitutional questions was exposed.

I do not suggest that the Court should never step ahead of the political branches in pursuit of a constitutional precept. *Brown v. Board of Education*, the 1954 decision declaring racial segregation in public schools offensive to the equal protection principle, is the case that best fits the bill. Past the midpoint of the twentieth century, apartheid remained the law-enforced system in several states, shielded by a constitutional interpretation the Court itself advanced at the turn of the century—the "separate but equal" doctrine.

In contrast to the legislative reform movement in the states, contemporaneous with *Roe*, widening access to abortion, prospects in 1954 for state legislation dismantling racially segregated schools were bleak. That was so, I believe, for a reason that distances race discrimination from discrimination based on sex. Most women are life partners of men; women bear and raise both sons and daughters. Once women's own consciousness was awakened to the unfairness of allocating opportunity and responsibility on the basis of sex, education of others—of fathers, husbands, sons as well as daughters—could begin, or be reinforced, at home. When blacks were confined by law to a separate sector, there was no similar prospect for educating the white majority.

In most of the post-1970 gender-classification cases, . . . the Court . . . approved the direction of change through a temperate brand of decisionmaking, one that was not extravagant or divisive. *Roe*, on the other hand, halted a political process that was moving in a reform direction. . . .

LEE v. WEISMAN (1992)

Middle and high school principals in Providence, Rhode Island invited members of the clergy from around the city to give invocation and benediction prayers as part of their schools' graduation ceremonies. A principal invited a rabbi to offer a prayer at a particular graduation ceremony. This rabbi was given a pamphlet describing official guidelines for the prayer's nonsectarian composition. The practice was challenged as an establishment of religion by government, a violation of the First Amendment.

JUSTICE KENNEDY delivered the opinion of the Court. . . .

. . . It is beyond dispute that, at a minimum, the Constitution guarantees that government may not coerce anyone to support or participate in religion or its exercise, or otherwise act in a way which "establishes a [state] religion or religious faith, or tends to do so." . . . The State's involvement in the school prayers challenged today violates these central principles.

That involvement is as troubling as it is undenied. A school official, the principal, decided that an invocation and a benediction should be given; this is a choice attributable to the State, and from a constitutional perspective it is as if a state statute decreed that the prayers must occur. The principal chose the religious partici- pant, here a rabbi, and that choice is also attributable to the State. The reason for the choice of the rabbi is not disclosed by the record, but the potential for divisiveness over the choice of a particular member of the clergy to conduct the ceremony is apparent. . . .

The State's role did not end with the decision to include a prayer and with the choice of the clergyman. Principal Lee provided Rab- bi Gutterman with a copy of the "Guidelines for Civic Occasions," and advised him that his prayers should be nonsectarian. Through these means the principal directed and controlled the content of the prayer. Even if the only sanction for ignoring the instructions were that the rabbi would not be invited back, we think no religious rep- resentative who valued his or her continued reputation and effec- tiveness in the community would incur the State's displeasure in this regard. It is a cornerstone principle of our Establishment Clause jurisprudence that "it is no part of the business of government to compose official prayers for any group of the American people to recite as a part of a religious program carried on by the govern- ment," *Engel v. Vitale* (1962), and that is what the school officials attempted to do.

Petitioners argue, and we find nothing in the case to refute it, that the directions of the content of the prayers were a good-faith attempt by the school to ensure that the sectarianism which is so often the flashpoint for religious animosity be removed from the graduation ceremony. The concern is understandable, as a prayer which uses ideas or images identified with a particular religion may foster a different sort of sectarian rivalry than an invocation or benediction in terms more neutral. The school's explanation, how- ever, does not resolve the dilemma caused by its participation. The question is not the good faith of the school in attempting to make the prayer acceptable to most persons, but the legitimacy of its undertaking that enterprise at all when the object is to produce a prayer to be used in a formal religious exercise which students, for all practical purposes, are obliged to attend.

The degree of school involvement here made clear that the gradu- ation prayers bore the imprint of the State and thus put school-age children who objected in an untenable position. We turn our attention now to consider the position of the students, both those who desire the prayer and she who did not. . . .

. . . What to most believers may seem nothing more than a reasonable requirement that the nonbeliever respect their religious practices, in a school context may appear to the nonbeliever or dissenter to be an attempt to employ the machinery of the State to enforce a religious orthodoxy.

We need not look beyond the circumstances of this case to see the phenomenon at work. The undeniable fact is that the school district's supervision and control of a high school graduation ceremony places public pressure, as well as peer pressure, on attending students to stand as a group, or at least, maintain respectful silence during the Invocation and Benediction. This pressure, though subtle and indirect, can be as real as any overt compulsion. Of course, in our culture standing or remaining silent can signify adherence to a view or simple respect for the view of others. And no doubt some persons who have no desire to join a prayer have little objection to standing as a sign of respect for those who do. But for the dissenter of high school age, who has a reasonable perception that she is being forced by the State to pray in a manner her conscience will not allow, the injury is no less real. There can be no doubt that for many, if not most, of the students at the graduation, the act of standing or remaining silent was an expression of participation in the Rabbi's prayer. That was the very point of the religious exercise. It is of little comfort to a dissenter, then, to be told for her the act of standing or remaining silent signifies mere respect, rather than participation. What matters is that, given our social conventions, a reasonable dissenter in this milieu could believe that the group exercise signified her own participation or approval of it.

Finding no violation under these circumstances would place objectors in the dilemma of participating, with all that implies, or protesting. We do not address whether that choice is acceptable if the affected citizens are mature adults, but we think the State may not, consistent with the Establishment Clause, place primary or secondary school children in this position. Research in psychology supports the common assumption that adolescents are often susceptible to pressure from their peers toward conformity, and that the influence is strongest in matters of social convention. . . .

JUSTICE SCALIA, dissenting, joined by CHIEF JUSTICE REHNQUIST, JUSTICE WHITE, and JUSTICE THOMAS. . . .

. . . In holding that the Establishment Clause prohibits invocations and benedictions at public-school graduation ceremonies, the Court—with nary a mention that it is doing so—lays waste a tradition that is as old as public-school graduation ceremonies themselves, and that is a component of an even more longstanding American tradition of nonsectarian prayers to God at public celebrations generally. As its instrument of destruction, the bulldozer of its social engineering, the Court invents a boundless, and boundlessly manipulable, test of psychological coercion. . . . Today's opinion shows more forcefully than volumes of argumentation why our Nation's protection, that fortress which is our Constitution, cannot possibly rest upon the changeable philosophical predilections of the Justices of this Court, but must have deep foundations in the historic practices of our people.

. . . The founders of our Republic knew the fearsome potential of sectarian religious belief to generate civil dissension and civil strife. And they also knew that nothing, absolutely nothing, is so inclined to foster among religious believers of various faiths a toleration—no, an affection—for one another than voluntarily joining in prayer together, to the God whom they all worship and seek. Needless to say, no one should be compelled to do that, but it is a shame to deprive our public culture of the opportunity, and indeed the encouragement for people to do it voluntarily. . . . To deprive our society of that important unifying mechanism, in order to spare the nonbeliever what seems to me the minimal inconvenience of standing or even sitting in respectful nonparticipation, is as senseless in policy as it is unsupported in law.

7

Foreign Policy

This section considers the challenges posed to free, constitutional government by the requirements of foreign policy.

FEDERALIST 23

Part of Publius's defense of an "energetic constitution" is a consideration of the "infinite" variety of "circumstances that endanger the safety of nations."

The principal purposes to be answered by Union are these; The common defence of the members; the preservation of the public peace, as well against internal convulsions as external attacks; the regulation of commerce with other nations and between the States; the superintendence of our intercourse, political and commercial, with foreign countries.

The authorities essential to the care of the common defence are these; to raise armies; to build and equip fleets; to prescribe rules for the government of both—to direct their operations; to provide for their support. These powers ought to exist without limitation: *Because it is impossible to foresee or define the extent and variety of national exigencies, or the correspondent extent & variety of the means which may be necessary to satisfy them.* The circumstances that endanger the safety of nations are infinite; and for this reason no constitutional shackles can wisely be imposed on the power to which the care of it is committed. This power ought to be co-extensive with all the possible combinations of such circumstances; and ought to be under the direction of the same councils, which are appointed to preside over the common defence.

This is one of those truths, which to a correct and unprejudiced mind, carries its own evidence along with it; and may be obscured, but cannot be made plainer by argument or reasoning. It rests upon axioms as simple as they are universal. The *means* ought to be proportioned to the *end*; the persons, from whose agency the attainment of any *end* is expected, ought to possess the *means* by which it is to be attained.

Whether there ought to be a Federal Government intrusted with the care of the common defence, is a question in the first instance open to discussion; but the moment it is decided in the affirmative, it will follow, that government ought to be clothed with all the powers requisite to the complete execution of its trust. And unless it can be shown, that the circumstances which may affect the public safety are reducible within certain determinate limits; unless the contrary of this position can be fairly and rationally disputed, it must be admitted, as a necessary consequence, that there can be no limitation of that authority, which is to provide for the defence and protection of the community, in any matter essential to its efficacy; that is, in any matter essential to the *formation, direction* or *support* of the NATIONAL FORCES. . . .

GEORGE WASHINGTON, FAREWELL ADDRESS (1796)

Upon leaving office, President Washington attempted to chart the foreign policy course for a nation "free, enlightened," and soon to be "great."

Observe good faith and justice towards all Nations. Cultivate peace and harmony with all. Religion and morality enjoin this conduct; and can it be that good policy does not equally enjoin it? It will be worthy of a free, enlightened, and, at no distant period, a great Nation, to give to mankind the magnanimous and too novel example of a People always guided by an exalted justice and benevolence. Who can doubt that in the course of time and things the fruits of such a plan would richly repay any temporary advantages which might be lost by a steady adherence to it? Can it be, that Providence has not connected the permanent felicity of a Nation with its virtue? The experiment, at least, is recommended by every sentiment which ennobles human Nature. Alas! is it rendered impossible by its vices?

In the execution of such a plan nothing is more essential than that permanent, inveterate antipathies against particular Nations and passionate attachments for others should be excluded; and that in place of them just and amicable feelings toward all should be cultivated. The Nation, which indulges towards another an habitual hatred, or an habitual fondness, is in some degree a slave. It is a slave to its animosity or to its affection, either of which is sufficient to lead it astray from its duty and its interest. Antipathy in one Nation against another, disposes each more readily to offer insult and injury, to lay hold of slight causes of umbrage, and to be haughty and intractable, when accidental or trifling occasions of dispute occur. Hence frequent collisions, obstinate, envenomed and bloody contests. The Nation, prompted by ill will and resentment sometimes impels to War the Government, contrary to the best calculations of policy. The Government sometimes participates in the national propensity, and adopts through passion what reason would reject; at other times; it makes the animosity of the Nation subservient to projects of hostility instigated by pride, ambition and other sinister and pernicious motives. The peace often, sometimes perhaps the Liberty, of Nations has been the victim.

So likewise, a passionate attachment of one Nation for another produces a variety of evils. Sympathy for the favourite nation, facilitating the illusion of an imaginary common interest, in cases where no real common interest exists, and infusing into one the enmities of the other, betrays the former into a participation in the quarrels and Wars of the latter, without adequate inducement or justification: It leads also to concessions to the favourite Nation of privileges denied to others, which is apt doubly to injure the Nation making the concessions; by unnecessarily parting with what ought to have been retained; and by exciting jealousy, ill will, and a disposition to retaliate, in the parties from who equal privileges are withheld: And it gives to ambitious, corrupted, or deluded citizens (who devote themselves to the favourite Nation) facility to betray, or sacrifice the interests of their own country, without odium, sometimes even with popularity; gilding with the appearances of a virtuous sense of obligation a commendable deference for public opinion, or a laudable zeal for public good, the base or foolish compliances of ambition, corruption or infatuation.

As avenues to foreign influence in innumerable ways, such attachments are particularly alarming to the truly enlightened and independent Patriot. How many opportunities do they afford to tamper with domestic factions, to practice the arts of seduction, to mislead public opinion, to influence or awe the public Councils! Such an attachment of a small or weak, towards a great and powerful Nation, dooms the former to be the satellite of the latter.

Against the insidious wiles of foreign influence, (I conjure you to believe me fellow citizens) the jealousy of a free people ought to be *constantly* awake; since history and experience prove that foreign influence is one of the most baneful foes of Republican Government. But that jealousy to be useful must be impartial; else it becomes the instrument of the very influence to be avoided, instead of a defense against it. Excessive partiality for one foreign nation and excessive dislike of another, cause those whom they actuate to see danger only on one side, and serve to veil and even second the arts of influence on the other. Real Patriots, who may resist the intrigues of the favourite, are liable to become suspected and odious; while its tools and dupes usurp the applause and confidence of the people, to surrender their interests.

The Great rule of conduct for us, in regard to foreign Nations is in extending our commercial relations to have with them as little *political* connection as possible. So far as we have already formed engagements let them be fulfilled, with perfect good faith. Here let us stop.

Europe has a set of primary interests, which to us have none, or a very remote relation. Hence she must be engaged in frequent controversies, the causes of which are essentially foreign to our concerns. Hence therefore it must be unwise in us to implicate ourselves, by artificial ties, in the ordinary vicissitudes of her politics, or the ordinary combinations and collision of her friendships, or enmities:

Our detached and distant situation invites and enables us to pursue a different course. If we remain one People, under an efficient government, the period is not far off, when we may defy material injury from external annoyance; when we may take such an attitude as will cause the neutrality we may at any time resolve upon to be scrupulously respected; when belligerent nations, under the impossibility of making acquisitions upon us, will not lightly hazard the giving us provocation; when we may choose peace or war, as our interest guided by our justice shall Counsel.

Why forego the advantages of so peculiar a situation? Why quit our own to stand upon foreign ground? Why, by interweaving our destiny with that of any part of Europe, entangle our peace and prosperity in the toils of European Ambition, Rivalship, Interest, Humour or Caprice?

'Tis our true policy to steer clear of permanent Alliances, with any portion of the foreign world. So far, I mean, as we are now at liberty to do it, for let me not be understood as capable of patronising infidelity to existing engagements (I hold the maxim no less applicable to public than to private affairs, that honesty is always the best policy). I repeat it therefore, let those engagements be observed in their genuine sense. But in my opinion, it is unnecessary and would be unwise to extend them.

Taking care always to keep ourselves, by suitable establishments, on a respectably defensive posture, we may safely trust to temporary alliances for extraordinary emergencies.

Harmony, liberal intercourse with all Nations, are recommended by policy, humanity, and interest. But even our Commercial policy should hold an equal and impartial hand: neither seeking nor granting exclusive favours or preferences; consulting the natural course of things; diffusing and diversifying by gentle means the streams of Commerce, but forcing nothing; establishing with Powers so disposed; in order to give to trade a stable course, to define the rights of our Merchants, and to enable the Government to support them; conventional rules of intercourse, the best that present circumstances and mutual opinion will permit, but temporary, and liable to be from time to time abandoned or varied, as experience and circumstances shall dictate; constantly keeping in view, that 'tis folly in one Nation to look for disinterested favours from another; that it must pay with a portion of its Independence for whatever it may accept under that character; that by such acceptance, it may place itself in the condition of having given equivalents for nominal favours and yet of being reproached with ingratitude for not giving more. There can be no greater error than to expect, or calculate upon real favours from Nation to Nation. 'Tis an illusion which experience must cure, which a just pride ought to discard.

In offering to you, my Countrymen these counsels of an old and affectionate friend, I dare not hope they will make the strong and lasting impression, I could wish; that they will control the usual current of the passions, or prevent our Nation from running the course which has hitherto marked the Destiny of Nations: But if I may even flatter myself, that they may be productive of some partial benefit, some occasional good; that they may now and then recur to moderate the fury of party spirit, to warn against the mischiefs of foreign Intrigue, to guard against the Impostures of pretended patriotism; this hope will be a full recompence for the solicitude for your welfare, by which they have been dictated.

FRANKLIN D. ROOSEVELT, "FOUR FREEDOMS" SPEECH (1941)

After World War I the United States sank into a mood of isolationism in foreign policy captured by the slogan "America first!" Beginning in 1937 President Roosevelt tried to alert the nation to the futility and irresponsibility of such isolationism. In this 1941 State of the Union address, Roosevelt appealed to American idealism by citing "four essential human freedoms" to which all people are entitled as a way of encouraging Americans to support the nations at war with the Axis powers of Germany, Italy, and Japan. His immediate goal was support for his lend-lease program of military aid for Great Britain and the Soviet Union.

. . . Let us say to the democracies:

We Americans are vitally concerned in your defense of freedom. We are putting forth our energies, our resources and our organizing powers to give you the strength to regain and maintain a free world. We shall send you in ever-increasing numbers, ships, planes, tanks, guns. That is our purpose and our pledge. . . .

Yes, and we must prepare, all of us prepare, to make the sacrifices that the emergency—almost as serious as war itself—demands. Whatever stands in the way of speed and efficiency in defense, in defense preparations at any time, must give way to the national need.

A free nation has the right to expect full cooperation from all groups. A free nation has the right to look to the leaders of business, of labor and of agriculture to take the lead in stimulating effort, not among other groups but within their own group. . . .

As men do not live by bread alone, they do not fight by armament alone. Those who man our defenses and those behind them who build our defenses must have the stamina and the courage which come from unshakable belief in the manner of life which they are defending. The mighty action that we are calling for cannot be based on a disregard for all the things worth fighting for.

The nation takes great satisfaction and much strength from the things which have been done to make its people conscious of their individual stakes in the preservation of democratic life in America. Those things have toughened the fiber of our people, have renewed their faith and strengthened their devotion to the institutions we make ready to protect.

Certainly, this is no time for any of us to stop thinking about the social and economic problems which are the root cause of the social revolution which is today a supreme factor in the world. For there is nothing mysterious about the foundations of a healthy and strong democracy.

The basic things expected by our people of their political and economic systems are simple. They are:

Equality of opportunity for youth and for others.

Jobs for those who can work.

Security for those who need it.

The ending of special privilege for the few.

The preservation of civil liberties for all.

The employment of the fruits of scientific progress in a wider and constantly rising standard of living.

These are the simple, the basic things that must never be lost sight of in the turmoil and unbelievable complexity of our modern world. The inner and abiding strength of our economic and political systems is dependent upon the degree to which they fulfill these expectations. . . .

I have called for personal sacrifice, and I am assured of the willingness of almost all Americans to respond to that call. A part of the sacrifice means the payment of more money in taxes. In my budget message I will recommend that a greater portion of this great defense program be paid for from taxation than we are paying for today. No person should try, or be allowed to get rich out of the program, and the principle of tax payments in accordance with ability to pay should be constantly before our eyes to guide our legislation.

If the Congress maintains these principles the voters, putting patriotism ahead of pocketbooks, will give you their applause.

In the future days which we seek to make secure, we look forward to a world founded upon four essential human freedoms.

The first is freedom of speech and expression—everywhere in the world.

The second is freedom of every person to worship God in his own way—everywhere in the world.

The third is freedom from want, which, translated into world terms, means economic understanding which will secure to every nation a healthy peacetime life for its inhabitants—everywhere in the world.

The fourth is freedom from fear, which, translated in world terms, means a world-wide reduction of armaments to such a point and in such a thorough fashion that no nation will be in a position to commit an act of physical aggression against any neighbor—anywhere in the world.

That is no vision of a distant millennium. It is a definite basis for a kind of world attainable in our own time and generation. That kind of world is the very antithesis of the so-called "new order" or tyranny which the dictators seek to create with the crash of a bomb.

To that new order we oppose the greater conception—the moral order. A good society is able to face schemes of world domination and foreign revolutions alike without fear.

Since the beginning of our American history we have been engaged in change, in a perpetual, peaceful revolution, a revolution which goes on steadily, quietly, adjusting itself to changing conditions without the concentration camp or the quicklime in the ditch. The world order which we seek is the cooperation of free countries, working together in a friendly, civilized society.

This nation has placed its destiny in the hands, heads and hearts of the millions of free men and women, and its faith in freedom under the guidance of God. Freedom means the supremacy of human rights everywhere. Our support goes to those who struggle to gain those rights and keep them. Our strength is our unity of purpose.

To that high concept there can be no end save victory.

HARRY S TRUMAN, SPECIAL MESSAGE TO CONGRESS ON GREECE AND TURKEY: THE TRUMAN DOCTRINE (1947)

President Truman asked Congress for $400 million in military and economic aid for Greece and Turkey to contain the expansion of communism. Congress approved the aid by a large majority after a bitter debate. At the heart of the controversy was Truman's belief that the United States should support the struggle of "free peoples" throughout the world.

. . . It is important to note that the Greek Government has asked for our aid in utilizing effectively the financial and other assistance we may give to Greece, and in improving its public administration. It is of the utmost importance that we supervise the use of any funds made available to Greece, in such a manner that each dollar spent will count toward making Greece self-supporting, and will help to build an economy in which a healthy democracy can flourish.

No government is perfect. One of the chief virtues of a democracy, however, is that its defects are always visible and under democratic processes can be pointed out and corrected. The government of Greece is not perfect. Nevertheless it represents 85 percent of the members of the Greek Parliament who were chosen in an election last year. Foreign observers, including 692 Americans, considered this election to be a fair expression of the views of the Greek people.

The Greek Government has been operating in an atmosphere of

chaos and extremism. It has made mistakes. The extension of aid by this country does not mean that the United States condones everything that the Greek Government has done or will do. We have condemned in the past, and we condemn now, extremist measures of the right or the left. We have in the past advised tolerance, and we advise tolerance now. . . .

To ensure the peaceful development of nations, free from coercion, the United States has taken a leading part in establishing the United Nations. The United Nations is designed to make possible lasting freedom and independence for all its members. We shall not realize our objectives, however, unless we are willing to help free peoples to maintain their free institutions and their national integrity against aggressive movements that seek to impose upon them totalitarian regimes. This is no more than a frank recognition that totalitarian regimes imposed upon free peoples, by direct or indirect aggression, undermine the foundations of international peace and hence the security of the United States.

The peoples of a number of countries of the world have recently had totalitarian regimes forced upon them against their will. The Government of the United States has made frequent protests against coercion and intimidation, in violation of the Yalta agreement, in Poland, Rumania, and Bulgaria. I must also state that in a number of other countries there have been similar developments.

At the present moment in world history nearly every nation must choose between alternative ways of life. The choice is too often not a free one.

One way of life is based upon the will of the majority, and is distinguished by free institutions, representative government, free elections, guarantees of individual liberty, freedom of speech and religion, and freedom from political oppression.

The second way of life is based upon the will of the minority forcibly imposed upon the majority. It relies upon terror and oppression, a controlled press and radio, fixed elections, and the suppression of personal freedoms.

I believe that it must be the policy of the United States to support free peoples who are resisting attempted subjugation by armed minorities or by outside pressures.

I believe that we must assist free peoples to work out their destinies in their own way.

I believe that our help should be primarily through economic stability and orderly political processes.

The world is not static, and the *status quo* is not sacred. But we cannot allow changes in the *status quo* in violation of the Charter of the United Nations by such methods as coercion, or by such subterfuges as political infiltration. In helping free and independent nations to maintain their freedom, the United States will be giving effect to the principles of the Charter of the United Nations.

It is necessary only to glance at a map to realize that the survival and integrity of the Greek nation are of grave importance in a much wider situation. If Greece should fall under the control of an armed minority, the effect upon its neighbor, Turkey, would be immediate and serious. Confusion and disorder might well spread throughout the entire Middle East.

Moreover, the disappearance of Greece as an independent state would have a profound effect upon those countries in Europe whose peoples are struggling against great difficulties to maintain their freedoms and their independence while they repair the damages of war.

It would be an unspeakable tragedy if these countries, which have struggled so long against overwhelming odds, should lose that victory for which they sacrificed so much. Collapse of free institutions and loss of independence would be disastrous not only for them but for the world. Discouragement and possibly failure would quickly be the lot of neighboring peoples striving to maintain their freedom and independence. . . .

The United States contributed $341,000,000,000 toward winning World War II. This is an investment in world freedom and world peace.

The assistance that I am recommending for Greece and Turkey amounts to little more than 1/10 of 1 percent of this investment. It is only common sense that we should safeguard this investment and make sure that it was not in vain.

The seeds of totalitarian regimes are nurtured by misery and want. They spread and grow in the evil soil of poverty and strife. They reach their full growth when the hope of a people for a better life has died.

We must keep that hope alive.

The free peoples of the world look to us for support in maintaining their freedoms.

If we falter in our leadership, we may endanger the peace of the world—and we shall surely endanger the welfare of this Nation.

Great responsibilities have been placed upon us by the swift movement of events.

I am confident that the Congress will face these responsibilities squarely.

GEORGE F. KENNAN, THE SOURCES OF SOVIET CONDUCT (1947)

With the Truman Doctrine and the Marshall Plan the United States had already begun a policy of "containing" Soviet expansion when, in July 1947, an article defending this policy appeared in the journal Foreign Affairs. *The title of the article was "The Sources of Soviet Conduct," and the author's name was given only as "X." Later the mysterious Mr. X was revealed as George F. Kennan, the head of the State Department's new policy planning staff, which was charged with the making of long-range plans for the conduct of American foreign policy.*

. . . [T]he Kremlin is under no ideological compulsion to accomplish its purposes in a hurry. Like the Church, it is dealing in ideological concepts which are of long-term validity, and it can afford to be patient. It has no right to risk the existing achievements of the revolution for the sake of vain baubles of the future. The very teachings of Lenin himself require great caution and flexibility in the pursuit of Communist purposes. Again, these precepts are fortified by the lessons of Russian history: of centuries of obscure battles between nomadic forces over the stretches of a vast unfortified plain. Here caution, circumspection, flexibility and deception are the valuable qualities; and their value finds natural appreciation in the Russian or the oriental mind. Thus the Kremlin has no compunction about retreating in the face of superior force. And being under the compulsion of no timetable, it does not get panicky under the necessity for such retreat. Its political action is a fluid stream which moves constantly, wherever it is permitted to move, toward a given goal. Its main concern is to make sure that it has filled every nook and cranny available to it in the basin of world power. But if it finds unassailable barriers in its path, it accepts these philosophically and accommodates itself to them. The main thing is that there should always be pressure, increasing constant pressure, toward the desired goal. There is no trace of any feeling in Soviet psychology that goal must be reached at any given time.

These considerations make Soviet diplomacy at once easier and more difficult to deal with than the diplomacy of individual aggressive leaders like Napoleon and Hitler. On the one hand it is more sensitive to contrary force, more ready to yield on individual sectors of the diplomatic front when that force is felt to be too strong, and thus more rational in the logic and rhetoric of power. On the other hand it cannot be easily defeated or discouraged by a single victory on the part of its opponents. And the patient persistence by which it is animated means that it can be effectively countered not by sporadic acts which represent the momentary whims of democratic opinion but only by intelligent long-range policies on the part of Russia's adversaries—policies no less steady in their purpose, and no less variegated and resourceful in their application, than those of the Soviet Union itself.

In these circumstances it is clear that the main element of any United States policy toward the Soviet Union must be that of a long-term, patient but firm and vigilant containment of Russian expansive tendencies. It is important to note, however, that such a policy has nothing to do without outward histrionics: with threats or blustering or superfluous gestures of outward "toughness." While the Kremlin is basically flexible in its reaction to political realities, it is by no means unamenable to considerations of prestige. Like almost any other government, it can be placed by tactless and threatening gestures in a position where it cannot afford to yield even though this might be dictated by its sense of realism. The

Russian leaders are keen judges of human psychology, and as such they are highly conscious that loss of temper and of self-control is never a source of strength in political affairs. They are quick to exploit such evidences of weakness. For these reasons, it is a *sine qua non* of successful dealing with Russia that the foreign government in question should remain at all times cool and collected and that its demands on Russian policy should be put forward in such a manner as to leave the way open for a compliance not too detrimental to Russian prestige. . . .

. . . Russia, as opposed to the Western world in general, is still by far the weaker party, . . . Soviet policy is highly flexible, and Soviet society may well contain deficiencies which will eventually weaken its own total potential. This would of itself warrant the United States entering with reasonable confidence upon a policy of firm containment, designed to confront the Russians with unalterable counterforce at every point where they show signs of encroaching upon the interests of a peaceful and stable world.

But in actuality the possibilities for American policy are by no means limited to holding the line and hoping for the best. It is entirely possible for the United States to influence by its actions the internal developments, both within Russia and throughout the international Communist movement, by which Russian policy is largely determined. This is not only a question of the modest measure of informational activity which this government can conduct in the Soviet Union and elsewhere, although that, too, is important. It is rather a question of the degree to which the United States can create among the peoples of the world generally the impression of a country which knows what it wants, which is coping successfully with the problems of its internal life and with the responsibilities of a World Power, and which has a spiritual vitality capable of holding its own among the major ideological currents of the time. To the extent that such an impression can be created and maintained, the aims of Russian Communism must appear sterile and quixotic, the hopes and enthusiasm of Moscow's supporters must wane, and added strain must be imposed on the Kremlin's foreign policies. For the palsied decrepitude of the capitalist world is the keystone of Communist philosophy. Even the failure of the United States to experience the early economic depression which the ravens of the Red Square have been predicting with such complacent confidence since hostilities ceased would have deep and important repercussions throughout the Communist world.

By the same token, exhibitions of indecision, disunity and internal disintegration within this country have an exhilarating effect on the whole Communist movement. At each evidence of these tendencies, a thrill of hope and excitement goes through the Communist world; a new jauntiness can be noted in the Moscow trend; now groups of foreign supporters climb on to what they can only view as the band wagon of international politics; and Russian pressure increases all along the line in international affairs.

It would be an exaggeration to say that American behavior unassisted and alone could exercise a power of life and death over the Communist movement and bring about the early fall of Soviet power in Russia. But the United States has it in its power to increase enormously the strains under which Soviet policy must operate, to force upon the Kremlin a far greater degree of moderation and circumspection than it has had to observe in recent years, and in this way to promote tendencies which must eventually find their outlet in either the break-up or the gradual mellowing of Soviet power. For no mystical, Messianic movement—and particularly not that of the Kremlin—can face frustration indefinitely without eventually adjusting itself in one way or another to the logic of that state of affairs.

Thus the decision will really fall in large measure in this country itself. The issue of Soviet-American relations is in essence a test of the over-all worth of the United States as a nation among nations. To avoid destruction the United States need only measure up to its own best traditions and prove itself worthy of preservation as a great nation.

Surely, there was never a fairer test of national quality than this. In the light of these circumstances, the thoughtful observer of Russian-American relations will find no cause for complaint in the Kremlin's challenge to American society. He will rather experience a certain gratitude to a Providence which, by providing the American people with this implacable challenge, has made their entire security as a nation dependent on their pulling themselves together and accepting the responsibilities of moral and political leadership that history plainly intended them to bear. . . .

DWIGHT D. EISENHOWER,
FAREWELL ADDRESS (1961)

Eisenhower was the first president to deliver a televised fare-well address, three days before the end of his second term. His departing speech is often compared with George Washington's in 1796. He urges that statesmen direct technological and international development according to American principle.

My fellow Americans:

Three days from now, after half a century in the service of our country, I shall lay down the responsibilities of office as, in traditional and solemn ceremony, the authority of the Presidency is vested in my successor.

This evening I come to you with a message of leave-taking and farewell, and to share a few final thoughts with you, my countrymen. . . .

Throughout America's adventure in free government, our basic purposes have been to keep the peace; to foster progress in human achievement, and to enhance liberty, dignity and integrity among people and among nations. To strive for less would be unworthy of a free and religious people. Any failure traceable to arrogance, or our lack of comprehension or readiness to sacrifice would inflict upon us grievous hurt both at home and abroad.

Progress toward these noble goals is persistently threatened by the conflict now engulfing the world. It commands our whole attention, absorbs our very beings. We face a hostile ideology—global in scope, atheistic in character, ruthless in purpose and insidious in method. Unhappily the danger it poses promises to be of indefinite duration. To meet it successfully, there is called for, not so much the emotional and transitory sacrifices of crisis, but rather those which enable us to carry forward steadily, surely and without complaint the burdens of a prolonged and complex struggle—with liberty the stake. Only thus shall we remain, despite every provocation, on our charted course toward permanent peace and human betterment.

Crises there will continue to be. In meeting them, whether foreign or domestic, great or small, there is a recurring temptation to feel that some spectacular and costly action could become the miraculous solution to all current difficulties. A huge increase in newer elements of our defense; development of unrealistic programs to cure every ill in agriculture; a dramatic expansion in basic and applied research—these and many other possibilities, each possibly promising itself, may be suggested as the only way to the road we wish to travel.

But each proposal must be weighed in the light of a broader consideration; the need to maintain balance in and among national programs—balance between the private and public economy, balance between cost and hoped for advantage—balance between the clearly necessary and the comfortably desirable; balance between our essential requirements as a nation and the duties imposed by the nation upon the individual; balance between actions of the moment and the national welfare of the future. Good judgment seeks balance and progress; lack of it eventually finds imbalance and frustration.

The record of many decades stands as proof that our people and their government have, in the main, understood these truths and have responded to them well in the face of stress and threat. But threats, new in kind or degree, constantly arise. I mention two only. . . .

Until the latest of our world conflicts, the United States had no armaments industry. American makers of plowshares could, with time and as required, makes swords as well. But now we can no longer risk emergency improvision of national defense; we have been compelled to create a permanent armaments industry of vast proportions. Added to this, three and a half million men and women are directly engaged in the defense establishment. We annually spend on military security more than the net income of all United States corporations.

This conjunction of an immense military establishment and a large arms industry is new in the American experience. The total influence—economic, political, even spiritual—is felt in every city, every State house, every office of the Federal Government. We recognize the imperative need for this development. Yet we must not fail to comprehend its grave implications. Our toil, resources and livelihood are all involved; so is the very structure of our society.

In the councils of government, we must guard against the acquisition of unwarranted influence, whether sought or unsought, by the military-industrial complex. The potential for the disastrous rise of misplaced power exists and will persist.

We must never let the weight of this combination endanger our liberties or democratic processes. We should take nothing for granted. Only an alert and knowledgeable citizenry can compel the proper meshing of the huge industrial and military machinery of defense with our peaceful methods and goals, so that security and liberty may prosper together.

Akin to, and largely responsible for the sweeping changes in our industrial-military posture, has been the technological revolution during recent decades.

In this revolution, research has become central; it also becomes more formalized, complex, and costly. A steadily increasing share is conducted for, by, or by the direction of, the Federal government.

Today, the solitary inventor, tinkering in his shop, has been over-shadowed by task forces of scientists in laboratories and testing fields. In the same fashion, the free university, historically the foun-tainhead of free ideas and scientific discovery, has experienced a revolution in the conduct of research. Partly because of the huge costs involved, a government contract becomes virtually a substi-tute for intellectual curiosity. For every old blackboard there are now hundreds of new electronic computers.

The prospect of domination of the nation's scholars by Federal employment, project allocations, and the power of money is ever present—and is gravely to be regarded.

Yet, in holding scientific research and discovery in respect, as we should, we must also be alert to the equal and opposite danger that public policy could itself become the captive of a scientific-technological elite.

It is the task of statesmanship to mold, to balance, and to inte-grate these and other forces, new and old, within the principle of our democratic system—ever aiming toward the supreme goals of our free society.

Another factor in maintaining balance involves the element of time. As we peer into society's future, we—you and I, and our government—must avoid the impulse to live only for today, plundering, for our own ease and convenience, the precious resources of tomorrow. We cannot mortgage the material assets of our grandchildren without risking the loss also of their political and spiritual heritage. We want democracy to survive for all generations to come, not to become the insolvent phantom of tomorrow. . . .

To all the people of the world, I once more give expression to America's prayerful and continuing aspiration:

We pray that peoples of all faiths, all races, all nations, may have their great human needs satisfied; that those now denied opportunity shall come to enjoy it to the full; that all who yearn for freedom may experience its spiritual blessings; that those who have freedom will understand, also, its heavy responsibilities; that all who are insensitive to the needs of others will learn charity; that the scourges of poverty, disease and ignorance will be made to disappear from the earth, and that in the goodness of time, all peoples will come to live together in a peace guaranteed by the binding force of mutual respect and love.

JIMMY CARTER, ADDRESS AT THE UNIVERSITY OF NOTRE DAME (1977)

This address is an optimistic statement concerning the future of human rights throughout the world. That optimism was the basis of President Carter's call for a new foreign policy, one no longer constrained by an "inordinate fear of Communism."

I want to speak today about the strands that connect our actions overseas with our essential character as a nation.

I believe we can have a foreign policy that is democratic, that is based on our fundamental values and that uses power and influence for humane purposes. We can also have a foreign policy that the American people both support and understand.

I have a quiet confidence in our own political system.

Because we know democracy works, we can reject the arguments of those rulers who deny human rights to their people.

We are confident that democracy's example will be compelling, and so we seek to bring that example closer to those from whom we have been separated and who are not yet convinced.

We are confident that democratic methods are the most effective, and so we are not tempted to employ improper tactics at home or abroad.

We are confident of our own strength, so we can seek substantial mutual reductions in the nuclear arms race.

We are confident of the good sense of our own people, and so we let them share the process of making foreign policy decisions. We can thus speak with the voices of 215 million, not just of a handful.

Democracy's great recent successes—in India, Portugal, Greece, Spain—show that our confidence is not misplaced.

Being confident of our own future, we are now free of that inordinate fear of Communism which once led us to embrace any dictator who joined us in our fear.

For too many years we have been willing to adopt the flawed principles and tactics of our adversaries, sometimes abandoning our values for theirs.

We fought fire with fire, never thinking that fire is better fought with water.

This approach failed, with Vietnam the best example of its intellectual and moral poverty.

But through failure we have found our way back to our own principles and values, and we have regained our lost confidence.

By the measure of history, our nation's 200 years are brief; and our rise to world eminence is briefer still. It dates from 1945, when Europe and the old international order both lay in ruins. Before then, America was largely on the periphery of world affairs. Since then, we have inescapably been at the center.

We helped to build solid testaments to our faith and purpose—

the United Nations, the North Atlantic Treaty Organization, the World Bank, the International Monetary Fund and other institutions. This international system has endured and worked well for a quarter of a century.

Our policy during this period was guided by two principles: a belief that Soviet expansion must be contained, and the corresponding belief in the importance of an almost exclusive alliance among non-Communist nations on both sides of the Atlantic.

That system could not last forever unchanged. Historical trends have weakened its foundation. The unifying threat of conflict with the Soviet Union has become less intensive, even though the competition has become more extensive.

The Vietnamese war produced a profound moral crisis, sapping worldwide faith in our policy. The economic strains of the 1970's have weakened public confidence in the capacity of industrial democracy to provide sustained well-being for its citizens, a crisis of confidence made even more grave by the covert pessimism of some of our leaders.

It is a familiar truth that the world today is in the midst of the most profound and rapid transformation in its entire history. In less than a generation the daily lives and the aspirations of most human beings have been transformed. Colonialism has nearly gone; a new sense of national identity exists in almost 100 new countries; knowledge has become more widespread; aspirations are higher. As more people have been freed from traditional constraints, more have become determined to achieve social justice.

The world is still divided by ideological disputes, dominated by regional conflicts and threatened by the danger that we will not resolve the differences of race and wealth without violence or without drawing into combat the major military powers. We can no longer separate the traditional issues of war and peace from the new global questions of justice, equity and human rights.

It is a new world, but America should not fear it. It is a new world, and we should help to shape it. It is a new world that calls for a new American foreign policy—a policy based on constant decency in its values and on optimism in its historical vision.

We can no longer have a policy solely for the industrial nations as the foundation of global stability, but we must respond to the new reality of a politically awakening world.

We can no longer expect that the other 150 nations will follow the dictates of the powerful, but we must continue—confidently— our efforts to inspire and to persuade and to lead.

Our policy must reflect our belief that the world can hope for more than simple survival and our belief that dignity and freedom are man's fundamental spiritual requirements.

Our policy must shape an international system that will last longer than secret deals.

We cannot make this kind of policy by manipulation. Our policy must be open and candid; it must be one of constructive global involvement, resting on these five cardinal premises:

First, our policy should reflect our people's basic commitment to promote the cause of human rights.

Next, our policy should be based on close cooperation among the industrial democracies of the world—because we share the same values and because together we can help to shape a more decent life for all.

Based on a strong defense capability, our policy must also seek to improve relations with the Soviet Union and with China in ways that are both more comprehensive and more reciprocal. Even if we cannot heal ideological divisions, we must reach accommodations that reduce the risk of war.

Also, our policy must reach out to the developing nations to alleviate suffering and to reduce the chasm between the world's rich and poor.

Finally, our policy must encourage all countries to rise above narrow national interests and work together to solve such formidable global problems as the threat of nuclear war, racial hatred, the arms race, environmental damage, hunger, and disease.

Since last January we have begun to define and to set in motion a foreign policy based on these premises, and I have tried to make these premises clear to the American people. Let me review what we have been doing and discuss what we intend to do.

First, we have reaffirmed America's commitment to human rights as a fundamental tenet of our foreign policy. In ancestry, religion, color, place of origin and cultural background, we Americans are as diverse a nation as the world has ever known. No common mystique of blood or soil unites us. What draws us together, perhaps more than anything else, is a belief in human freedom. We want the world to know that our nation stands for more than financial prosperity.

This does not mean that we can conduct our foreign policy by rigid moral maxims. We live in a world that is imperfect and will always be imperfect, a world that is complex and will always be complex. I understand fully the limits of moral suasion. I have no illusion that changes will come easily or soon. But I also believe that it is a mistake to undervalue the power of words and of the ideas that words embody. In our own history that power has ranged from Thomas Paine's "Common Sense" to Martin Luther King Jr.'s "I have a Dream." . . .

We can already see dramatic worldwide advances in the protection of the individual from the arbitrary power of the state. For us to ignore this trend would be to lose influence and moral authority in the world. To lead it will be to regain the moral stature we once had.

All people will benefit from these advances. From free and open competition comes creative change—in politics, commerce, science and the arts. From control comes conformity and despair.

The great democracies are not free because they are strong and prosperous. I believe they are strong and prosperous because they are free. . . .

More than 100 years ago, Abraham Lincoln said that our nation could not exist half slave and half free. We know that a peaceful world cannot long exist one-third rich and two-thirds hungry.

Most nations share our faith that, in the long run, expanded and equitable trade will best help developing countries to help themselves. But the immediate problems of hunger, disease, illiteracy and repression are here now.

The Western democracies, the OPEC nations and the developed Communist countries can cooperate through existing international institutions in providing more effective aid. This is an excellent alternative to war.

We have a special need for cooperation and consultation with other nations in this hemisphere. We do not need another slogan; although these are our close friends and neighbors, our links with them are the same links of equality that we forge with the rest of the world. We will be dealing with them as part of a new worldwide mosaic of global, regional and bilateral relations.

It is important that we make progress toward normalizing relations with the People's Republic of China. We see the American-Chinese relationship as a central element of our global policy, and China as a key force for global peace. We wish to cooperate closely with the creative Chinese people on the problems that confront all mankind. We hope to find a formula which can bridge some of the difficulties that still separate us.

Finally, let me say that we are committed to a peaceful resolution of the crisis in southern Africa. The time has come for the principle of majority rule to be the basis for political order, recognizing that in a democratic system the rights of the minority must also be protected. To be peaceful, change must come promptly. The United States is determined to work together with our European allies and the concerned African states to shape a congenial international framework for the rapid and progressive transformation of southern African society and to help protect it from unwarranted outside interference.

Let me conclude:

Our policy is based on a historical vision of America's role;

It is derived from a larger view of global change;

It is rooted in our moral values;

It is reinforced by our material wealth and by our military power;

It is designed to serve mankind;

And it is a policy that I hope will make you proud to be an American.

JEANE KIRKPATRICK, ADDRESS BEFORE THE AMERICAN ENTERPRISE INSTITUTE (1981)

Kirkpatrick, President Reagan's ambassador to the United Nations, criticizes Carter's foreign policy. She says that its superficial optimism masked a deeper resignation about the "inevitability" of "American decline." She goes on to describe the dangers and opportunities that faced the new Reagan administration.

The election of Ronald Reagan was a watershed event in American politics, which signaled the end of one major postwar period and the beginning of a new one.

This new period may be understood best, I think, as the third period of the postwar era. The first, which spanned two decades, began with the Soviet takeover of Eastern Europe and the subsequent creation of NATO and ended at some point in the late 1960s—probably at that moment in early 1968 when the establishment that had guided American foreign policy throughout the postwar era turned against our involvement in Vietnam. This first period has been called, for want of a better term, the period of the cold war.

Some critics of American foreign policy look back with dread and regret on the "dark years of the cold war" and express a morbid fear lest we reenter such a period. I must say that I have reservations about this view. In the context of the twentieth century, a century filled with horrors on a scale quite literally unprecedented in human history, the years of the cold war were a relatively happy respite during which free societies and democratic institutions were unusually secure. The West was united, strong, and self-assured. The United States and the democratic ethos we espoused were ascendent everywhere in the world, if not everywhere triumphant.

The circumstances in which we found ourselves during those years encouraged the expression of our national penchant for optimism, vision, and leadership. We were strong, we were prosperous. No country or group of countries could compete on equal terms with us economically or could successfully challenge our military power. Moreover, the major trends also seemed hopeful. With our help, our wartime allies and our adversaries had recovered swiftly from the war and had firmly established themselves as stable and prosperous industrial democracies. In Africa and Asia, one country after another attained independence and looked forward to the prospect of democratic development in close cooperation with the West. And in the Soviet bloc itself a series of political cries in Eastern Europe—in Hungary, in Czechoslovakia—coupled with an ideological crisis brought on by Khrushchev's denunciation of Stalin's terror gave substance to the hope that communism might indeed mellow if only we showed sufficient patience and fortitude. While we felt under no compulsion to delude ourselves about the inherently antagonistic nature of communism, we were confident that the free world—which was not at that time bracketed in derogatory quotation marks—would ultimately prevail. . . .

The hopes and expectations of the postwar period, as we now remember, were finally destroyed by the protracted and bitterly disillusioning conflict in Vietnam and by a sequence of political, economic, and cultural shocks that polarized our society and shattered the confidence of our ruling elites. It is not necessary to review in detail this second period in the postwar era, which began with the full emergence of the New Left in the late 1960s and ended with the defeat of Jimmy Carter and the victory of Ronald Reagan in the last election. Let us simply recall the major points.

This period, which has euphemistically been called the era of détente, was marked by the relentless expansion of Soviet military and political power and a corresponding contraction of American military and political power. It was marked as well by the rise, in what came to be called the Third World, of dictators espousing anti-American and anti-Western ideologies and by the rise in Western Europe of tendencies favoring a neutralist position in world affairs. Not least, this same period saw the emergence of OPEC as a major economic power whose monopoly pricing introduced inflationary shocks throughout the world economy—most disastrously in the very

"Third World" countries that were presumably linked by experience and ideology with the fraternal oil-producing states.

Within the United States, an attitude of defeatism, self-doubt, self-denigration, and self-delusion—an attitude that Solzhenitsyn called "the spirit of Munich"—displaced what had been a distinctly American optimism about the world and our prospects as a nation. For a time the proponents of defeatism cultivated an air of superior optimism. We had, so it was said, liberated ourselves from the fear of communism and were therefore free to identify with the "forces of change" that were sweeping the world. According to this point of view, it was futile to try to resist these forces, and it was reckless to do so as well since the effort to hold back the tides of change would bring the wrath of the world down upon our heads. Far better, it was said, to adopt an attitude of equanimity toward what only appeared to be the decline of American power but was in fact, in this view, a process of mature adjustment to reality. Such an attitude, in the words of a top official of the last administration, was really "a sign of growing American maturity in a complex world."

The seizure of the hostages in Iran and the Soviet invasion of Afghanistan destroyed this attitude of determined equanimity as completely as the events of the late 1960s had destroyed the hopes of the first postwar period. Looked at from this perspective, the election of Ronald Reagan was a victory for those who rejected the idea of the inevitability of America's decline. In this respect, President Reagan's election was a watershed that marked the end to a period of retreat. Similarly, the president's inauguration—endowed with unique significance by the simultaneous release of our hostages, which closed out the most humiliating episode in our history—signaled a new beginning for America.

The new period we have now entered is, I believe, an exceedingly dangerous one—perhaps the most dangerous we have faced—and its outcome is far from clear. It is not only conceivable that an affluent and technologically advanced democratic civilization may succumb to one that is distinctly inferior in the wealth and well-being of its people. This has occurred more than once in history. The decisive factor in the rise and fall of nations is what Machiavelli called *virtu*, meaning vitality and a capacity for collective action. In the battle with totalitarianism, a free society has enormous advantages of which we are all well aware. But without the political will not merely to survive but to prevail, these advantages count for naught.

We have now entered a period when the moral and political will of our nation will be tested as never before. If I am hopeful that we can meet this test, it is because of the new situation that exists as a result of Ronald Reagan's victory in the last election, as well as because of the effective causes of that victory, and because certain changes in the world have created new opportunities for our country and its allies. Still, the challenges we must face are awesome, and it is by no means a foregone conclusion that we will prevail in the tests that lie ahead.

Probably no administration in American history faced problems of foreign policy as serious, as far-flung, and as difficult as those that confronted the government of Ronald Reagan when it assumed office last January. What are euphemistically termed East-West problems had spread and intensified, and so had those called (with equal oversimplification) North-South. Further, most of the intellectual tools we had used to approach world problems had proved inadequate and had to be discarded. The massive, unprecedented, unflagging Soviet military buildup had created what Soviet theoreticians describe as a "new world correlation of forces"—which, if it does not feature Soviet military superiority, unquestionably is characterized by rough parity. It is characterized, that is, by the end of U.S. and Western military superiority. . . .

Menacing as they have been, Soviet strength and aggressiveness are by no means the only important problems confronting the Reagan administration—though critics often accuse us of thinking so. North-South relations have also become more troubled.

In some of the less-developed countries, separatism and fundamentalism exacerbate the problems of nation building, making it more difficult to develop national identifications and political institutions, more difficult to maintain civic peace, stable boundaries, and regional order. In many of these countries low growth or no growth, soaring energy costs, and proliferating trade barriers frustrate dreams and plans, leaving bitterness in their wake.

It has been several decades since the expectation of progress was juxtaposed to the facts of stagnation and poverty. Resignation has given way to rage. The result is new demands, new reproaches, new rights claimed, new duties assigned, creating little growth but many hard feelings. The fact that a "right" to development has been promulgated during the past year at the United Nations creates no new economic growth; it does, however, lay the foundation for newly felt entitlements and resentments.

Bad as they are, the problems of Soviet expansion and the problems of instability and poverty in what even I have come at the United Nations to call the Third World are at least familiar, and both have been made more difficult still by the decline of American power. But what *really* complicates the policy problems of the Reagan administration is the obsolescence of the familiar theories that have been relied on to deal with the problems.

Just as the cold war and the accompanying doctrine of limited war succumbed to the Vietnam experience, several popular theories about Soviet goals and policies were similarly disproved by the Soviet invasion of Afghanistan—among them, the two doctrinal cornerstones of détente.

The first of these cornerstones was the expectation that the proliferation of economic and cultural ties and rewards would function as incentives to restrain Soviet expansion. The main concept behind détente was the "linkage" of the military, the economic, and the political. The idea, as explained by Henry Kissinger, was "to move forward on a very broad front on many issues" in order to create many "vested interests" on both sides. That was the theory. Under that theory, unprecedented incentives were developed; yet unprecedented aggression nonetheless occurred.

A second conceptual casualty of the Carter period was the theory that "weaker is stronger"—according to which U.S. military superiority constitutes a provocation, which stimulates countermeasures and overreaction by the Soviets, leading them to ever greater arms efforts. It followed, then, according to this argument, that U.S. "restraint" in military buildup would quiet Soviet suspicions and produce reciprocal restraint. One version of this theory—that arms, being provocative, cannot produce security—is still heard. But the basic argument that U.S. restraint in military buildup would be matched by Soviet restraint has been stilled, at least for the present, by the weight of recent experience.

A third, related popular theory—the stimulus-response, frustration-aggression theory—also has fallen victim to Soviet expansionism. According to this theory, the Soviet Union behaved aggressively because it was frustrated by a sense of insecurity deriving from its relative weakness, much as an adolescent may be provoked to rebellion by frustration deriving from a sense of impotence. The solution to aggressive behavior, then, this theory argued, lay in creating a feeling of security by eliminating the impotence.

These theories are all examples of the mirror image approach to international relations, which assumes that all "superpowers," indeed all powers, are alike in fundamental respects, that their basic motives are peaceable and decent, and that undesirable or "bad" behavior is simply a reaction to some prior condition. Thus Soviet leaders desire not superiority but parity, not conquest but security, not power but safety.

This approach is nearly irresistible to an age and to a society like ours, which regularly deny the existence of evil and explain away its manifestations as a response of the weak to the strong. As there are no bad boys, so there are no bad governments. It is only necessary, the theory argues, to change the environment in order to alter the behavior. These theories not only rest on erroneous assumptions, but also nourish a spurious sense that it is possible to control one's adversary merely by altering one's own behavior.

Because their key assumptions are rooted in popular conceptions of human psychology and behavior, these theories have widespread appeal. A massive Soviet buildup and expansionist policies on a global scale were required to break their power—even temporarily.

The intellectual situation vis-à-vis problems of development closely parallels that concerning East-West relations. The problems of the less-developed nations persist and have grown worse, but it was clear by 1980 that the theories that have guided U.S. policies were utterly inadequate to cope with those problems.

Since World War II, when most of the new nations came into being, things have not, generally speaking, moved onward and upward, fulfilling dreams of inevitable historical progress. Polities have not become stronger and more democratic, nor economies more productive, nor societies more egalitarian and participatory. Moreover, the methods that had been widely relied on failed to produce the expected or desired results. National ownership, central planning, altruistic social incentives were all once believed to be better suited to the communal spirit of the Third World. But they produced bureaucracy, stagnation, and decay instead of the anticipated economic development. Determinism, socialism, and utopianism have proved no better guides to development policy than the grand theories concerning "superpower" behavior proved in dealing with the Soviet Union. One important, I believe fundamental, reason that the foreign policy of the Reagan administration seems to many to lack a comprehensive doctrine is that this administration's policy is not postulated on these conventional assumptions. We have not postulated our policy on these conventional assumptions and theories because they have become depleted and been discarded. But if we have rejected those theories, where does that leave us? Where does it leave those of us who must devise policies and make decisions?

The answer, I believe, is that both our methods and policies must be more respectful of historical experience and more pragmatic— while never confusing historical method with historicism or pragmatism with lack of principle.

In dealing with development, for example, respect for history means taking care to note what kinds of policies have actually promoted development, growth, and increased affluence in real societies, what kinds of policies have been associated with stagnation and chaos. In dealing with Soviet and Cuban behavior, we should also begin with the facts: facts of 85,000 Soviet troops in Afghanistan, of more than 35,000 Cuban troops in Africa, of Cuban arms, advisers, and ambitions in the Middle East and Central America, the fact of SS-20s in Europe, the fact that Soviet and Cuban armies function today in Ethiopia, Angola, Yemen, and elsewhere much like the Roman legions, which maintained the rule of a distant imperial power.

Finally, a new foreign policy must begin from the equally important, irreducible fact that the Soviet empire is decaying at its center, challenged above all by Poland's insistent demands for greater freedom and autonomy, and from the fact of the exhaustion of Marxism as an ideology capable of motivating men and women. Above all, perhaps, a new foreign policy must begin from the irreducible fact that the United States has nonnegotiable goals and non-negotiable moral commitments—and that these require our support for self-determination and for national independence, for the nurturing of regional order, for the protection of freedom wherever it exists and, within the limits of our power, skill, and opportunities, its promotion where it does not yet exist. . . .

RONALD REAGAN, ADDRESS TO THE BRITISH PARLIAMENT (1982)

This address reflects President Reagan's understanding of America's global responsibility during the final phase of the Cold War. He shared President Carter's optimism about the future of human liberty and the coming demise of communism. But he also made it clear that liberty's future depended upon America's and the West's resolve and military strength.

. . . America's time as a player on the stage of world history has been brief. I think understanding this fact has always made you patient with your younger cousins. Well, not always patient. I do recall that on one occasion Sir Winston Churchill said in exasperation about one of our most distinguished diplomats, "He is the only case I know of a bull who carries his china shop with him."

Witty as Sir Winston was, he also had that special attribute of great statesmen: the gift of vision, the willingness to see the future based on the experience of the past.

It is this sense of history, this understanding of the past, that I want to talk with you about today, for it is in remembering what we share of the past that our two nations can make common cause for the future.

We have not inherited an easy world. If developments like the Industrial Revolution, which began here in England, and the gifts of science and technology have made life much easier for us, they have also made it more dangerous. There are threats now to our freedom, indeed, to our very existence, that other generations could never even have imagined.

There is, first, the threat of global war. No President, no Congress, no Prime Minister, no Parliament, can spend a day entirely free of this threat. And I don't have to tell you that in today's world, the existence of nuclear weapons could mean, if not the extinction of mankind, then surely the end of civilization as we know it.

That is why negotiations of intermediate range nuclear forces now under way in Europe and the Start talks—Strategic Arms Reduction Talks—which will begin later this month, are not just critical to American or Western policy; they are critical to mankind. Our commitment to early success in these negotiations is firm and unshakable and our purpose is clear: reducing the risk of war by reducing the means of waging war on both sides.

At the same time, there is a threat posed to human freedom by the enormous power of the modern state. History teaches the danger of government that overreaches: political control takes precedence over free economic growth; secret police, mindless bureaucracy—all combining to stifle individual excellence and personal freedom.

Now I am aware that among us here and throughout Europe there is legitimate disagreement over the extent to which the public sector should play a role in a nation's economy and life. But on one point all of us are united: our abhorrence of dictatorship in all its forms but most particularly totalitarianism and the terrible inhumanities it has caused in our time: the great purge, Auschwitz and Dachau, the Gulag and Cambodia.

Historians looking back at our time will note the consistent restraint and peaceful intentions of the West. They will note that it was the democracies who refused to use the threat of their nuclear monopoly in the 40's and early 50's for territorial or imperial gain. Had that nuclear monopoly been in the hands of the Communist world, the map of Europe, indeed, the world, would look very different today. And certainly they will note it was not the democracies that invaded Afghanistan or suppressed Polish Solidarity or used chemical and toxin warfare in Afghanistan or Southeast Asia.

If history teaches anything, it teaches [that] self-delusion in the face of unpleasant facts is folly. We see around us today the marks of our terrible dilemma—predictions of doomsday, antinuclear demonstrations, an arms race in which the West must for its own protection be an unwilling participant. At the same time, we see totalitarian forces in the world who seek subversion and conflict around the globe to further their barbarous assault on the human spirit.

What, then, is our course? Must civilization perish—in a hail of fiery atoms? Must freedom wither—in a quiet, deadening accommodation with totalitarian evil? Sir Winston Churchill refused to accept the inevitability of war or even that it was imminent. He said: "I do not believe that Soviet Russia desires war. What they desire is the fruits of war and the indefinite expansion of their power and doctrines. But what we have to consider here today while time remains, is the permanent prevention of war and the establishment of conditions of freedom and democracy as rapidly as possible in all countries."

This is precisely our mission today: to preserve freedom as well as peace. It may not be easy to see, but I believe we live now at a turning point.

In an ironic sense, Karl Marx was right. We are witnessing today a great revolutionary crisis—a crisis where the demands of the economic order are colliding directly with those of the political order. But the crisis is happening not in the free, non-Marxist West, but in the home of Marxism-Leninism, the Soviet Union.

It is the Soviet Union that runs against the tide of history by denying freedom and human dignity to its citizens. It also is in deep economic difficulty. The rate of growth in the Soviet gross national product has been steadily declining since the 50's and is less than half of what it was then. The dimensions of this failure are astounding; a country which employs one-fifth of its population in agriculture is unable to feed its own people.

Were it not for the tiny private sector tolerated in Soviet agriculture, the country might be on the brink of famine. These private plots occupy a bare 3 percent of the arable land but account for nearly one-quarter of Soviet farm output and nearly one-third of meat products and vegetables.

Overcentralized, with little or no incentives, year after year the Soviet system pours its best resources into the making of instruments of destruction. The constant shrinkage of economic growth combined with the growth of military production is putting a heavy strain on the Soviet people.

What we see here is a political structure that no longer corresponds to its economic base, a society where productive forces are hampered by political ones.

The decay of the Soviet experiment should come as no surprise to us. Wherever the comparisons have been made between free and closed societies—West Germany and East Germany, Austria and Czechoslovakia, Malaysia and Vietnam—it is the democratic countries that are prosperous and responsive to the needs of their people.

And one of the simple but overwhelming facts of our time is this: of all the millions of refugees we have seen in the modern world, their flight is always away from, not toward, the Communist world. Today on the NATO line, our military forces face east to prevent a possible invasion. On the other side of the line the Soviet forces also face east—to prevent their people from leaving.

The hard evidence of totalitarian rule has caused in mankind an uprising of the intellect and will. Whether it is the growth of the new schools of economics in America or England or the appearance of the so-called new philosophers in France, there is one unifying thread running through the intellectual work of these groups: rejection of the arbitrary power of the state, the refusal to subordinate the rights of the individual to the superstate, the realization that collectivism stifles all the best human impulses.

Since the Exodus from Egypt, historians have written of those who sacrificed and struggled for freedom: the stand at Thermopylae, the revolt of Spartacus, the storming of the Bastille, the Warsaw uprising in World War II.

More recently we have seen evidence of this same human impulse in one of the developing nations in Central America. For months and months the world news media covered the fighting in El Salvador. Day after day, we were treated to stories and film slanted toward the brave freedom fighters battling oppressive Government forces on behalf of the silent, suffering people of that tortured country. . . .

. . . Around the world today, the democratic revolution is gathering new strength. In India, a critical test has been passed with the peaceful change of governing political parties. In Africa, Nigeria is moving in remarkable and unmistakable ways to build and strengthen its democratic institutions. In the Caribbean and Central America, 16 of 24 countries have freely elected governments. And in the United Nations 8 of 10 developing nations which have joined the body in the past five years are democracies.

In the Communist world as well, man's instinctive desire for freedom and self-determination surfaces again and again. To be sure, there are grim reminders of how brutally the police state attempts to snuff out this quest for self-rule: 1953 in East Germany, 1956 in Hungary, 1968 in Czechoslovakia, 1981 in Poland.

But the struggle continues in Poland, and we know there are even those who strive and suffer for freedom within the confines of the Soviet Union itself. How we conduct ourselves here in the Western democracies will determine whether this trend continues.

No, democracy is not a fragile flower; still it needs cultivating. If the rest of this century is to witness the gradual growth of freedom and democratic ideals, we must take actions to assist the campaign for democracy.

Some argue that we should encourage democratic change in right-wing dictatorships, but not in Communist regimes. To accept this preposterous notion—some well-meaning people have—is to invite the argument that, once countries achieve a nuclear capability, they should be allowed an undisturbed reign of terror over their own citizens. We reject this course.

As for the Soviet view, Chairman Brezhnev repeatedly has stressed that the competition of ideas and systems must continue and that this is entirely consistent with relaxation of tension and peace. We ask only that these systems begin by living up to their own constitutions, abiding by their own laws and complying with the international obligations they have undertaken. We ask only for a process, a direction, a basic code of decency—not for instant transformation.

We cannot ignore the fact that even without our encouragement, there have been and will continue to be repeated explosions against repression in dictatorships. The Soviet Union itself is not immune to this reality. Any system is inherently unstable that has no peaceful means to legitimize its leaders. In such cases, the very repressiveness of the state ultimately drives people to resist it—if necessary, by force.

While we must be cautious about forcing the pace of change, we must not hesitate to clear our ultimate objectives and to take concrete actions to move toward them. We must be staunch in our conviction that freedom is not the sole prerogative of a lucky few but the inalienable and universal right of all human beings. So states the United Nations' Universal Declaration of Human Rights—which, among other things, guarantees free elections.

The objective I propose is quite simple to state: To foster the infrastructure of democracy—the system of a free press, unions, political parties, universities—which allows a people to choose their own way, to develop their own culture, to reconcile their own differences through peaceful means.

This is not cultural imperialism; it is providing the means for genuine self-determination and protection for diversity. Democracy already flourishes in countries with very different cultures and historical experiences. It would be cultural condescension, or worse, to say that any people prefer dictatorship to democracy. . . .

I do not wish to sound overly optimistic, yet the Soviet Union is not immune from the reality of what is going on in the world. It has happened in the past: a small ruling elite either mistakenly attempts to ease domestic unrest through greater repression and foreign adventure or it chooses a wiser course—it begins to allow its people a voice in their own destiny.

Even if this latter process is not realized soon, I believe the renewed strength of the democratic movement, complemented by a global campaign for freedom, will strengthen the prospects for arms control and world at peace.

I have discussed on other occasions, including my address on May 9, the elements of Western politics toward the Soviet Union to safeguard our interests and protect the peace. What I am describing now is a plan and a hope for the long term—the march of freedom and democracy which will leave Marxism-Leninism on the ash heap of history as it has left other tyrannies which stifle the freedom and muzzle the self-expression of the people.

That is why we must continue our efforts to strengthen NATO even as we move forward with our zero-option initiative in the negotiations on intermediate range forces and our proposal for a one-third reduction in strategic ballistic missile warheads.

Our military strength is a prerequisite to peace, but let it be clear we maintain this strength in the hope it will never be used. For the ultimate determinant in the struggle now going on for the world will not be bombs and rockets but a test of wills and ideas—a trial of spiritual resolve: the values we hold, the beliefs we cherish, the ideals to which we are dedicated.

The British people know that, given strong leadership, time and a little bit of hope, the forces of good ultimately rally and triumph over evil. Here among you is the cradle of self-government, the mother of parliaments. Here is the enduring greatness of the British contribution to mankind, the great civilized ideas: individual liberty, representative government and the rule of law under God.
. . .

MALCOLM WALLOP, DEFENSE POLICY AFTER THE COLD WAR (1992)

Wallop served as a Republican senator from Wyoming from 1977 to 1995. He was known as a confident and aggressive proponent of a strong national defense. In these remarks made on the Senate floor, he argues that post-Cold War defense policy should be determined by the American national security and global interests, and not by budgetary considerations.

None of the congressional plans for reducing the defense budget below the Administration's request adequately supports a coherent concept of American global interests and a realistic assessment of what it will take to protect and project those interests in the years ahead.

The policy of containment, codified in 1950 in the historical document NSC-68, guided U.S. strategy and military policy for 40 years. Although U.S. defense spending and military strategy were far from constant during these four decades, the framework of American policy remained intact. This policy structure has not been abandoned as the Cold War moves into the pages of history, but its replacement has yet to emerge. In fact, it is difficult to avoid the conclusion that the Administration feels no need for such a new doctrine. In practical terms, however, until the American people recognize and accept containment's successor, there can be no agreement on strategy, force sizing and defense spending. Strategy in a policy vacuum cannot provide the unifying force that we now so desperately need.

This is not to say that debate is inappropriate. But if this debate focuses solely on budget bottom lines, as it has to date, then we are destined to make monumental decisions this year with our eyes firmly shut. Before we can make informed decisions on the defense budget, we must first answer two fundamental questions: Should America remain a superpower? And, can America afford to remain a superpower?

The end of the Cold War and the collapse of the Soviet Union leaves the United States as the sole remaining superpower. Although the existence of this situation is beyond dispute, there is less consensus as to the desirability of maintaining this status.

Before answers can be found, we must first consider what options are available. Three general alternatives are evident. The United States can seek to preserve its superpower status; it can attempt to foster a multipolar situation in which we are but one among several relatively equal power centers; or it can, as both the right and left suggest, lapse into isolationism and relative decline in the global balance of power.

Although few Americans openly endorse a policy of military inferiority for the United States, many of the isolationist arguments for slashing the defense budget, if implemented, could very well produce this outcome. Those who argue that U.S. foreign policy should focus exclusively on trade and other economic endeavors fail to grasp even the most basic tenets of geopolitics and international relations. Trade and foreign policy without the backing of military strength is nothing more than an extended hand begging for fair treatment. Without a global military presence and the ability to project power, America's maritime lifeline cannot be guaranteed and our ability to influence global events will disappear.

Because of the increasingly interdependent nature of the world economy, and the global reach of communications and military technology, the global presence of U.S. military power has become more important than ever. To those who assert that there is no threat to U.S. national security interests, I respond that with the world having become a smaller place, it has also become a more dangerous place—dangerous in a different perspective. In this world, even third-rate military powers will be able to threaten American cities with sudden and massive destruction. Terrorism by strategic weaponry is a real possibility. With America's economic vitality increasingly dependent upon things and events external to our borders, we cannot afford to turn our backs on the world. History is replete with examples—ancient and modern—of when nations took for granted the peace for which they had struggled long and hard. Without exception, the price for such complacency has been too high.

If it can be agreed that isolationism and military inferiority are not in the American interest, we must still decide whether to remain a superpower or reduce our global commitment to some level of military parity. If the latter course is chosen, the obvious question remains: Equal to what? Russia, the European Community, Argentina?

For decades, we have struggled merely to maintain a semblance of parity with the Soviet Union, and even this effort was decried by some as provocative. These same voices are now insisting that we abandon the military superiority that we have gained through winning the Cold War. Let us be honest. Those who ridicule the defense planning guidance as an attempt to create a Pax Americana are merely displaying their traditional discomfort with American military status. After all, the Pentagon plan does not advocate an increase in American military capability. It seeks only to preserve the advantages Americans have paid for. In fact, it actually calls for a sizeable reduction in American military capabilities—more than a 25 percent reduction in force structure and defense spending by 1997.

But those who seek to preserve U.S. military superiority must still answer the question: Why not equal? To put this question in perspective, we must acknowledge that those who advocate military parity for the United States are themselves the ones recommending a change in the U.S. posture. To reach equality will require that we step down from a position we now hold. Even if American withdrawal from the world scene were only partial, it does not require much imagination to see that a vacuum would be left. As in the rest of nature, in the realm of politico-military affairs, vacuums are inevitably filled.

Why not simply rely on the United Nations or some other form of collective security to fill this vacuum? The answer is simple. Without U.S. military and political leadership, collective security is nothing but a dream.

We could not have achieved the collective security to go to Iraq without the fact that we were, in the first place, strong enough to do it on our own, had that been necessary.

Preserving American military strength and global reach is essential if we as a Nation are going to continue to attract allies. America's superpower status is a stabilizing magnet holding together our alliances and the ad hoc collective security arrangements that we will undoubtedly need in the future. Without this guiding and unifying force, international power will once again fracture, generating competition and conflict.

If the United States does not remain engaged in Europe, Asia and throughout the world, we will simply be inviting the kind of balance of power struggles that plagued Europe for centuries. History has not come to an end and the sources of conflict have not been eliminated.

There are seven wars currently engaged in on the European and mid-Asian continent today.

Even in Europe, the guns that went silent in 1945 can once again be heard. Economic integration and the spread of democracy provide a stabilizing force in the world, but nationalism, militarism and jealousies of every dimension remain. The reemergence of an expansionist power driven by a hostile ideology cannot be dismissed. As Charles De Gaulle said, "The future lasts a long time."

The world recognizes the U.S. military power as a force of freedom and stability. In fact, the United States is the one power in the world whose superpower status would not be viewed with mistrust. We seek no territory of domination; our power is benign and stabilizing and is recognized as such. Only aggressive and expansionist powers need fear American leadership and military strength.

Yes, a soaring Federal deficit, an economy lingering in recession and numerous domestic ills are not matters to be taken lightly. But slashing defense will not solve these problems and may actually exacerbate them in the near term by adding to unemployment, by undermining a weak economic recovery and by reducing American technological competitiveness.

Even under the Administration's current plan, some two million jobs, both in DOD [Department of Defense] and the private sector, will be lost by 1996. If the defense budget is cut by another $100 billion, as some of my colleagues have proposed, as many as 3.3 million jobs could be lost.

It is thus clear that defense cuts cannot be rationalized as a means of solving near-term domestic problems. Defense is already being reduced at a dramatic rate. In fact, the defense budget has been declining in real terms since 1985. According to the Administration's budget plan, by Fiscal Year 1997, defense outlays will fall to 3.4 percent of GNP and about 16 percent of Federal outlays, a cumulative decline in outlays of 26 percent since Fiscal Year 1985. During this same period, domestic entitlements will grow by about 33 percent and domestic discretionary outlays will increase by about 8 percent.

By 1997, the level of defense expenditure will have declined to a level reminiscent of the 1930s, a time when the United States was not even a superpower. And as history reveals, our retreat from international responsibilities during the 1930s contributed to the emergence of militaristic states in Europe and the Pacific seeking to fill the power vacuums they encountered.

Can we afford not to remain a superpower? The price of retreat is not in firewalls, and it is not peace dividends, but it is hugely expensive in the refire of a military engine. Worse than that, the price of retreat is paid in American blood, and it is easily shucked out of sight in a debate like this and at a moment like this.

But ask any American whether he wants to see our country a beggar on the world stage for security. Ask any American if he wishes to see us dependent on somebody else for our access to the seas, for the support of our allies, for the support of our communications, for our access to space, and that American will tell the senator "no."

RICHARD NIXON, *BEYOND PEACE* (1994)

Nixon, the only president to resign rather than be impeached, spent his post-presidential years attempting to restore his reputation, largely through his prolific and astute analyses of contemporary affairs. The excerpt below comes from his last book, Beyond Peace, *completed shortly before his death in 1994.*

There are those who now argue that communism was never a real threat and that our efforts in the Cold War were unnecessary, even wasteful, since the Soviet Union would have collapsed anyway as a result of its internal contradictions and its failure to fulfill the boast that it would overtake capitalism. By 1986, when I first met with Mikhail Gorbachev, twenty-seven years after my "kitchen debate" with Khrushchev, the question had become not when the Soviet Union would overtake us but whether it would survive at all without drastic economic reforms. Had we done nothing, the argument goes, the results of the Cold War would have been exactly the same.

It is true that communism would eventually have collapsed, because it was and remains a false faith. Talking about Russian people, John Foster Dulles presciently observed forty years ago, "People who understand the intricacies of the atom will eventually see the fatal flaws in communism." As history demonstrates, evil ideas inevitably fail because they are fundamentally at odds with human nature, but until they fail, they can do enormous damage to humanity. Evil regimes have prevailed for long periods of time and have won significant victories. Ultimately, however, unless they expand, they will die. In the Cold War, the United States and the West blocked the expansion of the idea of communism. Our active resistance to communist aggression, and the weapons of economic power we brought to bear on the communist regimes, ensured that communism would be defeated years, perhaps decades, before it would have collapsed on its own.

Our efforts during the Cold War prevented communism from spreading into Western Europe and also blunted its expansion in what was then called the Third World, particularly in Afghanistan, the only Third World nation where the Red Army committed its forces. The much-maligned military buildup under President Reagan placed enormous strains on the Soviet system to compete, which it ultimately could not do. That program, as well as the efforts of all the Cold War Presidents from Truman to Bush, prevented Soviet communism from making further gains and thus hastened its collapse. In doing so we saved millions from misery and tyranny.

We and our allies can be proud of our role in the Cold War. But the defeat of communism was a double-edged sword. Surveying the carnage in the aftermath of the Battle of Waterloo in 1815, where fifty thousand men fell in one day, Wellington said that there was "only one thing worse than winning a battle, and that was losing it." Historically there is always a period of exhaustion after a military victory. Victory in the Cold War was not just military. It was a complex ideological, political, and economic triumph. Our exhaustion is therefore felt in all of these dimensions simultaneously.

Throughout the Cold War, we looked forward to a time when we might live in a peaceful world, with harmonious international relations, prosperous economies reaping the benefits of unlimited global trade, the expansion of freedom and human rights, and the opportunity to enjoy life. These promises of peace crystallized into an idealized vision of a post-Cold War future. The fact that it has not been realized has produced a pervasive, enervating sense of anticlimax. The reality of peace is that it is only the foundation upon which a more prosperous and just world can be built. This effort will require just as much determination, vision, and patience as the defeat of communism required.

Yet a potentially devastating fallout of our post-Cold War letdown is that the American people have grown tired of world leadership. They were reluctant to have it thrust upon them in the first place. At a dinner I gave for him shortly before I went to China in 1972, Andre Malraux observed that the United States is the first nation in history to become a world power without trying to become one. We are essentially isolationist and become involved in foreign conflicts not simply when our interests are at stake but when we also believe we are engaged in a great idealistic cause.

Following World War II, the United States abandoned its traditional peacetime isolationism to wage the Cold War against communism around the world. We did so because we believed we were engaged in an ideological conflict with profound moral consequences. Many now believe that it is time for others to carry the burden of leadership abroad and that we should turn our attention and resources to our problems at home. This was candidate Clinton's major theme and the primary reason President Bush, a foreign policy expert, lost the election of 1992.

Most Americans thought that our victory in the Cold War, with its peace dividend, would help us solve our domestic problems. The opposite has occurred. The end of the Cold War has exacerbated our problems at home. Foreign challenges unite us. Domestic challenges divide us. What we must realize is that domestic and foreign policies are like Siamese twins—one cannot survive without the other. The American people will not support a strong foreign policy unless we have a strong economy at home. Conversely, a weak economy, as we learned in the thirties, almost inevitably leads to a weak foreign policy—with potentially devastating consequences. It is no accident that fascists rose to power in a Europe stricken by a depression aggravated by our shortsighted trade policies. Periods of prolonged peace are generally periods of stagnation. No one would say that war is good for a country, but it is undeniable that the United States has been at its best when confronted with aggression or some other significant international challenge (our space effort after the shock of Sputnik is a case in point). Most of our greatest Presidents were war Presidents. Our greatest bursts of increased productivity and scientific advancement have occurred during war. To meet the challenges we face in the post-Cold War era, we must marshal the same resources of energy, optimism, and common purpose that thrive during war and put them to work at home and abroad during an era when our enemy will be neither communism not Nazism but our own self-defeating pessimism.

Charles de Gaulle once said, "France was never her true self unless she was engaged in a great enterprise." This is true of the United States as well. Great causes push us to heights, as a nation and as individuals, that would not otherwise be achieved. Without a great cause to galvanize America, the very unity of our nation will be at risk as we struggle to meet the challenges of the coming century.

If America is to remain a great nation, what we need today is a mission beyond peace.

Appendix

The Constitution of the United States of America

We, the People of the United States, in order to form a more perfect union, establish justice, insure domestic tranquility, provide for the common defence, promote the general welfare, and secure the blessings of liberty to ourselves and our posterity, do ordain and establish this Constitution for the United States of America.

ARTICLE I

Section 1

All legislative powers herein granted shall be vested in a Congress of the United States, which shall consist of a Senate and House of Representatives.

Section 2

The House of Representatives shall be composed of members chosen every second year by the people of the several states, and the electors in each state shall have the qualifications requisite for electors of the most numerous branch of the state legislature.

No person shall be a representative who shall not have attained to the age of twenty-five years, and been seven years a citizen of the United States, and who shall not, when elected, be an inhabitant of that state in which he shall be chosen.

Representatives and direct taxes shall be apportioned among the several states which may be included within this Union, according to their respective numbers, which shall be determined by adding to the whole number of free persons, including those bound to service for a term of years, and excluding Indians not taxed, three-fifths of all other persons. The actual enumeration shall be made within three years after the first meeting of the Congress of the United States, and within every subsequent term of ten years, in such manner as they shall by law direct. The number of representatives shall not exceed one for every thirty thousand, but each state shall have at least one representative; and until such enumeration shall be made, the state of New-Hampshire shall be entitled to chuse three, Massachusetts eight, Rhode-Island and Providence Plantations one, Connecticut five, New-York six, New-Jersey four, Pennsylvania eight, Delaware one, Maryland six, Virginia ten, North-Carolina five, South-Carolina five, and Georgia three.

When vacancies happen in the representation from any state, the Executive authority thereof shall issue writs of election to fill such vacancies.

The House of Representative shall chuse their Speaker and other officers; and shall have the sole power of impeachment.

Section 3

The Senate of the United States shall be composed of two senators from each state, chosen by the legislature thereof, for six years; and each senator shall have one vote.

Immediately after they shall be assembled in consequence of the first election, they shall be divided as equally as may be into three classes. The seats of the senators of the first class shall be vacated at the expiration of the second year, of the second class at the expiration of the fourth year, and of the third class at the expiration of the sixth year, so that one-third may be chosen every second year; and if vacancies happen by resignation, or otherwise, during the recess of the Legislature of any state, the Executive thereof may make temporary appointments until the next meeting of the Legislature, which shall then fill such vacancies.

No person shall be a senator who shall not have attained to the age of thirty years, and been nine years a citizen of the United States, and who shall not, when elected, be an inhabitant of that state for which he shall be chosen.

The Vice-President of the United States shall be President of the senate, but shall have no vote, unless they be equally divided.

The Senate shall chuse their other officers, and also a President pro tempore, in the absence of the Vice-President, or when he shall exercise the office of President of the United States.

The Senate shall have the sole power to try all impeachments. When sitting for that purpose, they shall be on oath or affirmation. When the President of the United States is tried, the Chief Justice shall preside: And no person shall be convicted without the concurrence of two-thirds of the members present.

Judgment in cases of impeachment shall not extend further than to removal from office, and disqualification to hold and enjoy any office of honor, trust or profit under the United States; but the party convicted shall nevertheless be liable and subject to indictment, trial, judgment and punishment, according to law.

Section 4

The times, places and manner of holding elections for senators and representatives, shall be prescribed in each state by the legislature thereof; but the Congress may at any time by law make or alter such regulations, except as to the places of chusing Senators.

The Congress shall assemble at least once in every year, and such meeting shall be on the first Monday in December, unless they shall by law appoint a different day.

Section 5

Each house shall be the judge of the elections, returns and qualifications of its own members, and a majority of each shall constitute a quorum to do business; but a smaller number may adjourn from day to day, and may be authorized to compel the attendance of absent members, in such manner, and under such penalties as each house may provide.

Each house may determine the rules of its proceedings, punish its members for disorderly behaviour, and, with the concurrence of two-thirds, expel a member.

Each house shall keep a journal of its proceedings, and from time to time publish the same, excepting such parts as may in their judgment require secrecy; and the yeas and nays of the members of either house on any question shall, at the desire of one-fifth of those present, be entered on the journal.

Neither house, during the session of Congress, shall, without the consent of the other, adjourn for more than three days, nor to any other place than that in which the two houses shall be sitting.

Section 6

The senators and representatives shall receive a compensation for their services, to be ascertained by law, and paid out of the treasury of the United States. They shall in all cases, except treason, felony and breach of the peace, be privileged from arrest during their attendance at the session of their respective houses, and in going to and returning from the same; and for any speech or debate in either house, they shall not be questioned in any other place.

No senator or representative shall, during the time for which he was elected, be appointed to any civil office under the authority of the United States, which shall have been created, or the emoluments whereof shall have been encreased during such time; and no person holding any office under the United States, shall be a member of either house during his continuance in office.

Section 7

All bills for raising revenue shall originate in the house of representatives; but the senate may propose or concur with amendments as on other bills.

Every bill which shall have passed the house of representatives and the senate, shall, before it become a law, be presented to the president of the United States; if he approve he shall sign it, but if not he shall return it, with his objections to that house in which it shall have originated, who shall enter the objections at large on their journal, and proceed to reconsider it. If after such reconsideration two-thirds of that house shall agree to pass the bill, it shall be sent, together with the objections, to the other house, by which it shall likewise be reconsidered, and if approved by two-thirds of that house, it shall become a law. But in all such cases the votes of both houses shall be determined by yeas and nays, and the names of the persons voting for and against the bill shall be entered on the journal of each house respectively. If any bill shall not be returned by the President within ten days (Sundays excepted) after it shall have been presented to him, the same shall be a law, in like manner as if he had signed it, unless the Congress by their adjournment prevent its return, in which case it shall not be a law.

Every order, resolution, or vote to which the concurrence of the Senate and House of Representatives may be necessary (except on a question of adjournment) shall be presented to the President of the United States; and before the same shall take effect, shall be approved by him, or, being disapproved by him, shall be repassed by two-thirds of the Senate and House of Representatives, according to the rules and limitations prescribed in the case of a bill.

Section 8

The Congress shall have power

To lay and collect taxes, duties, imposts and excises, to pay the debts and provide for the common defence and general welfare of the United States; but all duties, imposts and excises shall be uniform throughout the United States;

To borrow money on the credit of the United States;

To regulate commerce with foreign nations, and among the several states, and with the Indian tribes;

To establish an uniform rule of naturalization, and uniform laws on the subject of bankruptcies throughout the United States;

To coin money, regulate the value thereof, and of foreign coin, and fix the standard of weights and measures;

To provide for the punishment of counterfeiting the securities and current coin of the United States;

To establish post offices and post roads;

To promote the progress of science and useful arts, by securing for limited times to authors and inventors the exclusive right to their respective writings and discoveries;

To constitute tribunals inferior to the supreme court;

To define and punish piracies and felonies committed on the high seas, and offences against the law of nations;

To declare war, grant letters of marque and reprisal, and make rules concerning captures on land and water;

To raise and support armies, but no appropriation of money to that use shall be for a longer term than two years;

To provide and maintain a navy;

To make rules for the government and regulation of the land and naval forces;

To provide for calling forth the militia to execute the laws of the union, suppress insurrections and repel invasions;

To provide for organizing, arming, and disciplining, the militia, and for governing such part of them as may be employed in the service of the United States, reserving to the States respectively, the appointment of the officers, and the authority of training the militia according to the discipline prescribed by Congress;

To exercise exclusive legislation in all cases whatsoever, over such district (not exceeding ten miles square) as may, by cession of particular States, and the acceptance of Congress, become the seat of the government of the United States, and to exercise like authority over all places purchased by the consent of the legislature of the state in which the same shall be, for the erection of forts, magazines, arsenals, dock-yards, and other needful buildings;—And

To make all laws which shall be necessary and proper for carrying into execution the foregoing powers, and all other powers vested by this constitution in the government of the United States, or in any department or officer thereof.

Section 9

The migration or importation of such persons as any of the states now existing shall think proper to admit, shall not be prohibited by the Congress prior to the year one thousand eight hundred and eight, but a tax or duty may be imposed on such importation, not exceeding ten dollars for each person.

The privilege of the writ of habeas corpus shall not be suspended, unless when in cases of rebellion or invasion the public safety may require it.

No bill of attainder or ex post facto law shall be passed.

No capitation, or other direct, tax shall be laid, unless in proportion to the census or enumeration herein before directed to be taken.

No tax or duty shall be laid on articles exported from any state. No preference shall be given by any regulation of commerce or revenue to the ports of one state over those of another: nor shall vessels bound to, or from, one state, be obliged to enter, clear, or pay duties in another.

No money shall be drawn from the treasury, but in consequence of appropriations made by law; and a regular statement and account of the receipts and expenditures of all public money shall be published from time to time.

No title of nobility shall be granted by the United States:—And no person holding any office of profit or trust under them, shall, without the consent of the Congress, accept of any present, emolument, office, or title, of any kind whatever, from any king, prince, or foreign state.

Section 10

No state shall enter into any treaty, alliance, or confederation; grant letters of marque and reprisal; coin money; emit bills of credit; make any thing but gold and silver coin a tender in payment of debts; pass any bill of attainder, ex post facto law, or law impairing the obligation of contracts, or grant any title of nobility.

No state shall, without the consent of the Congress, lay any imposts or duties on imports or exports, except what may be absolutely necessary for executing its inspection laws; and the net produce of all duties and imposts, laid by any state on imports or exports, shall be for the use of the Treasury of the United States; and all such laws shall be subject to the revision and controul of the Congress. No state shall, without the consent of Congress, lay any duty of tonnage, keep troops, or ships of war in time of peace, enter into any agreement or compact with another state, or with a foreign power, or engage in war, unless actually invaded, or in such imminent danger as will not admit of delay.

ARTICLE II

Section 1

The executive power shall be vested in a president of the United States of America. He shall hold his office during the term of four years, and, together with the vice-president, chosen for the same term, be elected as follows.

Each state shall appoint, in such manner as the legislature thereof may direct, a number of electors, equal to the whole number of senators and representatives to which the state may be entitled in the Congress: but no senator or representative, or person holding an office of trust or profit under the United States, shall be appointed an elector.

The electors shall meet in their respective states, and vote by ballot for two persons, of whom one at least shall not be an inhabitant of the same state with themselves. And they shall make a list of all the persons voted for, and of the number of votes for each; which list they shall sign and certify, and transmit sealed to the seat of the government of the United States, directed to the president of the senate. The president of the senate shall, in the presence of the senate and house of representatives, open all the certificates, and the votes shall then be counted. The person having the greatest number of votes shall be the president, if such number be a majority of the whole number of electors appointed; and if there be more than one who have such majority, and have an equal number of votes, then the house of representatives shall immediately chuse by ballot one of them for president; and if no person have a majority, then from the five highest on the list the said house shall in like manner chuse the president. But in chusing the president, the votes shall be taken by states, the representation from each state having one vote; a quorum for this purpose shall consist of a member or members from two-thirds of the states, and a majority of all the states shall be necessary to a choice. In every case, after the choice of the president, the person having the greatest number of votes of the electors shall be the vice-president. But if there should remain two or more who have equal votes, the senate shall chuse from them by ballot the vice-president.

The Congress may determine the time of chusing the electors, and the day on which they shall give their votes; which day shall be the same throughout the United States.

No person except a natural born citizen, or a citizen of the United States, at the time of the adoption of this constitution, shall be eligible to the office of president; neither shall any person be eligible to that office who shall not have attained to the age of thirty-five years, and been fourteen years a resident within the United States.

In case of the removal of the president from office, or of his death, resignation, or inability to discharge the powers and duties of the said office, the same shall devolve on the vice-president, and the Congress may by law provide for the case of removal, death, resignation or inability, both of the president and vice-president, declaring what officer shall then act as president, and such officer shall act accordingly, until the disability be removed, or a president shall be elected.

The president shall, at stated times, receive for his services, a compensation, which shall neither be encreased nor diminished during the period for which he shall have been elected, and he shall not receive within that period any other emolument from the United States, or any of them.

Before he enter on the execution of his office, he shall take the following oath or affirmation:—"I do solemnly swear (or affirm) that I will faithfully execute the office of president of the United States, and will to the best of my ability, preserve, protect and defend the constitution of the United States."

Section 2

The president shall be commander in chief of the army and navy of the United States, and of the militia of the several States, when called into the actual service of the United States; he may require the opinion, in writing, of the principal officer in each of the executive departments, upon any subject relating to the duties of their respective offices, and he shall have power to grant reprieves and pardons for offences against the United States, except in cases of impeachment.

He shall have power, by and with the advice and consent of the senate, to make treaties, provided two-thirds of the senators present concur; and he shall nominate, and by and with the advice and consent of the senate, shall appoint ambassadors, other public ministers and consuls, judges of the supreme court, and all other officers of the United States, whose appointments are not herein otherwise provided for, and which shall be established by law. But the Congress may by law vest the appointment of such inferior officers, as they think proper, in the president alone, in the courts of law, or in the heads of departments.

The president shall have power to fill up all vacancies that may happen during the recess of the senate, by granting commissions which shall expire at the end of their next session.

Section 3

He shall from time to time give to the Congress information of the state of the union, and recommend to their consideration such measures as he shall judge necessary and expedient; he may, on extraordinary occasions, convene both houses, or either of them, and in case of disagreement between them, with respect to the time of adjournment, he may adjourn them to such time as he shall think proper; he shall receive ambassadors and other public ministers; he shall take care that the laws be faithfully executed, and shall commission all the officers of the United States.

Section 4

The president, vice-president and all civil officers of the United States, shall be removed from office on impeachment for, and conviction of, treason, bribery, or other high crimes and misdemeanors.

ARTICLE III

Section 1

The judicial power of the United States, shall be vested in one supreme court, and in such inferior courts as the Congress may from time to time ordain and establish. The judges, both of the supreme and inferior courts, shall hold their offices during good behaviour, and shall, at stated times, receive for their services, a compensation, which shall not be diminished during their continuance in office.

Section 2

The judicial power shall extend to all cases, in law and equity, arising under this constitution, the laws of the United States, and treaties made, or which shall be made, under their authority;—to all cases affecting ambassadors, other public ministers and consuls; to all cases of admiralty and maritime jurisdiction; to controversies to which the United States shall be a party; to controversies between two or more States, between a state and citizens of another state, between citizens of different States, between citizens of the same state claiming lands under grants of different States, and between a state, or the citizens thereof, and foreign States, citizens or subjects.

In all cases affecting ambassadors, other public ministers and consuls, and those in which a state shall be party, the supreme court shall have original jurisdiction. In all the other cases before mentioned, the supreme court shall have appellate jurisdiction, both as to law and fact, with such exceptions, and under such regulations as the Congress shall make.

The trial of all crimes, except in cases of impeachment, shall be by jury; and such trial shall be held in the state where the said crimes shall have been committed; but when not committed within any state, the trial shall be at such place or places as the Congress may by law have directed.

Section 3

Treason against the United States, shall consist only in levying war against them, or in adhering to their enemies, giving them aid and comfort. No person shall be convicted of treason unless on the testimony of two witnesses to the same overt act, or on confession in open court.

The Congress shall have power to declare the punishment of treason, but no attainder of treason shall work corruption of blood, or forfeiture except during the life of the person attainted.

ARTICLE IV

Section 1

Full faith and credit shall be given in each state to the public acts, records, and judicial proceedings of every other state. And the Congress may by general laws prescribe the manner in which such acts, records and proceedings shall be proved, and the effect thereof.

Section 2

The citizens of each state shall be entitled to all privileges and immunities of citizens in the several states.

A person charged in any state with treason, felony, or other crime, who shall flee from justice, and be found in another state, shall, on demand of the executive authority of the state from which he fled, be delivered up, to be removed to the state having jurisdiction of the crime.

No person held to service or labour in one state, under the laws thereof, escaping into another, shall, in consequence of any law or regulation therein, be discharged from such service or labour, but shall be delivered up on claim of the party to whom such service or labour may be due.

Section 3

New states may be admitted by the Congress into this union; but no new state shall be formed or erected within the jurisdiction of any other state; nor any state be formed by the junction of two or more states, or parts of states, without the consent of the legislatures of the states concerned as well as of the Congress.

The Congress shall have power to dispose of and make all needful rules and regulations respecting the territory or other property belonging to the United States; and nothing in this Constitution shall be so construed as to prejudice any claims of the United States, or of any particular state.

Section 4

The United States shall guarantee to every state in this union a Republican form of government, and shall protect each of them against invasion; and on application of the legislature, or of the executive (when the legislature cannot be convened) against domestic violence.

ARTICLE V

The Congress, whenever two-thirds of both houses shall deem it necessary, shall propose amendments to this constitution, or, on the application of the legislatures of two-thirds of the several states, shall call a convention for proposing amendments, which, in either case, shall be valid to all intents and purposes, as part of this constitution, when ratified by the legislatures of three-fourths of the several states, or by conventions in three-fourths thereof, as the one or the other mode of ratification may be proposed by the Congress; Provided, that no amendment which may be made prior to the year one thousand eight hundred and eight shall in any manner affect the first and fourth clauses in the ninth section of the first article; and that no state, without its consent, shall be deprived of its equal suffrage in the senate.

ARTICLE VI

All debts contracted and engagements entered into, before the adoption of this Constitution, shall be as valid against the United States under this Constitution, as under the confederation.

This constitution, and the laws of the United States which shall be made in pursuance thereof; and all treaties made, or which shall be made, under the authority of the United States, shall be the supreme law of the land; and the judges in every state shall be bound thereby, any thing in the constitution or laws of any state to the contrary notwithstanding.

The senators and representatives beforementioned, and the members of the several state legislatures, and all executive and judicial officers, both of the United States and of the several States, shall be bound by oath or affirmation, to support this constitution; but no religious test shall ever be required as a qualification to any office or public trust under the United States.

ARTICLE VII

The ratification of the conventions of nine States, shall be sufficient for the establishment of this constitution between the States so ratifying the same.

Done in Convention, by the unanimous consent of the States present, the seventeenth day of September, in the year of our Lord one thousand seven hundred and eighty-seven, and of the Independence of the United States of America the twelfth. In witness whereof we have hereunto subscribed our Names.

AMENDMENT I [I-X adopted in 1791]

Congress shall make no law respecting an establishment of religion, or prohibiting the free exercise thereof; or abridging the freedom of speech, or of the press; or the right of the people peaceably to assemble, and to petition the Government for a redress of grievances.

AMENDMENT II

A well regulated Militia, being necessary to the security of a free State, the right of the people to keep and bear Arms, shall not be infringed.

AMENDMENT III

No Soldier shall, in time of peace be quartered in any house, without the consent of the Owner, nor in time of war, but in a manner to be prescribed by law.

AMENDMENT IV

The right of the people to be secure in their persons, houses, papers, and effects, against unreasonable searches and seizures, shall not be violated, and no Warrants shall issue, but upon probable cause, supported by Oath or affirmation, and particularly describing the place to be searched, and the persons or things to be seized.

AMENDMENT V

No person shall be held to answer for a capital, or otherwise infamous crime, unless on a presentment or indictment of a Grand Jury, except in cases arising in the land or naval forces, or in the Militia, when in actual service in time of War or public danger; nor shall any person be subject for the same offence to be twice put in jeopardy of life or limb; nor shall be compelled in any criminal case to be a witness against himself, nor be deprived of life, liberty, or property, without due process of law; nor shall private property be taken for public use, without just compensation.

AMENDMENT VI

In all criminal prosecutions, the accused shall enjoy the right to a speedy and public trial, by an impartial jury of the State and district wherein the crime shall have been committed, which district shall have been previously ascertained by law, and to be informed of the nature and cause of the accusation; to be confronted with the witnesses against him; to have compulsory process for obtaining witnesses in his favor, and to have the Assistance of Counsel for his defence.

AMENDMENT VII

In Suits at common law, where the value in controversy shall exceed twenty dollars, the right of trial by jury shall be preserved, and no fact tried by a jury, shall be otherwise re-examined in any Court of the United States, than according to the rules of the common law.

AMENDMENT VIII

Excessive bail shall not be required, nor excessive fines imposed, nor cruel and unusual punishments inflicted.

AMENDMENT IX

The enumeration in the Constitution, of certain rights, shall not be construed to deny or disparage others retained by the people.

AMENDMENT X

The powers not delegated to the United States by the Constitution, nor prohibited by it to the States, are reserved to the States respectively, or to the people.

AMENDMENT XI [1798]

The Judicial power of the United States shall not be construed to extend to any suit in law or equity, commenced or prosecuted against one of the United States by Citizens of another State, or by Citizens or Subjects of any Foreign State.

AMENDMENT XII [1804]

The Electors shall meet in their respective states, and vote by ballot for President and Vice-President, one of whom, at least, shall not be an inhabitant of the same state with themselves; they shall name in their ballots the person voted for as President, and in distinct ballots the person voted for as Vice-President, and they shall make distinct lists of all persons voted for as President, and of all persons voted for as Vice-President, and of the number of votes for each, which lists they shall sign and certify, and transmit sealed to the seat of the government of the United States, directed to the President of the Senate;—The President of the Senate shall, in the presence of the Senate and House of Representatives, open all the certificates and the votes shall then be counted;—The person having the greatest number of votes for President, shall be the President, if such number be a majority of the whole number of Electors appointed; and if no person have such majority, then from the persons having the highest numbers not exceeding three on the list of those voted for as President, the House of Representatives shall choose immediately, by ballot, the President. But in choosing the President, the votes shall be taken by states, the representation from each state having one vote; a quorum for this purpose shall consist of a member or members from two-thirds of the states, and a majority of all the states shall be necessary to a choice. And if the House of Representatives shall not choose a President whenever the right of choice shall devolve upon them, before the fourth day of March next following, then the Vice-President shall act as President, as in the case of the death or other constitutional disability of the President.—The person having the greatest number of votes as Vice-President, shall be the Vice-President, if such number be a majority of the whole number of Electors appointed, and if no person have a majority, then from the two highest numbers on the list, the Senate shall choose the Vice-President; a quorum for the purpose shall consist of two-thirds of the whole number of Senators, and a majority of the whole number shall be necessary to a choice. But no person constitutionally ineligible to the office of President shall be eligible to that of Vice-President of the United States.

AMENDMENT XIII [1865]

Section 1

Neither slavery nor involuntary servitude, except as a punishment for crime whereof the party shall have been duly convicted, shall exist within the United States, or any place subject to their jurisdiction.

Section 2

Congress shall have power to enforce this article by appropriate legislation.

AMENDMENT XIV [1868]

Section 1

All persons born or naturalized in the United States, and subject to the jurisdiction thereof, are citizens of the United States and of the State wherein they reside. No State shall make or enforce any law which shall abridge the privileges or immunities of citizens of the United States; nor shall any State deprive any person of life, liberty, or property, without due process of law; nor deny to any person within its jurisdiction the equal protection of the laws.

Section 2

Representatives shall be apportioned among the several States according to their respective numbers, counting the whole number of persons in each State, excluding Indians not taxed. But when the right to vote at any election for the choice of electors for President and Vice President of the United States, Representatives in Congress, the Executive and Judicial officers of a State, or the members of the Legislature thereof, is denied to any of the male inhabitants of such State, being twenty-one years of age, and citizens of the United States, or in any way abridged, except for participation in rebellion, or other crime, the basis of representation therein shall be reduced in the proportion which the number of such male citizens shall bear to the whole number of male citizens twenty-one years of age in such State.

Section 3

No person shall be a Senator or Representative in Congress, or elector of President and Vice President, or hold any office, civil or military, under the United States, or under any State, who, having previously taken an oath, as a member of Congress, or as an officer of the United States, or as a member of any State legislature, or as an executive or judicial officer of any State, to support the Constitution of the United States, shall have engaged in insurrection or rebellion against the same, or given aid or comfort to the enemies thereof. But Congress may by a vote of two-thirds of each House, remove such disability.

Section 4

The validity of the public debt of the United States, authorized by law, including debts incurred for payment of pensions and bounties for services in suppressing insurrection or rebellion, shall not be questioned. But neither the United States nor any State shall assume or pay any debt or obligation incurred in aid of insurrection or rebellion against the United States, or any claim for the loss or emancipation of any slave; but all such debts, obligations and claims shall be held illegal and void.

Section 5

The Congress shall have power to enforce, by appropriate legislation, the provisions of this article.

AMENDMENT XV [1870]

Section 1

The right of citizens of the United States to vote shall not be denied or abridged by the United States or by any State on account of race, color, or previous condition of servitude.

Section 2

The Congress shall have power to enforce this article by appropriate legislation.

AMENDMENT XVI [1913]

The Congress shall have power to lay and collect taxes on incomes, from whatever source derived, without apportionment among the several States, and without regard to any census or enumeration.

AMENDMENT XVII [1913]

The Senate of the United States shall be composed of two Senators from each State, elected by the people thereof, for six years; and each Senator shall have one vote. The electors in each State shall have the qualifications requisite for electors of the most numerous . branch of the State legislatures.

When vacancies happen in the representation of any State in the Senate, the executive authority of such State shall issue writs of election to fill such vacancies: *Provided*, That the legislature of any State may empower the executive thereof to make temporary appointments until the people fill the vacancies by election as the legislature may direct.

This amendment shall not be so construed as to affect the election or term of any Senator chosen before it becomes valid as part of the Constitution.

AMENDMENT XVIII [1919]

Section 1

After one year from the ratification of this article the manufacture, sale, or transportation of intoxicating liquors within, the importation thereof into, or the exportation thereof from the United States and all territory subject to the jurisdiction thereof for beverage purposes is hereby prohibited.

Section 2

The Congress and the several States shall have concurrent power to enforce this article by appropriate legislation.

Section 3

This article shall be inoperative unless it shall have been ratified as an amendment to the Constitution by the legislatures of the several States, as provided in the Constitution, within seven years from the date of the submission hereof to the States by the Congress.

AMENDMENT XIX [1920]

The right of citizens of the United States to vote shall not be denied or abridged by the United States or by any State on account of sex.

Congress shall have power to enforce this article by appropriate legislation.

AMENDMENT XX [1933]

Section 1

The terms of the President and Vice President shall end at noon on the 20th day of January, and the terms of Senators and Representatives at noon on the 3d day of January, of the years in which such terms would have ended if this article had not been ratified; and the terms of their successors shall then begin.

Section 2

The Congress shall assemble at least once in every year, and such meeting shall begin at noon on the 3d day of January, unless they shall by law appoint a different day.

Section 3

If, at the time fixed for the beginning of the term of the President, the President elect shall have died, the Vice President elect shall become President. If a President shall not have been chosen before the time fixed for the beginning of his term, or if the President elect shall have failed to qualify, then the Vice President elect shall act as President until a President shall have qualified; and the Congress may by law provide for the case wherein neither a President elect nor a Vice President elect shall have qualified, declaring who shall then act as President, or the manner in which one who is to act shall be selected, and such person shall act accordingly until a President or Vice President shall have qualified.

Section 4

The Congress may by law provide for the case of the death of any of the persons from whom the House of Representatives may choose a President whenever the right of choice shall have devolved upon them, and for the case of the death of any of the persons from whom the Senate may choose a Vice President whenever the right of choice shall have devolved upon them.

Section 5

Sections 1 and 2 shall take effect on the 15th day of October following the ratification of this article.

Section 6

This article shall be inoperative unless it shall have been ratified as an amendment to the Constitution by the legislatures of three-fourths of the several States within seven years from the date of its submission.

AMENDMENT XXI [1933]

Section 1

The eighteenth article of amendment to the Constitution of the United States is hereby repealed.

Section 2

The transportation or importation into any State, Territory, or possession of the United States for delivery or use therein of intoxicating liquors, in violation of the laws thereof, is hereby prohibited.

Section 3

This article shall be inoperative unless it shall have been ratified as an amendment to the Constitution by conventions in the several States, as provided in the Constitution, within seven years from the date of the submission hereof to the States by the Congress.

AMENDMENT XXII [1951]

Section 1

No person shall be elected to the office of the President more than twice, and no person who has held the office of President, or acted as President, for more than two years of a term to which some other person was elected President shall be elected to the office of the President more than once. But this Article shall not apply to any person holding the office of President when this Article was proposed by the Congress, and shall not prevent any person who may be holding the office of President, or acting as President, during the term within which this Article becomes operative from holding the office of President or acting as President during the remainder of such term.

Section 2

This article shall be inoperative unless it shall have been ratified as an amendment to the Constitution by the legislatures of three-fourths of the several States within seven years from the date of its submission to the States by the Congress.

AMENDMENT XXIII [1961]

Section 1

The District constituting the seat of Government of the United States shall appoint in such manner as the Congress may direct:

A number of electors of President and Vice President equal to the whole number of Senators and Representatives in Congress to which the District would be entitled if it were a State, but in no event more than the least populous State; they shall be in addition to those appointed by the States, but they shall be considered, for the purposes of the election of President and Vice President, to be electors appointed by a State; and they shall meet in the District and perform such duties as provided by the twelfth article of amendment.

Section 2

The Congress shall have power to enforce this article by appropriate legislation.

AMENDMENT XXIV [1964]

Section 1

The right of citizens of the United States to vote in any primary or other election for President or Vice President, for electors for President or Vice President, or for Senator or Representative in Congress, shall not be denied or abridged by the United States or any State by reason of failure to pay any poll tax or other tax.

Section 2

The Congress shall have power to enforce this article by appropriate legislation.

AMENDMENT XXV [1967]

Section 1

In case of the removal of the President from office or of his death or resignation, the Vice President shall become President.

Section 2

Whenever there is a vacancy in the office of the Vice President, the President shall nominate a Vice President who shall take office upon confirmation by a majority vote of both Houses of Congress.

Section 3

Whenever the President transmits to the President pro tempore of the Senate and the Speaker of the House of Representatives his written declaration that he is unable to discharge the powers and duties of his office, and until he transmits to them a written declaration to the contrary, such powers and duties shall be discharged by the Vice President as Acting President.

Section 4

Whenever the Vice President and a majority of either the principal officers of the executive departments or of such other body as Congress may by law provide, transmit to the President pro tempore of the Senate and the Speaker of the House of Representatives their written declaration that the President is unable to discharge the powers and duties of his office, the Vice President shall immediately assume the powers and duties of the office as Acting President.

Thereafter, when the President transmits to the President pro tempore of the Senate and the Speaker of the House of Representatives his written declaration that no inability exists, he shall resume the powers and duties of his office unless the Vice President and a majority of either the principal officers of the executive department or of such other body as Congress may by law provide, transmit within four days to the President pro tempore of the Senate and the Speaker of the House of Representatives their written declaration that the President is unable to discharge the powers and duties of his office. Thereupon Congress shall decide the issue, assembling within forty-eight hours for that purpose if not in session. If the Congress, within twenty-one days after receipt of the latter written declaration, or, if Congress is not in session, within twenty-one days after Congress is required to assemble, determines by two-thirds vote of both Houses that the President is unable to discharge the powers and duties of his office, the Vice President shall continue to discharge the same as Acting President; otherwise, the President shall resume the powers and duties of his office.

AMENDMENT XXVI [1971]

Section 1

The right of citizens of the United States, who are eighteen years of age or older, to vote shall not be denied or abridged by the United States or by any State on account of age.

Section 2

The Congress shall have power to enforce this article by appropriate legislation.

AMENDMENT XXVII [1992]

No law, varying the compensation for the services of the Senators and Representatives, shall take effect, until an election of Representatives shall have intervened.

About the Editors

Peter Augustine Lawler is professor of political science at Berry College, Georgia. Among his publications is *The Restless Mind: Alexis de Tocqueville on the Origin and Perpetuation of Human Liberty* (Rowman and Littlefield). He is coeditor of *The American Experiment: Essays on the Theory and Practice of Liberty* (Rowman and Littlefield).

Robert Martin Schaefer is assistant professor of political science at the University of Mobile, Alabama. He has published essays on political philosophy and public administration, and is coeditor of *The American Experiment: Essays on the Theory and Practice of Liberty.*